WHITE WORKING-CL

Multicultural community-building and change

Harris Beider

First published in Great Britain in 2015 by

Policy Press
University of Bristol
1-9 Old Park Hill
Bristol
BS2 8BB
UK
t: +44 (0)117 954 5940
pp-info@bristol.ac.uk
www.policypress.co.uk

North America office:
Policy Press
c/o The University of Chicago Press
1427 East 60th Street
Chicago, IL 60637, USA
t: +1 773 702 7700
f: +1 773-702-9756
sales@press.uchicago.edu
www.press.uchicago.edu

British Library Cataloguing in Publication Data
A catalogue record for this book is available from the British Library

Library of Congress Cataloging-in-Publication Data
A catalog record for this book has been requested

ISBN 978-1-4473-1396-0 paperback
ISBN 978-1-4473-1395-3 hardcover
ISBN 978-1-4473-1398-4 ePub
ISBN 978-1-4473-1399-1 Kindle

Cover design by Clifford Hayes Design
Front cover image: Getty Images
Printed and bound in Great Britain by CMP, Poole
Policy Press uses environmentally responsible print partners

Contents

Acknowledgements

There was a time when I used to hate white people in general and white working-class people in particular. Growing up in inner-city Birmingham, which was the warm embodiment of a multicultural community, providing shelter and support in equal measure. Moving to a large state secondary school located in peripheral public sector housing yanked away my cocoon-like existence as I was exposed to the cold reality of visceral racism for the first time. The perpetrators were my fellow students from white working-class backgrounds, who made it clear that I was not welcome in their school and community. The story could have ended here: a 12-year-old second-generation son of Pakistani migrants with a pathological hatred of whiteness and white working-class people. Yet, there is another story to be told beyond this point. It is about how other students – yes, also white and working-class – became my friends and how their families welcomed me into their homes, showering me with hospitality. This story is about how we shared experiences, supported each other in our formative teenage years and enjoyed music and life. There is no need to be misty-eyed and nostalgic. The racist students continued to be vile and violent, and racism continues to be a lived experience for many. However I ceased to hate white people and white working-class people. Little did I know that I would be given the opportunity to discuss white working-class perspectives on multiculturalism in a book rather than being restricted literally to the school of hard knocks.

This book would not have been possible without the support of the Joseph Rowntree Foundation and Open Society Foundation. By awarding research grants, both foundations gave me space to frame ideas on white working-class views on social change. At the Joseph Rowntree Foundation, Anne Harrop and Bana Gora provided unstinting support and encouragement to transform data and frameworks into a coherent research monograph. Similarly, Nazia Hussain and Tufyal Choudhary challenged, pushed and prodded to secure a publication that complemented the pioneering *At Home in Europe* programme sponsored by the Open Society Foundation. Both these projects connected me with more than 150 people who were willing to share their experiences on multiculturalism and change in such a direct and supportive way. I want to place on record my thanks to these anonymous individuals for their time and thoughts.

Sculpting the manuscript into its finished form has been helped by two people. I want to thank Arlene Conn, who has been my friend and colleague for over six years. Her perspectives on white working class communities, identity and place in modern America helped me immeasurably in framing my ideas for the book. Arlene played a pivotal role in her work on the book and her contributions both improved the work and advanced it in a significant way. Catalina Neculai reviewed the final draft at speed, and with a critical eye, that bordered on forensic intensity at a time when she had competing interests. To both Arlene and Cat, thank you so much for your time and dedication to the task.

Coventry University and latterly the Centre for Trust, Peace and Social Relations have been my academic home since 2008. The University and Centre have given me space and support to develop my research ideas, and formal and informal discussions with colleagues have helped to take ideas forward. Kusminder Chahal and Heaven Crawley are not simply my erstwhile colleagues at the Centre, but close confidantes whose capacity for collegiality continues to impress.

This book has benefitted enormously from the time I have spent at various research institutions in the US. Many friends and colleagues across the pond have created opportunities to discuss ideas in this book. Janet Smith at University of Illinois at Chicago, Andrew Greenlee and Stacy Harwood at University of Illinois at Urbana-Champaign, Rob Chaskin at the University of Chicago, Nicole Marwell at City University of New York, and Sue Popkin at The Urban Institute organised seminars at their institutions. I am proud to record my thanks to Ester Fuchs at Columbia University in the City of New York. Ester has supported me in many ways, including in 2014/15 by providing a welcoming academic home at the School of International and Public Affairs. My Columbia students and colleagues made my time in New York City an unforgettable experience.

My family will be pleased that this book project is over. They have had to endure frequent absences upstairs in the study alongside my absent-mindedness when all that seemed to occupy me was the white working class and multiculturalism. To Jemima, Alys, Jess and Thom, I promise to be a fun father, and to Sarah, I can never say thank you enough for your love and support. You are my ultimate soulmate.

Dedication

Peter Hayes, you will always be remembered with fondness by your family and friends

ONE

Towards a definition of the white working class

Rationale and aims of the book

White working-class communities are commonly reduced to a
negative rump most typically by media commentators, politicians
and academics; an undifferentiated block who are welfare-dependent,
leading chaotic and dysfunctional lives, and resolutely against social
and economic change. Culturally, they are perceived as rooted in
nostalgia for an idealised past that never existed, and, politically, they
are viewed as unwavering supporters of racist political organisations that
emerged onto the national stage in the debate on multiculturalism and
immigration. The objectives of this book are to increase the knowledge
and understanding of white working-class communities' perspectives on
multiculturalism and change from a range of standpoints. These are from
white working-class communities themselves who participated in two
projects across four case study sites, critically assessing the representation
of white working-class communities and themes associated with
multiculturalism in modern cinema and television, which is our most
accessible art form, and widening the discussion away from Britain to
consider how white working-class perspectives on multiculturalism
have been discussed in both Europe and the US. Creating a platform for
grassroots perspectives, considering the lens of cinema and television,
and looking at the overlaps in politics and practice from an international
lens leads to an informed and much more rational debate on white
working-class communities and multiculturalism. None of this is reduce
white working-class communities to being either racist extremists or
paragons of anti-racism. People who identify with these communities
may reflect the national opinion on immigration control, which has
been the majority opinion since 1964 in Britain irrespective of the
state of the economy or who the governing party is.

The white working class need not be demonised or lionised in
relation to their views on multiculturalism and immigration. Rather,
the imperative is to recognise the need to reassess and provide a more
balanced characterisation in general and, more specifically, to dispel

a popular impression that the white working class are supporters of extremist political parties.

Creating a counter-narrative is important in a debate on class and its relationship to terms surrounding immigration, such as 'multiculturalism', 'cohesion' and 'integration'. These ideas, which have become part of the British government jargon to describe society ('multiculturalism') or to ascribe policy solutions ('cohesion' and 'integration'), have become noxious in an increasingly racialised national debate. Indeed, they have been assigned meanings by a range of characters, including politicians, the mass media, researchers and policymakers, and the impact has been to problematise minority communities.

The views of white working-class communities have been filtered through this high-level web, which spins a story that never completely or accurately captures a balanced representation. Their views may be known but they have never been given a direct voice. Supporting a new framework that provides a platform for the thoughts, ideals and concerns of white working-class communities themselves, along with interdisciplinary and international perspectives, provides new ways to better understand these communities and multiculturalism and change.

Preamble

Deconstructing 'white' and 'working class' and the application of definitions to social and research debates in Britain will be a key focus of the introduction. Stereotypical definitions of the white working class have been relied upon too readily to justify political positioning, or the formation of public policy on 'hot button' issues such as welfare reform, criminal justice and immigration.

Debates on class are many and varied. It is not the intent of this book to dissect the theoretical underpinning of class. More interesting is understanding the class system and how it has transitioned from occupation and income to a wider and, some would say, more malleable definition that is based on culture, contacts and different forms of capital. Those who view this transition as helpful suggest that definitions of class are being modernised to reflect the reality of inequality in the 21st century. However, those who emphasise an economic explanation point to the inherent methodological challenges in a cultural approach.

White working-class communities are seen as a detached entity shaped by different social norms, living in areas of concentrated poverty and requiring special programmes to enable inclusion into wider society. Whiteness can be as an invisible and pervasive point of privilege that structures and shapes societal norms. These create a scenario through which working-class communities can be seen as a 'dirty' but visible white, negatively illuminated by their style, behaviours and conduct. Any early privilege is assumed to be diminished by pathology. In yet another direction, there are scholars who suggest that the working class has become 'whiter' in recent times. In part, this is influenced by 'whiteness studies' in the US, which put forward the premise that 19th-century European migrants to America were not initially seen as white, or the 'white' of native-born Americans, but became so because of assimilation.

Defining the white working class is necessarily complex and complicated. Adopting a position, whether primarily based on economics, culture or mix of factors, is readily challenged. A workable and acceptable definition must be shaped and constructed by these many factors, which include occupation, income, culture, ideology, geography and politics. In constructing a definition of the white working class, we need to be mindful of the impact of these influences, which vary in time and place.

The shifting meaning of class

Class has been a slippery and difficult concept. Its meaning has shifted and this can be charted from a historical perspective. The historian E.P. Thompson (1964) pointed to the definitional challenges of class in his impressive treatise *The making of the English working class*, stating:

> 'Working classes' is a descriptive term, which evades as much as it defines ... and class happens when some men, as a result of common experiences (inherited and shared), feel and articulate the identity of their interests as between themselves, and as against other men whose interests are different from (and usually opposed to) theirs. (Thompson, 1964: 9)

The reference to 'working classes' as being an elusive term is taken for granted in the definition. Yet, Thompson also points to a shared common identity and experiences that bring a group of people together due to shared and reciprocal interests.

In Britain, ruminating on class has been described as an obsession, bordering on a 'disease' (Halsey, 1995). If it is an obsession, then the British have been pondering about how to group people for a long time. The industrialisation of Britain generated debate about classification according to occupation. Partly, this was focused on statistical grouping and making sense of the working population, but also on understanding how interventions to address health conditions such as infant mortality could be implemented in a pre-welfare state Britain (Rose, 1995; Rose and Pevalin, 2001). At the start of the 20th century, the British government understood that it needed to act to improve health outcomes for poor people. In 1913, the *Registrar General's Social Classes* (RGSC) was published in a first attempt to stratify groups according to occupation. The Registrar clustered occupations into upper, middle and working classes and also according to health, hygiene and 'good standing' (Rose and Pevalin, 2001). The last point demonstrates the partisanship of class organisation: upper classes can look after their health and are deemed hygienic, while those in working-class occupations were not especially reliable or trustworthy.

During the 1910s, these crass assumptions could be understandable given the class conflict and political mobilisation at the time. However, the fact that the social class scale remained largely unchanged until the 1970s is of concern. The classification has even more murky origins in the eugenics movement, which encouraged or discouraged reproduction based on a presumption of desirable or undesirable traits. Assumptions regarding inherent intelligence, and the perceived danger posed by the poor, were an important part of the construct (albeit to rebut these claims) of the social classes in 1913. As Rose and Pevalin (2001: 5) confirm: 'eugenicist assumptions about society as a graded hierarchy of inherited natural abilities reflected in the skill level of occupations, remained embedded in the official, and most commonly used, measure of social class in Britain for 90 years'.

'Knowing your place' in the class categorisation extends beyond government statistics and into popular culture. One of the more frequently repeated images of class was shown in *The Frost Report* on 7 April 1966. This was a popular and sharply satirical view of Britain. Three actors of differing height (Cleese [6 foot, 5 inches], representing the upper class; Barker [5 foot, 8 inches], representing the middle class; and Corbett [5 foot, 1 inch], representing the working class) were positioned next to each other in descending height order. The following narrative then took place:

Cleese: [In bowler hat, black jacket and pinstriped trousers.] I look down on him [indicates Barker] because I am upper-class.

Barker: [Pork-pie hat and raincoat.] I look up to him [Cleese] because he is upper-class; but I look down

	on him [Corbett] because he is lower-class. I am middle-class.
Corbett:	[Cloth cap and muffler.] I know my place. I look up to them both. But I don't look up to him [Barker] as much as I look up to him [Cleese], because he [Cleese] has got innate breeding.
Cleese:	I have got innate breeding, but I have not got any money. So sometimes I look up [bends knees, does so] to him [Barker].
Barker:	I still look up to him [Cleese] because although I have money, I am vulgar. But I am not as vulgar as him [Corbett] so I still look down on him [Corbett].
Corbett:	I know my place. I look up to them both; but while I am poor, I am honest, industrious and trustworthy. Had I the inclination, I could look down on them. But I don't.
Barker:	We all know our place, but what do we get out of it?
Cleese:	I get a feeling of superiority over them.
Barker:	I get a feeling of inferiority from him [Cleese], but a feeling of superiority over him [Corbett].
Corbett:	I get a pain in the back of my neck.

The contradictions and complications related to class may be deduced from this exchange but so too the resilience and perseverance of the working class. In this way, class is more than simply occupation in Britain: it is an elaborate navigation system designed to help guide people to their intrinsic position in the societal hierarchy. Predictably, it confirms to the working class their standing at the bottom of the pecking order.

In the 1950s, the National Readership Survey (NRS) developed a classification driven by the need for better information on consumer trends. Social grade (as distinct from social class) was based on the occupation of the head of household, leading to six groups: A and B (higher and intermediate managerial, administrative, professional occupations); C1 (supervisory, clerical and junior managerial, administrative, professional occupations); C2 (skilled manual occupations); and D and E (semi-skilled and unskilled manual occupations, unemployed, lowest-grade occupations). Initially at least, these social categories formed the basis of predicting consumer behaviour. For example, Britain's newspapers were divided into different groups with grades A and B taking the more highly regarded publications such as *The Times* and *The Guardian*, while grades C2, D and E were linked with tabloids like *The Sun* and *The Daily Mirror*. The problems include the reification of different groups based on occupation. Despite significant changes in the workforce, including the entry of women in large numbers into the workplace, the decline of the manufacturing industry and an increase in different sectors of the economy such as service-related occupations (see Savage et al, 2012), the NRS continued to be used for consumer surveys and was even expanded for use in market research.

Taking the shifting meaning of class further to the 1990s, the National Statistics Socio-Economic Classification (NS-SEC) adapted previous iterations to a modern and more varied workforce. It has become the standard for social stratification, being initially introduced for the 2001 Population Census. The categorisation itself is composed of 17 groupings, which can be further reduced to the three categories of higher, intermediate and lower occupations (Rose and Pevalin, 2005). The NS-SEC continues to focus on occupation, as well as the type of work undertaken. However, the changing nature of the economy as a result of deindustrialisation, globalisation and restructuring has had an impact on the working-class groupings. Consequently, they have become progressively smaller. As Payne (2013: 14) summarises:

> These classes suggest a potentially more informative picture of Britain today, following the collapse of the old working class and their institutions, than the traditional schema. When the economic activities of agricultural production or manufacturing industry in a society go into decline – so far a universal sociological law – their characteristic social relations, processes and institutions are also inevitably necessarily modified. As I observed recently, there is no place for the old working class social institutions of employment protection through strong trade unions and long craft apprenticeships; moral values learned in Non-Conformist Chapels; social solidarity through kinship, neighbouring and friendship in residential concentrations of occupational communities; intellectual development through evening classes and the WEA [Workers' Educational Association]; and political expression through a Left of Centre Labour Party.

The decline of working-class occupations in Britain has also been confirmed by longitudinal studies such as the British Social Attitudes survey. Since 1983, the number of people working in middle-class occupations (according to NS-SEC) has increased from 47% to 59% (BSA, 2013). This should not be confused with subjective identification related to social class. In the same survey, 60% of people described themselves as working class (BSA, 2013) even though they may actually be included in social-economic groups A, B and C1.

The statistical basis for defining the working class still rests with occupation. The modifications since the RGSC in 1913, to NRS in the 1950s, and then to NS-SEC have reflected changes in Britain since the turn of the 20th century from an industrial to a post-industrial society. It could be argued that the statistical classification, which is based on detailed empirical evidence, still shows a category of occupations, albeit devoid of references to those in higher occupations who are deemed to derive from 'good standing'. These occupational classifications make polemical observations unnecessary, even in a modern Britain where occupational hierarchy is based on the premise of social mobility.

Class continues to be of great interest in the UK. In January 2011, the BBC launched *The Great British Class Survey* in partnership with researchers at the University of Manchester and the Open University. This was based on neither government-sanctioned occupational categories, as was the case of the RGSC, or the sociological or skill-based criteria and occupations used in the widely applied NS-SEC framework. The survey was focused on broadening discussion from the traditional parameters of income and occupation to incorporate cultural notions of class, such as social relations, leisure activities and cultural pursuits. This study stemmed from the cultural class analysis popularised by the French academic Pierre Bourdieu (1984). Rather than simply focusing on occupation to understand social inequality, Bourdieu looked at the overlap and interplay between economic, social and cultural capital (Savage et al, 2005, 2012). Economic capital is concerned with income levels and general wealth; social capital relates to the extent to which social networks are generated from contacts and connections that may further privilege or disadvantage groups; and cultural capital is linked to people's interests outside of work, such as preferences in music, media, cuisine and other cultural pursuits.

The Great British Class Survey led to 161,000 online surveys being completed by June 2011 (Savage et al, 2012). Drawing on data, and framed within a cultural class analysis, new class groups were identified and these reflected levels of economic, social and cultural capital, including a small *elite* (which is high in all three forms of capital), an established middle class and a technical middle class with the former distinguished from the latter by (among other things) greater social and cultural capital.

In this schema, the working class has become fragmented into three groups: the traditional working class, emergent service workers and the precariat. First, there is a 'traditional working class', who tend to be homeowners and have moderate levels of capital in all three measures. Jobs commonly held in this group include administrators, van drivers and electricians. This group has been described as 'a residue of earlier historical periods … embodying characteristics of the '"traditional working class" … a "throwback" to an earlier phase in Britain's social history, as part of an older generational formation' (Savage et al, 2012: 240).

The second group are 'emergent service workers', who are relatively poor in terms of income but richer in cultural and social capital. This is because people who comprise this class – bar staff, nursing auxiliaries, call centre workers – generally tend to be younger than the traditional class group and have acquired 'lowbrow' tastes in music, the internet and sporting pursuits.

The third and final group has been termed the 'precariat', denoting precarious employment conditions, as well as very low levels of economic, social and cultural capital. This is the most deprived group in *The Great British Class Survey*. People in this group, if not unemployed, are typically van drivers (again in the first group mentioned earlier), cleaners and care workers. The precariat has been hit hardest by the 2008 recession and the continuing impact of globalisation. Standing (2011; 2014) describes this group as a 'dangerous class'. He continues:

> Most in it do not belong to any professional or craft community; they have no social memory on which to call, and no shadow of the future hanging over their deliberations with other people, making them opportunistic. The biggest dangers are social illnesses and the risk that populist politicians will play on their fears and insecurities to lure them onto the rocks of neo-fascism, blaming 'big government' and 'strangers' for their plight. We are witnessing this drift, increasingly disguised by clever rebranding, as in the case of the True Finns, Swedish Democrats and French National Front. They have natural allies in the US Tea Party, the Japanese copycats, the English Defence League and the originals, Berlusconi's neo-fascist supporters. (Standing, 2011)

The Great British Class Survey generated intense debate inside and outside the academic community. By suggesting that class may be viewed beyond the parameters of income and occupation to include social and cultural capital (as well as economic capital), it shifted the discussion from an economic to a cultural modelling. Such a radical change has led to criticism of the framing of the model and especially the typologies, indicators for capital and sampling (see Mills, 2014). Others have been critical of the groupings designed by Savage et al (2014). For example, Bradley (2014) suggests that the research led to an oversimplification of working-class culture. The traditional working class, new service workers and, specifically, the precariat are viewed as a passive and limited group uninterested in almost everything and incapable of consuming 'high' culture. In short, *The Great British Class Survey* is a deficit-sum model.

As we have seen, class is a contested concept. Initially associated with various levels of standing, status and health in Edwardian Britain, the focus on occupations and hierarchy continued to shape socio-economic classification until the late 20th century (Szreter, 1984; Savage et al, 2014), with six classes based on occupational esteem. In 2001, a new schema on class was introduced by NS-SEC and increased the number to 17 and differentiated between employers and employees, routine and non-routine work, and those with a labour and service contract (see Rose and Pevalin, 2003). In effect it recognised that skills, and not simply occupation, were important in providing an accurate picture of social stratification in Britain. The criticism was that NS-SEC did not consider the agency and symbolism of culture and networks in shaping inequality (Skeggs, 2004). The shift from income and occupation to different forms of culture is the most recent manifestation that attempts to make sense of the post-industrial and global society we inhabit.

Class has moved from economy to culture. During these transitions, the working class has also been attributed with different labels – the lumpen proletariat, underclass and precariat – while the one constant is their placement at the bottom of the hierarchy. Although a multidimensional cultural analysis may only recently have been identified, the poorest segment of the working class has been viewed as challenging and problematic from the outset of classification. This has been amplified with input by the media, satirised in television programming and chronicled in popular literature. 'Chavs' may be a recent label but similar unflattering discriminations have also been attributed in the past (Jones, 2011). Moreover, policy has been proxy for singling out the working class: council housing (Hanley, 2007), welfare dependence (Murray, 1996) and social exclusion (Mandelson, 1997).

The invocation of class can be seen as a vessel that becomes filled with the prevailing norms and reification handed down by government and inculcated by the media. This is not to suggest that culture is redundant in shaping stratification, being especially important in relation to reproducing 'common sense' pathologies of working-class communities that frame people as a problem. Indeed, the emphasis on culture feeds a 'clash of cultures' narrative between suspect groups: a backward, antagonistic and shrinking working class and a growing, threatening and culturally different minority population that characterised the politics of community cohesion under New Labour (2001–10) and continued as the politics of integration under the Coalition government (2001-15) The politics of community cohesion under New Labour (2001–10) continued as the politics of integration under the Coalition government (2010–15). Class becomes heightened and shaped by cultural factors; it is constantly evolving. The occupational class schema that defined much of the popular debate from 1913 to the 1980s may have provided a sense of clarity but it also became redundant in explaining stratification as Britain moved from an industrial to a post-industrial society. Moreover, the occupational category also carried cultural tropes enmeshed in a hierarchical framing of job worth. Working-class occupations really did 'know their place'.

Class is a slippery concept and is open to many subjective interpretations. The problem is the contested nature of the working class, made much more complicated when attempting to deconstruct 'white' (the subject of our inquiry), which has meandered in meaning since Thompson and his colleagues charted its rise.

Whiter than white: the meaning of whiteness

Recent attempts to deconstruct the terms 'white' and 'whiteness' have focused on its dominance and basis of privilege in society. A definition of whiteness is put forward by Hartigan (2005: 1): '"Whiteness" … asserts the obvious and overlooked fact that whites are racially interested and motivated. Whiteness both names and critiques hegemonic beliefs and practices that designate white people as "normal" and racially "unmarked"'. The unmarked quality of whiteness and the dominance it has on discourse that Hartigan refers to in this quote have been taken up by other writers on the subject. For example, Dyer (2006) considers the visual imaginary of whiteness, being influenced by critical cultural theorists such as Stuart Hall (1995).

Whiteness occupies a privileged position because it is masked, as well as unmarked, and does not come under the type of political scrutiny that has become the norm for visible minority communities. The focus for Dyer is both the interrogation of whiteness and its deconstruction from its dominant position. Being white is paradoxical. At one level, whiteness is not marked as 'whites are everywhere in representation ... they seem not to be represented to themselves as whites' (Dyer, 2006: 3). In comparison with minority communities , white people do not need to address racist stereotypes that disadvantage them in housing, education and employment markets. In contrast to Muslims, neither do white people need to respond to the racialisation that shines a searching light on their loyalty or discussions of how they are a threat to the country in terms of values, 'norms' and identity (CIC, 2007; Beider, 2012). Dyer's analysis states that white people are given liberty to be themselves because they are the normalised and hegemonic group in society, the litmus test that all others are measured against. At another level, being white creates an opportunity to be diverse in many different ways, hence Dyer's explanation that the nuances associated with whitenesss help 'to be presented as an apparently attainable, flexible, varied category while setting up an always moveable criterion of inclusion, the ascribed whiteness of your skin' (Dyer, 2006: 57).

The affirmation of white and whiteness as dominant yet unremarkable, as masked yet pervasive, and defined as an ethnicity only when whiteness is measured against minorities is compelling yet limited. In part, the analysis does not go deeper and analyse intra-class divides within whiteness based on, for example, income, power and access to social networks. Taking into account the impact of these factors into whiteness could enable whiteness to become marked and visible for white working-class communities.

The challenge of deconstructing whiteness has also been discussed by Clarke and Garner (2009). While agreeing with the view that whiteness is an unmarked yet dominant category, they nevertheless suggest a complexity and nuance that is missing from perspectives such as Dyer's (2006) that see it as a homogeneous basis of power. In this way, the limits of being a raced category need to be explored when discussing low-income communities. This includes discussion of class and place (Clarke and Garner, 2009: 3). In this cultural framing, the problematic other should also be explored (Hanley, 2007; Jones, 2011).

Dyer, while determined to expose whiteness as a privileged and powerful force, put forward the idea that working-class white people are specifically represented in film in a much less translucent way. There is some demarcation within whiteness. In definitional terms at least, whiteness is complex. Being white, by comparison to being a minority, denotes a position of preference within society and yet the working class have been tagged as a problematic and challenging group. They are hyper-visible in modern Britain. To this end, some have discussed the possibilities of using class as a way of not only marking whiteness, but also internally separating distinct components. Specifically, working-class whiteness may be construed as 'extreme', whereas middle-class whiteness is 'ordinary' (Lawler, 2012). Some have suggested that working-class whiteness has become 'dirty' and marked as a troubled 'other' (Haylett, 2001; Skeggs, 2009). It is not privileged, but problematic (Tyler, 2008; Garner, 2011; Jones, 2011), and it is quite a distance from the view taken by Dyer (1988, 2006) as a pervasive, all-powerful ordinariness.

Whiteness studies

Recently, there has been an increase in the number of scholars who have turned their attention to the collective field of 'whiteness studies'. Many of the leading proponents are based in the US (Roediger, 1991; Ignatiev, 1995) and largely adopt a historical perspective. The key assertion is that some European migrants to the US during the 19th century were not viewed as white and only achieved this status through assimilation and acceptance into social and political structures over a period of time.

There has been limited interest in the UK in 'whiteness studies' but there has been an emergence of whiteness and class (Bonnett, 1998, 2008; Garner, 2007, 2011). For example, Bonnett suggests that the construction of whiteness in Britain was a bourgeois enterprise that largely excluded the working class. As he described it, they had 'marginal' whiteness. Bonnett downplays the role that non-white immigration played in white identity formation as being too simplistic, instead viewing the white working class as part of the larger homogeneous majority group. The point is made in the following:

> Another seductively simple interpretative error also requires our attention … just as tempting to imagine for the assertion of white working class whiteness in Britain was non-white immigration: white identity arrived in working class politics when, and because 'people of colour' arrived in Britain … it is presupposed that the 'white working class' is an unproblematic category: that the white working class were white, always knew they were white, and merely required the presence of non-white communities/competition in order to start mobilizing around this 'fact'. (Bonnett, 1998: 317–318)

The marginalisation of the working class in terms of white identity shows an overlap with the concept of 'dirty whiteness' and 'clean whiteness', illustrating the complexity of whiteness and class. The idea that whiteness is not an amorphous category, but, instead, composed of different segments that may, at times, be competing and also complementary, has been debated in recent studies on working-class identity in Britain. For example, Rhodes (2011) discusses peripheral whiteness related to the working class in contrast to the mainstream whiteness of middle-class white people. Jones (2011) and Hanley (2007) invoke images of white working-class communities as detached groups almost ring-fenced from participating in mainstream society. Garner (2007) suggests that whiteness cannot be viewed as a fixed entity and also needs to be freed from the constraints of race relations based on the relationships between white and minority communities. Whiteness is not a fixed identity and should include a number of complex frames such as gender, age and place that nuance views on the way that communities relate to each other and to government. In studies on the extreme Right in Britain, Rhodes challenges the conjoining of the terms 'white' and 'working class' (Rhodes, 2010, 2011). The problem with this link is that it leads to a cultural conflation of white working-class communities as unreconstructed, unconditional supporters of the far Right. For example white middle-class communities are not held to account for racist practices that exclude minority communities from senior positions in the world of work, nor the way that purchasing power is used to move homes so as to better access schools that are less diverse in terms of ethnicity. Focusing simply on racial identity misses a number of critical dimensions, including social inequality (this links to ideas on the importance of class rather than whiteness [see Bottero, 2009], as well as the problems of multiculturalism in racing and excluding the white working class [see Haylett, 2001]).

Comparing 'whiteness studies' in the UK to those in the US may be premature. There are significant differences between the two countries in terms of the history of migration, paths to citizenship, political representation and ideology. The greater concern with 'whiteness studies' in the US is that they downplay the importance of white privilege and the extent of racism shown to communities of colour (for a good overview, see Fox and Guglielmo, 2012). For example, being an immigrant from Ireland, Italy or Spain to 19th-century America who encounters prejudice should in no way be compared to the more disturbing experiences of Native Americans, African-Americans, Chinese Americans and Japanese Americans who were variously terrorised, murdered and interned. European migrants did have the privilege of being part of the white category, however 'dirty', 'peripheral' or 'marginal'. Nonetheless, there have been important and valuable contributions to increasing the understanding of the white working class. Clearly, there needs to be resistance to attempts to construct this group as being culturally problematic and unconditional supporters of the extreme Right. Reification is generally flawed and this applies to the white working class and visible minorities. Numerous studies have testified to the richness and diversity within white working-class communities (Rogaly and Taylor, 2009; Beider, 2011, 2014; Garner, 2011; Skey, 2011).

The neglect and demonisation of the white working class in Britain cannot be compared to the racism and racialisation that shapes the everyday experiences of minorities. Yet, in some of the most recent studies of white working-class communities, a criticism is made of anti-racism (Bonnett, 1998) and multiculturalism (Haylett, 2001; Bottero, 2009). Some of these perspectives are important but there is a risk that criticism of multiculturalism then becomes a process to target minority communities in the current political climate. The retreat from multiculturalism and replacement with community cohesion under New Labour and integration under the Coalition government means that there is a much less tolerant view of immigration and difference. Those that are rightly critical of multiculturalism for excluding white working-class communities need to put forward ideas on how progressive politics could be built. This is about recognising the importance of race as a point of agency, as well as a means to social resistance.

Remembering class

The return of class to politics has been welcomed, but less so the conjoining of whiteness. The coupling of white and working class is problematic according to Bottero (2009). Rather than focusing on the issues of economic class inequality, the discussion digresses into a cultural interpretation of a white working-class position that not only pits it against minority communities who share similar class positions, but that is also against multiculturalism and change. The white working class are raced and classed. Here, whiteness is not only dirty, but dangerous, scrabbling almost feral-like alongside minority communities for scarce welfare resources, social housing and jobs. Bottero suggests that the real question is not so much this superficial pitting and framing, but understanding how inequalities arise in the first instance. Countering the acceptance of the simple existence of the white working class, a call is made to understand nuance and counter unhelpful social constructions based on ethnicity: 'There is a danger courted by the current discussions of the "white working class" as disadvantage is reframed as ethnic identity, and a stereotype of the white poor emerges, squeezing class inequality out the picture altogether' (Bottero, 2009: 14).

The shifting debate on the white working class from class to culture was accelerated by interventions from commentators such as Murray (1996). His analysis was laden with a heavy and unrelentingly negative view of the white working class. Communities and neighbourhoods became identified as being problematic, dysfunctional and dangerous. The diagnosis and the solutions were not about the impact of the deindustrialisation and deregulation that left many who worked in manual professions out of work, insecure and in poverty. Rather, the focus was on how social reforms led to the moral decay of Britain. The problematic state of the white working class was, instead, the result of an overgenerous welfare state, a decrease in common norms and an increase in crime. Being white and working-class was framed and viewed as being problematic (for a wider discussion, see Sveinsson, 2009; see also Levitas, 1998). Murray suggested that Britain was experiencing a white working-class problem that was getting worse. In fact, he referred to the white working class as an underclass, being detached from the mainstream and 'common values': 'There are many ways to identify an underclass. I will concentrate on 3 phenomena that have turned out to be early warning signals in the US: illegitimacy, violent crime, and drop out from the labour force' (Murray, 1996: 34).

Striking imagery accompanies Murray's rhetoric. He was concerned about how this feckless white working-class group seemed as a 'disease' and how visiting this group was akin to dropping into a 'plague area' (Murray, 1996: 43). It could therefore be argued that this framing of white working-class communities shaped a policy response that focused on cultural pathologies, which were characterised by public housing estates mired in criminal behaviour, generational welfare dependency, drug abuse and women as single parents. The policy response leads to a labelling of collective and dysfunctional practices as out of step with societal norms but also other class groups. This was the 'dirty whiteness' that had become detached and separated from the mainstream through an exaggerated emphasis on cultural erosion.

A marked and ethnicised white working class that is at the periphery (Rhodes, 2011) or that is marginalised (Webster, 2008) needs to be explored. Hanley (2007), in a personal account of growing up in a public housing estate in Birmingham, pinpoints how this type of accommodation went from being aspirational to being the place where people did not want to end up:

> Estates have come to mean more as ciphers for a malingering society than as places where people actually live. In the eyes of many people, council estates are little more than holding cages for the feral and lazy.... On the most marginalized estates, 60 per cent of adults are out of work, and yet those same adults find themselves blamed for the poor conditions in which they live. This is no longer a society that you can be proud, that your home has been provided by the state: it doesn't work like that anymore, not when you, the council tenant, exist in a minority of 12 per cent. (Hanley, 2007: 146)

The white working class is further divided but on this occasion by tenure, creating bounded spaces that kept people away and out of sight from the rest of society. In addition, government housing policies further deepened the divide between public housing tenants and homeowners. Specifically, the scheme known as 'Right to Buy' and embodied in the Housing Act 1980 allows secure tenants the ability to buy their home from the local authority at a significantly discounted rate (see Malpass and Murie, 1999; Mullins and Murie, 2006). Generally good-quality social housing stock was sold under 'Right to Buy', with more than 1 million council houses moving from public to private ownership within the first 10 years of the scheme. Councils did not replace this stock. The impact on communities was devastating, being marked by low levels of investment in increasingly deteriorating infrastructure in many council estates. Furthermore, a concentration of poverty resulted when new homeowners sold their homes and moved to contiguous private sector markets while, at the same time, council housing waiting lists mushroomed because the units sold were not replaced in order to address new needs (Hanley, 2007).

White working-class communities became marked not only as a cultural other, but as groups who were spatially excluded from societal norms. Webster (2008: 305) describes this existence as the 'ghettoization of the working class estates'. The existence of the 'walled places', out of site, focused the attention of government to extend housing privatisation in different ways. These included selling the remaining council estates to housing associations (not-for-profit housing organisations funded by a mix of private and public investment) through large-scale voluntary stock transfers. The promise of investment in declining assets, as well as the Right to Buy, were deemed by council tenants to be more advantageous than was the spectre of losing the vote at the ballot box (Mullins and Murie, 2006). People living in these spaces are judged by their whiteness (even though some are diverse in terms of ethnicity and tenure) and attached with cultural traits:

> Walled people are happily described as 'chav scum' estates, as 'places of last resort' and as 'dumping grounds' ... their 'failure' is not only contagious but morally repugnant ... most of all they serve to give concrete spatial reality to the existence of marginalized whiteness in the eyes of everyone else and as irredeemably associated with dangerous and criminal places. (Webster, 2008: 305)

The term 'underclass', when combined with its prevalence in council estates that are annexed and marked by the poor and white, suggests a view of a people who are cut off from the rest of society. They need to be managed and contained but cannot be reformed. This perspective changed when Tony Blair was elected Labour prime minister in the landslide election victory of 1997. A modernising Labour government also introduced a new label to describe those who were of low income. No longer an 'underclass', but 'socially excluded', the working class needed to be programmed to join 'mainstream' British society. Developing interventions that were targeted to close the gap between the poorest neighbourhoods in the country and the rest of the country, the process of social exclusion was to be coordinated centrally by the Social Exclusion Unit (SEU) within the Cabinet Office (see DCLG, 2001). As a precursor to this new programme, Peter Mandelson, the arch moderniser in the government, spoke at a Fabian meeting in 1997. He scaled the problem facing the new government at the close of the 20th century by rather ironically referencing working-class communities:

> We are people who are used to being represented as problematic. We are the long term, benefit-claiming, working-class poor, living through another period of cultural contempt. We are losers, no hopers, low life scroungers. Our culture is yob culture. The importance of welfare provisions to our lives has been denigrated and turned against us; we are welfare dependent and our problems won't be solved by giving us higher benefits. We are perverse in our failure to succeed, dragging our feet over social change, wanting the old jobs back, still having

babies instead of careers, stuck in outdated class and gender moulds. We are the challenge that stands out above all others, the greatest social crisis of our times. (Mandelson, 1997, quoted in Haylett, 2001: 6–9)

Minority communities were also part of the SEU plan, with specific programmes aimed at addressing racial disadvantage. It was clear from Mandelson that the focus was to be on white working-class communities. The inference being that the working class needed to be modernised and reformed in order to be brought into the 21st century in a similar way to how 'Old' Labour became New Labour. In the framing of social exclusion, Mandelson reduced the white working class as not only problematic generally, but also an almost luddite and recalcitrant group, out of step and out of touch with modern Britain. Another way to look at this classification is to compare the white working class, which is operating outside the borders of modern society, with the middle class, which has embraced an inclusive and modern culture (Skeggs, 2009). The white working class is defined as culturally deficient (Haylett, 2001), peripheral (Rhodes, 2011) and a 'dirty white' compared to its pristine middle-class superior relation (Skeggs, 2009).

Social exclusion could be viewed as transforming white working-class cultural behaviours to fit into a practice of working and living that would serve the needs of modern Britain. This was not just about de-concentrating poverty, but about integrating these groups into mainstream society. White working-class communities had become an embarrassment to the sheen of New Labour. They needed to rise to the expectations of citizenship by transitioning from welfare dependency and single parenthood to raised aspirations and movement to employment (however low-skilled and low-paid), modelling new behaviours and lifestyles and accessing the spirit of bootstrap capitalism. This was not simply economic renewal, but social renewal bent on addressing the cultural challenges of people who lived in poor places. As Haylett (2001: 364) concludes:

Here exclusion is partly about poverty but importantly also goes beyond an economic predicament. Inclusion to 'normal' society is predominantly cultural: it is inclusion to the culture of the nation ... the values, aspiration, and ways of living of the rest of 'us'.

Again, white working-class communities are unmasked as being problematic. They are marked by being segregated within 'walled' estates and reified with a set of cultural deficiencies. To Murray, they are an 'underclass', and for Mandelson, they are part of the challenge of social exclusion. The modernisation process for the white working class was mediated by policies of welfare reform and social inclusion. They are also portrayed as backward by their opposition and hostility towards multiculturalism. This is in contrast to middle-class communities, who are viewed as being progressive and modern (Haylett, 2001; Webster, 2008; Nayak, 2009). In this analysis, multiculturalism becomes a vehicle to increase the marginalisation of white working-class groups rather than celebrating difference and diversity. The irrational racism of the white working class is linked to low levels of education, backwardness and sheer vulgarity. The contestation is discussed on the terrain of white working-class cultural remoteness from dominant norms in British society, where acceptance of a multicultural society excludes people as being part of the nation. The problem with this analysis is that *multiculturalism* is seen as a contributory factor to demonisation and keeps the focus on culture rather than the impact of deindustrialisation, deregulation and specific policies, such as the Right to Buy. In attempting to put forward a class analysis as the reason why white working-class communities are viewed as a problematic 'other', there is a risk that the achievements of multiculturalism are erased and the concept is caballed under the admitted weakness of cultural explanations. For example, consider the following:

> The logic of conflict inherent within class relations cannot be restructured via a multiculturalism whose dominant rhetorics of inclusion, equality of opportunity, and antidiscrimination are addressed by identity relations and ideals of integration and diversity ... by way of conclusion I want to suggest that the representation of poor whites within the discourse of 'multicultural modernization' can be considered as a modern form of imperialism, with class-racist elements. (Haylett, 2001: 365)

The analysis needs to be reviewed. Invoking class to ridicule and exclude debates on multiculturalism runs the risk of supporting policies such as community cohesion and integration whose implementation has paralleled the rise of extreme Right activity. Reductionism of this type, intended or not, should be resisted.

Framing class and whiteness as uncluttered categories is too simple a deduction. These are complex terms, attributed with cultural meaning by media commentators such as Murray and politicians drawn from different political parties. Therefore, 'white working class' is as nuanced as any other categorisation. In asserting the merit of considering 'white working class' as a defined entity, it would be a mistake to simply suggest that its privilege and power has been erased. Whiteness, though complex, remains a dominant force in a racialised society. It continues to be the norm that frames debate in policy and politics, especially with regard to themes of immigration and race. Hate crimes based on race and religion continue to disproportionately impact minority communities. The most recent statistics show only 0.1% of the victims were affiliated with white communities compared to 1.3% from minority communities (Home Office, 2013: 23).Of cases involving racially motivated crime taken to court 71.6% of the defendants were White British (Crown Prosecution Service, 2014: 4). Moreover, the situation has deteriorated rather than improved recently, but one consistency is that the victims are minorities and the perpetrators are white people (Chahal and Julienne, 2000). 'Stop and search' is a tactic that is predominantly utilised in minority communities. Between 1999 and 2007, there was a 120% increase in stop and search actions for minority communities compared to only 7% for white communities (*The Guardian*, 2013a). There may be a corollary between class and place but the more compelling link is with race. Whiteness, irrespective of class, continues to be the norm, a norm that protects and masks in contrast to the 'abnormal', unprotected and unmasked state in which minorities exist in society.

Conclusion

In this opening chapter, whiteness and working class have been explored. Taken together, the white working class has been presented as a single, unified group, lacking in variation without regard to income, tenure or place. In this homogeneous state, the white working class is filled with cultural tropes and expected to behave in a predictable way. The group is possessed with fixed and troubled identities that mark them as a dangerous 'other', as well as against the prevailing norms expected of productive Britons. The white working class is pitted by some commentators against minority communities in a 'clash of cultures', as two suspect and problematic groups competing for limited resources, with the latter blamed by the former for their lowly predicament. The dominant narrative is culturally framed, borrowing from negative stereotypes. Hence, members of the white working class are essentialised as representing the lumpen proletariat, devoid of rational thinking, backward and resistant to change. They are a class of people hostile to multiculturalism and immigration.

The pathway to a definitive meaning of the white working class is cluttered and complex. Some counter that class is essential to the definition of the working class and that there is a danger that it is becoming yet another ethnic category. Of course, it is important to reject a one-dimensional view of the white working class. Conceptually, theoretically and in practice, identity is nuanced. The white working class is as complex, diverse and differentiated as any other group in society. In responding to the sometimes frenzied debates on the United Kingdom Independence party (UKIP) after the 2014 European elections, it is important to propose views on white working class and identity that suggest a much more subtle, not to say complex, view that is the reality rather than the impression. So, there is not one white working class, but many, and these can be negative and include scroungers, the welfare-dependent and an undeserving lumpen proletariat that has come to the forefront in the context of welfare reform and policies. The white working class is also comprised of the more commendable hard-pressed and hard-working families that use their social capital and resilience to sustain neighbourhoods and communities through recession and change. Either way, they are a group that is diverse and shaped by changing demographic, economic and cultural trends. Conversely, political parties and the media use the complexity of the term to socially construct an idealised position that may suit their own objectives for immediate and long-term ends.

This first chapter has focused on the complexity and nuance associated with the 'white working class'. The following chapter outline summarises the remainder of the book.

Chapter Two: The political exclusion of the white working class

The second chapter delves into the debates on how the white working class became reduced to 'a rabble' from being viewed as an important part of the building of modern Britain. Multiculturalism will be explored in terms of whether it has reduced the salience of the white working class in the debates on identity and change. The contention is that it was not multiculturalism that led to a reduced voice, but shifting policy and political debates. Recently, there has been a decline of multiculturalism and its transformation into much more racialised debates based on community cohesion and integration. Community cohesion, which emerged after the riots of 2001 in Burnley, Oldham and Bradford, will be viewed as problematic due to its emphasis on norms, culture and visible minority communities. Low-income white communities were key protagonists in the riots but strangely absent from community cohesion. This follows a tradition within academic studies on race where the white working class has been silent, or set as an adversarial opponent of migrants, as well as hostile towards immigration. Multiculturalism was not the problem as much as changing economic and political priorities. This chapter will suggest that the rise of New Labour paralleled the loss of this voice. After the 2010 election, class has had somewhat of a comeback in Labour politics with the increasing influence of Blue Labour and the rise of UKIP in the 2014 elections based on the strategy of appealing to white working-class voters. Invoking memory, loss and disenfranchisement could easily lead to the reification of white working-class communities as backward, resistant to change and in support of extreme positions. The new visibility of whiteness need not be reactionary to multiculturalism.

Chapter Three: White working class and racist? An exploration

The popular discourse on white working-class communities is that they have been in the vanguard of racism, as seen within the context of a number of social issues, including immigration and its impact on national identity, housing and employment. This has been exacerbated by national interventions from politicians who have championed the slogan 'British jobs for British workers' or who have decried the failure of 'state multiculturalism'. This much we know of the politics of racism: the end game is 'protecting' the white working class from the excesses of multiculturalism and, in so doing, securing their short-term political support. More germane, the chapter will discuss the view that white working-class communities default to hostility to both immigration and the concept of multiculturalism. It has been a recurrent theme in policy and, to a certain extent, academic literature. Initially, the focus will be depictions in popular culture, especially in film and television, in the 1950s and 1960s that transition white working-class characterisation from being almost heroic to problematic. We will then look at examples that have been framed, in part, as popular white working-class interventions on multiculturalism and change – the 1958 Race Riots in Notting Hill, the response to Enoch Powell's 'Rivers of Blood' speech in 1968 and the emergence of punk and the rise of 2 Tone in Coventry. The two earlier examples are better known and extensively documented as white working-class racism. The latter two, and especially 2 Tone, are less well known and discussed but have been viewed locally as a union of diverse elements of the working class coming together to celebrate difference. These two events demonstrate how the pathology of whiteness and class are treated differently to inform a distinct and reified narrative.

Chapter Four: International perspectives on whiteness, class and politics

The narratives of disconnection, loss and change are not restricted to Britain. Despite differences in population, politics and ideology, similar experiences have been played out in many parts of Europe and the US in relation to the white working class. This chapter will consider the politics of white working-class communities in the context of countries that are becoming ethnically diverse as a result of immigration. The US is also an interesting case study because of the rise of the political movement known as the 'Tea Party'. This has been characterised as a popular revolt against established politicians and its supporters are largely white working-class voters concerned about immigration, economic stability and social change. The narrative echoes the rise of UKIP in the UK and political movements in Europe. However, the chapter will suggest a reality that is somewhat different, with the Tea Party defined as middle-class and a local insurgency, while political parties in Europe speak to a different constituency.

Chapter Five: A reactionary voice: nuanced views on multiculturalism

This will be the first of two chapters based on research conducted in four different locations in the UK. These give a grassroots perspective on multiculturalism and change, which appears to be at odds with the view that white working-class communities are collectively supporters of the far Right and opposed to multiculturalism. People interviewed were disconnected from politicians at the national level but also at the local level, where it was perceived that their political leaders failed to provide public goods and services. Jobs had been lost, housing was difficult to access and cuts had been made to local services, but they did not view this through the prism of immigration. This was not a reactionary voice. Instead, nuanced, complex and sometimes contradictory views were expressed.

Chapter Six: Integrated and equal: similar challenges and opportunities

The second of the two fieldwork chapters will rely on field research to illustrate the weakness of national policy frameworks such as community cohesion, which was touted as a model to bring communities together. Community cohesion focused on the disconnect between people and their government and yet it was viewed as remote and bureaucratic to the lived experiences of the communities engaged. Policies were seen as imposing doctrinaire solutions that favoured some groups and not others and there was a lack of clarity on concepts. The common failure was the perception that policies were 'top-down' when the need was for 'bottom-up', with consideration to solutions that also took into account locality. The research commits itself to a long-term and strategic approach to viewing multiculturalism and change rather than one that is driven by ad hoc, short-term political expediency. Moreover, the research also demonstrated how white working-class communities rejected the politics of extremism. Instead, people wanted fairness, not favours, and projects embedded in lived experiences. Therefore, Chapters Five and Six illustrate the gaps between policy, research and local practice.

Chapter Seven: Reshaping white working-class identities: inclusive and progressive

The final chapter will attempt to construct a different narrative on white working-class politics related to multiculturalism and change. Commonalities exist with minority communities in terms of class, values and space, as well as personal interactions, such as relationships and marriage, in the context of work or school. White working-class communities have also been at the forefront of collective bargaining actions through trade unions and have played a critical role in demonstrating a desire for anti-racism in popular movements such as 2 Tone. This suggests that white working-class communities can be viewed as being inclusive and progressive on multiculturalism. However, we need to remember that polling on immigration has revealed that most social classes in Britain favour greater restrictions on immigration. The message that needs to be emphasised is that white working-class communities should be regarded as being as diverse as any other group in society in response to issues of immigration. There is a need for institutions to reconnect and promote coalitions of interest between different groups at a grassroots level. This agenda for change reinforces the role of the state as facilitator rather than driver. The book will conclude by encouraging ongoing discussion and debate on these complex and controversial issues.

TWO

Multiculturalism and the exclusion of the white working class

Introduction

How did the white working class come to be seen as 'a rabble' when it was once perceived as the bedrock in the building of modern Britain? This question will be explored in the context of multiculturalism and, more specifically, whether its rise paralleled the decline of the voice of the white working class. Our contention is that it was not multiculturalism that led to the marginality of this group in the debates on identity and social change, but shifting policy and political priorities.

Recently, there has been plenty of discussion in political and academic debates about the decline in multiculturalism. Its place as a policy framework has been taken initially by community cohesion and latterly integration. Community cohesion, which emerged after the riots of 2001 in Burnley, Oldham and Bradford, may be viewed as problematic due to its emphasis on nebulous norms and culture as well as problematic differences in visible minority communities. Low-income white communities were key protagonists in the riots but were largely absent from the slew of government-sponsored reports that were published soon afterwards. In itself, this is not surprising given that academic research on race has tended to frame the white working class as either silent, or an adversarial opponent of migrants and hostile towards immigration.

This chapter will suggest that deindustrialisation and the rise of New Labour were among the key drivers for the loss of the white working-class voice and not multiculturalism. In particular, the political strategy of maximising middle-class votes by occupying a centrist position in politics confined the white working class to the political margins. However, Labour's defeat in the 2010 general election led to a renewed interest in the white working class. This can be seen in the influence of the 'Blue Labour' grouping, with its emphasis on communitarian and class values, as well as in the success of the ultra-nationalist UKIP, which while formerly viewed as a refuge for right-wing Conservatives in the south-east of England, changed its strategy to appeal to white working-class voters who had traditionally voted Labour, with a good deal of success in the 2014 elections.

There is a danger that this renewed interest in working-class politics and identity may be politically and socially counterproductive. In the search for quick fixes, invoking the memory of an idealised working-class past, eroded through the loss of institutions like the public house and the working men's club and electoral disenfranchisement, runs the risk of a nostalgic return to the reification of white working-class communities as being backward, resistant to change and supporters of extreme positions. The heightened interest in whiteness and the working class need not be reactionary towards multiculturalism.

Multiculturalism replacing class

One of the problems in discussing multiculturalism is the tendency for it to be conflated in public policy discussions and subsequently used and abused by those seeking specific political ends (Blunkett, 2002; Goodhart, 2004; Cameron, 2011). Just as discussions about the 'white working class' lack a solid definition, 'multiculturalism' morphs into a slippery concept that becomes an easy target on which to pin increasing levels of residential segregation based on ethnicity and the breakdown of trust between white working-class and minority communities (Cantle, 2005; Phillips, 2005).

Multiculturalism, in its many guises and applications, has to be reviewed. The inconspicuousness silencing or muting of the working class may support a 'common sense' agenda for detractors, but the reality is somewhat different. The voice of the white working class was loud, barbed and arguably distorted in widely viewed programmes such as *Till Death Us Do Part* (1965), where the main character were portrayed as a racist, older white working-class man. These slanted versions of white working-class life reinforced a reified narrative of the problems of multiculturalism within a context of societal change during the 1960s and 1970s, which was also a period when TV became widely popular and a lens to depict society. The cultural representation of white working-class communities is addressed in Chapter Four.

Moving to the 2000s, some have suggested that multiculturalism, and the way in which it has been portrayed by government and the media, may have led to the diminution of white working-class communities (Haylett, 2001; Dench et al, 2006; Webster, 2008). This is not to say that these interventions in popular culture, drama and documentary are of the same tone and virulence as policy and political interventions (eg Goodhart, 2004; Cameron, 2011). However, the critique may become part of an overall sweep to undermine and dismantle multiculturalism, leading the way for racialised public discourse with the white working class as both agency and victim.

Defining multiculturalism is therefore challenging. A number of academics have attempted to come to terms with its meaning in different types of policy interventions ('The Crick Report' [Qualifications and Curriculum Authority, 1998]; 'The Parekh Report' [The Runnymede Trust, 2000]). Ostensibly, the Crick Report was concerned with establishing citizenship education in the school curriculum. It also defined Britain as a multicultural country that celebrates and, indeed, takes pride in the differences between communities:

> We see a multicultural society as one made up of a diverse range of cultures and identities, and one that emphasises the need for a continuous process of mutual engagement and learning about each other with respect, understanding and tolerance – whether in social, cultural, educational, professional, political or legal spheres. Such societies, under a framework of common civic values and common legal and political institutions, not only understand and tolerate diversities of identity but should also respect and take pride in them. (Qualifications and Curriculum Authority, 1998: 10)

Crick also rails against fixed and essentialised categories and instead puts forward the idea of people having fluid or multiple identities (Qualifications and Curriculum Authority, 1998). The tenor of the report suggests that the British history taught in schools should be modernised to include a review of how immigrants have helped to shape the country. The themes of Crick were picked up by 'The Commission on the Future of Multi-Ethnic Britain', coordinated by The Runnymede Trust – the race relations think tank – and supported by the New Labour administration that came to power following its landslide election victory of 1997. This is also sometimes referred to as the Parekh Report after its chairman, Bikhu Parekh. One of the most quoted passages from the report on multiculturalism inferred that Britain, and being British, was not simply a bounded category sealed by the borders of the nation-state, but much more nuanced. Multiculturalism in Britain had created new and fluid identities: 'Britain is both a community of citizens and a community of communities, both a liberal and a multicultural society, and needs to reconcile their sometimes conflicting requirements' (Parekh, 2000: preface).

The Parekh Report underpins its key message of the reality of different and diverse communities that need to be treated with respect within a set of liberal principles, including recognising difference, addressing racial disadvantage and linking multiculturalism within a human rights framework (Parekh, 2000). In a separate contribution to the report, Parekh expounds on the Commission's findings when he suggests that:

> multiculturalism is about the proper terms of relationship between different cultural communities. The norms governing their respective claims, including the principles of justice, cannot be derived from one culture alone but through an open and equal dialogue between them ... by definition a multicultural society consists of several cultures or cultural communities with their own distinct systems of meaning and significance and views on man and the world. (Parekh, 2000: 13)

The Parekh Report is viewed as a credible and serious affirmation of multiculturalism (see Amin, 2002; Madood, 2007; Rattansi, 2012). It embraced the tradition of difference and a view of Britain composed of a mosaic of communities and identities, which is a description of multiculturalism. Moreover, identity was not shaped by whiteness or a dominant monoculture, but was fluid and contextualised according to locality, ideology and history. In the following passage, the report discusses Britain not as a single homogeneous entity, but as marked by many different and sometimes overlapping communities:

> Britain needs to be, certainly, 'One Nation' – but understood as a community of communities and a community of citizens, not a place of oppressive uniformity based on a single substantive culture. Cohesion in such a community derives from widespread commitment to certain core values, both between communities and within them: equality and fairness; dialogue and consultation; toleration, compromise and accommodation; recognition of and respect for diversity; and – by no means least – determination to confront and eliminate racism and xenophobia. (The Runnymede Trust, 2000: 56)

Recognition of the '*One Nation*' concept advances the idea of an inclusive and progressive national entity. Interestingly, it has been invoked by both the Conservative and Labour parties to develop a style of policies that seek to address social inequality.[1] This does not advocate for a majority culture – such as whiteness – as the basis for national identity, but argues for explicit recognition of difference and diversity. In this way, it is counter to subsequent government interventions on the reduced value of multiculturalism and the emergence of community cohesion (Home Office, 2001) and integration (DCLG, 2012,). Here, there is relatively little discussion of Britain as being composed of a 'community of communities'. On the contrary, established and emerging minorities need to adapt to core national values focused on an essentialised view of British identity. In these new narratives, multiculturalism becomes not so much something to aspire to, but an obstacle preventing a cohesive and integrated country. Of course, increased levels of ethnic diversity were viewed by some as challenging notions of national identity, values and social mores (Home Office, 2001; Goodhart, 2004; Cameron, 2011).

The final element in the '*community of communities*' reference is the commitment to addressing racism. A key theme of this book is that the replacement of multiculturalism, initially with community cohesion and later with integration has led to a much more racialised public policy debate. The focus has been less on tackling racism and more on highlighting the adverse impact of immigration, the welfare burden of refugees and asylum seekers, and the involvement of British Muslims in violent extremism. The electoral success of racist parties like the British National Party (BNP) at the 2009 European elections or ultra-nationalist groupings such as UKIP at the same elections in 2014, media fixation on negative stories about immigrants and minority communities, and the push by national politicians for stricter immigration controls result in a febrile political environment in marked contrast to support for anti-racism during the 1980s and 1990s.

Addressing racism as part of the ethos of multiculturalism is important because the concept has been criticised as being based on a passive culturalism rather than a strong anti-racist framework. Kymlicka, a strong advocate of multiculturalism, suggests a more complex history rooted in the recognition of universal human rights and the need to hold to account dominant and unequal norms and hierarchies (Kymlicka, 2012). This progressive and activist perspective rejects the projection of multiculturalism as simply a celebration of cultural difference, which fixes on music, cuisine and the arts as uncritical symbolism (see Alibhai-Brown, 2000). Seen in this context, multiculturalism is not only benign, but also potentially problematic because it may place minority rights and identity above majority communities. Alternatively, in the human rights approach, multiculturalism is rooted in the civil rights and protest movements that were the catalyst for decolonisation after 1945, the mobilisation against racism and discrimination, and the campaign for minority rights. Multiculturalism thus becomes less a description of difference and more an agency for social change.

The Parekh Report addresses whiteness as being an important, but not exclusive, part of English or even British identity. Whiteness is given as the default racial code for British identity: 'Britishness, as much as Englishness, has systematic, largely unspoken, racial connotations. Whiteness nowhere features as an explicit condition of being British, but it is widely understood that Englishness, and therefore by extension Britishness, is racially coded' (The Runnymede Trust, 2000: para 3.4). The inference, and certainly the way in which the findings were received by a resolutely nationalist press, was that British identity equated to white identity. Interestingly, the reference to 'largely unspoken, racial connotations' could be interpreted as the invisible dominant norm of whiteness that bounds and conveys privilege to groups marked by this identity, including the white working class. Again, the report emphasised that multiculturalism may lead to a more inclusive country. Minority groups, who had not been viewed as part of nation-building, could be valued for their contribution to British life (see, eg, Fryer, 1984). The framing of British identity as being predicated on whiteness was deconstructed by the Commission's report.

Therefore, the Commission on the Future of Multi-Ethnic Britain remains the most coherent and sustained undertaking on multiculturalism. In promoting the idea that the country was a 'community of communities', recognising that identity had been bound to whiteness and that racism was prevalent, the Commission gave credence to the reality of a multicultural society in the latter half of the 20th century and gave hope to what Britain could be in the 21st century. As the statement on multiculturalism was published, some suggested that working-class whiteness during the early period of the New Labour government in 1997 was marked by references to backwardness, chaotic lifestyles and archaic and dangerous public spaces, such as public sector council estates. Arguably, the dominant narrative during this period was of working-class people being welfare-dependent with large families and uncontrollable children, of teenage women having babies, and of a dominant culture of unemployment in neighbourhoods composed of social housing that were closed to outsiders and beset with violence (Hanley, 2007; Haylett, 2001; Jones, 2011; Lawler, 2012). Certainly, before the 2001 riots and the emergence of community cohesion (Home Office, 2001), following the Parekh Report and also the Macpherson Report into the murder of the black teenager Stephen Lawrence in 1993 (Home Office, 1999) the national perspective viewed Britain as a modern, diverse, multicultural and inclusive country. Those who did not accept this viewpoint, or who felt uneasy about multiculturalism, were seen as backward and marginal (Haylett, 2001). As we shall discuss in Chapters Five and Six, the national framing of communities as being fixed and in conflict with each other is not borne out by the actual experiences of people living in working-class neighbourhoods.

To some, 'multiculturalism' is a limp term describing cultural interaction in Britain. However, this ignores human rights and downplays anti-racism in shaping the concept. A good example of the overlap between these two approaches is the campaign for a better deal for minority communities on social housing (see Harrison, 1995; Beider, 2007, 2012). For most of the post-1945 period, colonial immigrants from the Caribbean and Indian subcontinent had been locked out of social housing by a racialised political climate and racist discrimination in housing allocation practised by local authorities (Rex and Tomlinson, 1979; Beider, 2012). The combination of national frameworks and local implementation disadvantaged minority communities and impacted on life chances and outcomes as minority communities lived in overcrowded and poor-quality private sector housing (see Daniel, 1968). The campaign to improve housing conditions was based on anti-racism practice and securing a multicultural society for Britain. It was led locally by black-led housing associations (see Harrison, 1995) and nationally by the Federation of Black Housing Organisations (Beider, 2012). These early, radical roots of multiculturalism pre-dated the 1981 and 1985 riots in Britain's inner cities, and the subsequent government-sponsored policies designed to address discrimination against people and the renewal of neighbourhoods. These were an example of grassroots multiculturalism campaigns that are in sharp contrast with the way in which recent government interventions have viewed the concept. As Kundnani (2012: 157) notes:

> by the 1980s there were at least two ideas of multiculturalism in Britain, often in conflict with each other: a 'top-down' multiculturalism which was about managing communities, and a 'bottom up' multiculturalism which was about shared political struggle. For the former, culture and ethnicity were the main ways in which minority identity was conceived, while blackness as a positive political identity was seen as problematic.

The dichotomy is not only 'bottom-up' and 'top-down', but also spatial. For example, the way in which multiculturalism is discussed and implemented in London may be different to that in Birmingham or Newcastle. The importance of locality to perceptions of multiculturalism has been emphasised by research conducted by Ipsos Mori, which consistently revealed the spatial disparities regarding questions of difference and diversity, with respondents in London much more progressive on issues of immigration and multiculturalism than in other parts of the country (see Ipsos Mori, 2014). London, and other major British cities, being ethnically diverse and supportive of multiculturalism appears to have been verified by the 2014 European election results, which showed UKIP gaining only 16% of the vote in London compared to 27% in the wider country (see BBC, 2014). Multiculturalism may play out differently based on people, politics and ideology (see Kymlicka, 2012). Critics of multiculturalism sometimes view the concept as one-dimensional. This makes it easier to dismiss or demonise multiculturalism because the concept may be distorted when a rationale is given to explain the disconnection and discontentment with politicians and the government. In short, multiculturalism is a convenient distraction for inadequate political leadership.

Taken a step further, multiculturalism, in its many formats and themes, should be viewed not as being undeviated, but as being uneven and messy (Parekh, 2000; Madood, 2007; Bloemraadd et al, 2008). The problematic framing of multiculturalism by successive governments since the 2001 riots makes it easier to blame the concept rather than government for white working-class resentment, anger and exclusion (Sveinsson, 2009). After all, the politics of race and immigration since 1945 has been studded with 'moral panics' about the problems of managing increased levels of multiculturalism, including the 1958 Notting Hill race riots, the 'Rivers of Blood Speech' in 1968 and Margaret Thatcher's assertion in 1978 that citizens were concerned with Britain being *'swamped'* with immigrants (Solomos, 2003 Tomlinson, 2013). These three events, 10 years apart, are symptomatic of how multiculturalism has been challenged by referencing the concerns of *'ordinary people'*. Uneasiness about the competition for jobs and housing or anxiety about the dilution of a white British identity and culture is easily invoked by referencing working-class concerns. They are the victims of both immigration and multiculturalism (Dench et al, 2006; Gillborn, 2009). It is almost as if in the debates on the white working class and difference, class can only become prominent if multiculturalism is reduced in importance. This is the underlying assumption of The Runnymede Trust publication *Who cares about the white working class?*:

> the issue of class is not a problem of structure, but a problem of culture ... there is no working class anymore ... unless we are talking about multiculturalism, in which case the working class resurfaces from the depths of British history ... it is permissible to use class as a stick to beat multiculturalism. (Sveinsson, 2009: 4)

Reverse privilege is put forward to explain the resentment felt by the white working class. In this way, white privilege in employment and welfare markets has been inversed by multiculturalism and the perceived unfair advantage it gives to minority communities. To this end, Kenny (2011) has discussed the recognition claims by the white working class and points to the challenges for a political system in mediating competing interests. Others suggest that multiculturalism provides a platform for minority communities to gain voice and recognition and relegates the concerns of white working-class communities (Collins, 2005). The problem is compounded when grievances and concerns related to the increased competition for resources are viewed by policymakers as being based on maintaining a privileged status at the expense of overriding needs by groups who are nationalistic, racist or both. Being viewed as backward and bigoted further weakens claims by white working-class communities (National Community Forum, 2009).

As discussed earlier, the invisibility of whiteness may be deemed as the norm compared to the visibility of minority communities (Dyer, 2006). It is only when class is interjected that whiteness is recognised, or when whiteness becomes 'dirty' (Skeggs, 2005). The white working class was branded as 'dirty whiteness' through references to chaotic lives lived in annexed council estates a comfortable distance apart from the acceptable norms of invisible or 'clean whiteness'. Jones (2011) has illustrated how the media contributes to the construct of this visible working-class whiteness by discussing the details of the case of Karen Matthews. Matthews, along with a friend and a member of the family, was convicted of kidnapping her own daughter, Shannon, while pretending to be a concerned mother, in the hope that she would receive donations by concerned supporters. Karen Matthews became the poster child for the 'dirty whiteness' of the working class: a woman living on benefits in a council flat in Dewsbury in northern England, having given birth to seven children from five different fathers (*The Observer*, 2008; Jones, 2011). Compared to this chaotic lifestyle, the cool modernism of multiculturalism and its embrace by middle-class communities and consumers merely emphasised the outmoded world inhabited by the white working class (Haylett, 2001; Lawler, 2012). In this way, 'dirty whiteness' and its contribution to the debates on multiculturalism, identity and societal change is framed as lacking credibility. The depiction of white working-class communities is underpinned by unreconstructed racism, laced with an idealised view of the past that never existed. Again, this is compared by media commentators with middle-class adaptability on difference and diversity. Nayak (2009: 29) suggests that 'In contrast to the parochial whiteness thought to be inhabited by sections of the working class, the bourgeoisie tend to be envisaged as mobile, cosmopolitan citizens no longer rooted to archaic images of whiteness'.

The apparent acceptance of multiculturalism by the middle class compared with working-class rejection is constructed around the themes of social mobility, income and cultural taste. Above all, it is bounded by structural inequality. The middle class have greater spending power to enjoy international holidays, sample different types of cuisine and appreciate multicultural aesthetics. On balance, this may be too simplistic and it further stereotypes white working-class communities. However, recent research shows that negative attitudes on immigration cut across class boundaries (Ipsos Mori, 2014). In general, working-class groups, defined by C2, D and E or the new expanded categories based on social networks and cultural class (BBC Class Survey, 2013), tend to record higher levels of support in response to questions posed on firmer immigration controls (Ford and Goodwin, 2014; Kaufman and Harris, 2014). This seems to indicate that a significant section of the white working class vote for political parties of the Right and are persuaded to do so because of cultural factors related to the impact of immigration, loss of identity and increasing competition for jobs.

White working–class anti–immigrant sentiment is not new. In the 1960s, the influential Labour politician Richard Crossman acknowledged the vulnerability of the Labour Party to immigration in his 'Diaries' (Crossman, 1991). However, recent research using a mixed methodology, including in-depth interviewing, shows that working-class communities hold a range of views on multiculturalism and social change (Garner, 2011; Pearce and Milne, 2010; Beider, 2011, 2014). This will be explored in depth later on in the book.

Declining multiculturalism

According to Kymlicka (2012), the view that multiculturalism is in decline has become an unfortunate 'master narrative'. Some theorists have suggested that there has been a 'wholesale retreat' (Joppke, 2004), while others have announced its 'death' (Kundnani, 2002, 2012). Alongside the academic debate, political leaders across the European Union have made openly hostile pronouncements on multiculturalism. For example, in a 2010 speech given to a youth meeting of her Christian Democratic Party, German Chancellor Angela Merkel stated that multiculturalism and the idea of people of different cultures living side by side '*had utterly failed*',[2] and former French President Nicolas Sarkozy suggested in 2011 that newcomers who did not integrate into French society were '*not welcome*'.[3] In between, and to complete the commentary from the leaders of the three most powerful European countries, the British Prime Minister David Cameron attacked multiculturalism at a security conference held in Munich in 2011:

> Under the doctrine of State multiculturalism, we have encouraged different cultures to live separate lives, apart from each other and the mainstream. We have failed to provide a vision of society to which they feel they want to belong. We have even tolerated these segregated communities behaving in ways that run counter to our values. So when a white person holds objectionable views – racism, for example – we rightly condemn them. But when equally unacceptable views or practices have come from someone who isn't white, we've been too cautious, frankly even fearful, to stand up to them. (Cameron, 2011)

It is important to emphasise the context of these three interventions by the political leaders of Germany, France and Britain. The political shadow was provided by the threat of immigration into Europe and the spectre of Islam. After the attacks in New York City and Washington DC on 11 September 2001, the '*War on Terror*' and the Anglo-American led invasions in Iraq and Afghanistan, the terrorist bombings in Madrid in 2004 and London in 2005, Islam and specifically Muslims were framed as the problematic 'other' (Kundnani, 2007). Multiculturalism, viewed as promoting respect for different cultures, or a 'community of communities', was seen as being responsible for supporting European citizens who instigated terror campaigns against the countries of their birth. Not only is this viewed as detrimental to majority white identity

(Goodhart, 2004), but it also challenges the security of the nation-state (Kundnani, 2007).

Multiculturalism may not be in retreat, but it has certainly been in decline from its peak in 2000 with the publication of the Parekh Report. Ironically, the weakening of multiculturalism has created space for the white working class to be redeemed. In the apparent decline, retreat or death of multiculturalism, the white working class may be able to shed their problematic status. They are no longer part of 'dirty whiteness', but may now be viewed as fully contributing members to a new re-racialised (Schwartz, 1996) 'British identity', an identity that has become a central metaphor in the post-11 September domestic landscape. New Labour attempted to reclaim the white working-class 'rabble' with policies of social exclusion (Murray,1996) and the Conservative–Liberal Democrat Coalition discussed how the 'feral underclass' could be disciplined by initiatives such as 'Troubled Families' (Clarke, 2011). Both cases could be viewed as attempts to reintegrate the white working class from the political wilderness. These are deliberate government interventions that recognise that this group needs attention and support in order to become part of the social structure of the country.

Since 2001, the sharply racialised public policy environment has supported the road to redemption for the white working class. During this period, multiculturalism has ceased to be a marker for a modern Britain (Haylett, 2001). Indeed, British Muslims have become the new toxic group for sections of the media, allowing the 'dirty whiteness' to be laundered and cleaned in the process. This shift was not as much about class as ethnicity and the role that it played in mobilising different social-economic groups against a common enemy. After all, British Muslims continue to be among the most disadvantaged sections of society (Garner and Bhattacharya, 2011). White working-class communities could be viewed as having a stronger claim on identity than British Muslims. This is likely to continue given the success of the UKIP strategy that targeted white working-class communities in the 2014 elections. Admittedly, they are pathologised by the media and continue to be viewed as problematic (Sveinsson, 2009; Jones, 2011). However, unlike British Muslims, they have never been considered as a national threat, nor affiliated with terrorism.

Before reflecting on the role and impact of community cohesion in public policy from 2001, it is worth noting that there was a time when multiculturalism was perceived in a positive and progressive light. The publication of the Parekh Report was seen as a plan for managing difference as Britain moved into the 21st century (The Runnymede

Trust, 2000). There was explicit recognition that British identity was not simply about whiteness and that it needed to expand to recognise and include the reality of difference in a country comprised of a *'community of communities'* (The Runnymede Trust, 2000). As noted previously, the government was putting forward the vision of Britain as a modern, diverse country in 2000, and yet only 12 months later, after the 2001 riots, the Parekh Report recommendations were shelved and a much harsher and racialised climate was ushered in.

Although the Parekh Report was an important statement and endorsement of multiculturalism, the Macpherson Report, which delved into the murder of the black teenager Stephen Lawrence, should be viewed as a high point for race relations in post-1945 Britain (Home Office, 1999). The narrative is well known: a failed police investigation into the murder in 1993 initially resulted in the perpetrators escaping conviction. The publication of the report, whose influence extended beyond the urban landscape of South-East London where the crime was initially committed, redefined what constitutes a racist incident and defined institutional racism. Public sector organisations were held to account by the government on race equality as never before (see Bourne, 2001; Kundnani, 2002).

Britain was shocked by the conclusions reached in the Macpherson Report. In the pre-11 September, pre-community cohesion public policy space, media reactions were especially interesting. Surprisingly, one of the leading and progressive voices in the debate was the Conservative-supporting publication *The Daily Mail*. The paper launched a *Justice for Stephen Lawrence* campaign that was partly premised on finding evidence to convict his killers (Neal, 2003). In a reversal of the traditional racialised imaginary, the Lawrence family was viewed as the personification of British values – decent, hard-working and aspirational – while the five suspects were seen as the embodiment of 'dirty whiteness' – violent racist thugs, a criminal underclass, low achievers. Here was the white working class fulfilling every negative stereotype. The suspects lived in working-class South-East London on the Brooke estate. This was viewed as depressing public sector housing with a racist reputation that excluded anyone who was not white and working-class. As *The Daily Mail* reported in 1998: 'Sitting outside multicultural London this is an area blighted by racism, sometimes crude and violent, sometimes casual and unthinking but always lurking there like a malignant cancer' (cited in Murji and Solomos, 2005: 174). The causation implied by *The Daily Mail* is clear: association by residency defines you as racist. The deviancy of white working-class people living in detached council estates was perceived as being a threat to societal norms and modern multiculturalism (Hylatt, 2001; Nayak, 2009). *The Daily Mail* classed as well as raced the white working class in coming to these conclusions. Their whiteness and residence were exposed as being at odds with Britain. McLaughlin (2005: 175) summarised the approach: 'Readers were left in little doubt that the intrinsic violently racist culture of the semi-suburban racist working class estate that had bred the five suspects was a place at odds with not just nearby multicultural London but Middle England'.

Neal suggests that media coverage of the Lawrence suspects showed the shifting narratives on race and identity. The newspaper coverage of the 1981 riots in inner-city neighbourhoods, which largely involved minority groups and the police (Scarman, 1981; Benyon and Solomos, 1987), focused on masculinity, threats and violence from black communities. By 1999, the Lawrence family had won respect for their campaign to find justice for their dead son and the opprobrium was heaped onto the deviance and violence of white working-class men, represented in the five suspects:

> Black bodies in February 1999 were inscribed with dignity, courage, restraint and most significantly lawfulness … it was white bodies that signified danger, lawfulness … the five suspected men were … 'reassuring' or 'easy villains' … figures whose racism could be identified with a particular form of white masculinity that was distanced from 'mainstream society'.… *The Times* … discussed their' revolting racism' … and gave details … of their deviant/'underclass' family backgrounds. (Neal, 2003: 68)

In both the Macpherson and Parekh Reports it is white identity that is regarded as being problematic and needing to adapt and change to modern Britain. In the aftermath of the Macpherson Report, at the micro-level, institutions were implored to review and address the scale of racism; at the macro-policy level, white working-class neighbourhoods were viewed as being deviant and dangerous places. The Parekh Report called for a reframing of national identity that included the experiences of non-white Britons. This, together with public recognition of multiculturalism (The Runnymede Trust, 2000) and the extent of racism (Home Office, 1999), should have led to the reshaping of Britain as a progressive, multicultural society embracing the new century. Instead, it marked an onslaught against multiculturalism led by successive governments, supported by voices drawn from the Right, as well as what could once be formally described as the Left.

Community cohesion was the most significant policy intervention into race relations during the time of the Labour government, which was first elected in 1997 and then ejected in 2010 (Home Office, 2001). Of course, both the Parekh and Macpherson Reports were important statements on multiculturalism and racism but these interventions were pre-11 September. Beyond 2001, race, identity and security became intertwined, leading to a sustained period of racialised discourse (Kundnani, 2002; Cheong et al, 2007).

After the 2001 summer disturbances in Burnley, Oldham and Bradford, the Labour government led by Tony Blair commissioned an inquiry to identify the causes of the riots and recommend solutions (Home Office, 2001). This report, along with individual inquiries based in Bradford (Ouseley, 2001), Oldham (Ritchie, 2001) and Burnley (Clarke, 2001), established a common narrative for the disturbances that subsequently transformed debates on multiculturalism. The emphasis in each of the reports, to a lesser or greater extent, was on fragmented communities divided along faith and ethnic lines living in poor towns and cities (Back et al, 2002; Ratcliffe, 2013).

Admittedly, many of the reports noted that the riots took place in areas with high levels of socio-economic disadvantage. Towns like Burnley and Oldham and cities such as Bradford were transitioning into a post-industrial state that had been many decades in the making (Amin, 2002). This being said, the causes of the riots were not attributed to economic, but cultural, factors. Specifically, the notion was that Asian[4] and white working-class communities had self-segregated even though they lived in contiguous neighbourhoods. The emergence of the phrase '*parallel lives*' in the community cohesion literature was coined, describing entrenched levels of segregation. The Home Office (2001) report clearly viewed this as being about cultural distance. In putting forward the thesis of '*parallel lives*', community cohesion was sounding the death knell of multiculturalism. For example, let us consider the following extract from the report:

> Whilst the physical segregation of housing estates and inner city areas came as no surprise, the team was particularly struck by the depth of polarisation of our town and cities. The extent to which these physical divisions were compounded by so many aspects of our daily lives was very evident. Separate educational arrangements, community and voluntary bodies, employment, places of worship, language, social and cultural networks, means that many communities operate on the basis of a series of parallel

lives. These lives often do not seem to touch at any point, let alone overlap and promote any meaningful exchanges. (Home Office, 2001: 9)

Community cohesion then pitted the white working class against British Muslims on the basis of cultural, but also spatial, boundaries. Clearly, the inference was that the former lived in 'housing estates' while the latter were located in 'inner-city areas'. The imagery of segregated communities playing out as a localised '*clash of civilisations*' (Huntington, 1993) is evident in many of the reports. The culprit was not jobs, racism or even addressing the many challenges of post-industrialisation; it was simply multiculturalism, which was depicted as deepening the divisions between white working-class and Asian communities (Home Office, 2001; Back et al, 2002). Given that the problem was community fragmentation, the solution was to be found in creating spaces for cultural contact within the frame of common values (Home Office, 2001). Yet, a definition of community cohesion, or, more accurately, a cohesive community, was not provided until 2002 when the Local Government Association provided practical guidance to local authorities. Here, a cohesive community had a number of features:

There is a common vision and a sense of belonging for all communities; the diversity of people's different backgrounds and circumstances are appreciated and valued; those from different backgrounds have similar life opportunities; and strong and positive relationships are being developed between people from different backgrounds in the workplace, in schools and within neighbourhoods. (Local Government Association, 2002: 6)

Nevertheless, the government acknowledged that white working-class communities felt excluded from local investment plans, as well as the wider debates on multiculturalism, as the following quote from a government minister at the time shows:

We must, absolutely, continue to tackle and challenge racist behaviour and discrimination and, of course, as part of that work we have to question why it is that often black and ethnic minority people who experience poor housing have poor achievement at school and high levels of unemployment. But I do think that nothing is more dangerous than giving the impression that this is a process driven by statistics rather than a process that is for people. That all the efforts are targeted at those communities that are most statistically deprived to the exclusion of other communities, particularly the white community or those parts of the white community that suffer similar levels of deprivation.... Now I am not saying this is what happens at the moment, but the perception of that being the case is not something we can ignore. (Denham, 2002)

From this point, community cohesion and a culturalist approach became the dominant policy framework for race and identity through to the end of the Labour government's term in 2010. Initially, the focus was on sharpening the definition of community cohesion, devising practical guidance for organisations to implement strategies and assessing impact. As with the first reports on the 2001 disturbances, the emphasis was to develop common values and norms between different communities (Local Government Association, 2002). A non-government panel was established to advise the government following the riots. Its work concluded with a final report, *The end of parallel lives?* (Home Office, 2004), which recommended mainstreaming community cohesion into public services (Cantle, 2005). The Home Office (2005) publication *Improving opportunity, strengthening society* continued the strong emphasis on common norms and increasing interaction between different groups. Creating community cohesion was one of the four key themes, alongside addressing inequality, promoting inclusiveness and tackling racism and extremism.

Taking this further, the themes of common norms and values, together with integration, underlay the report of the Commission on Integration and Cohesion (CIC). This report was published by the Labour government following the London bombings of 7 July 2005 in an attempt to address issues of cohesion, integration and extremism. The report further solidified the notions of cultural estrangement between entrenched and embedded ethnic communities. The solution was building a '*shared vision*' that pulled disparate communities together under a sense of mutual self-obligation (CIC, 2007). This was viewed as a further significant move away from multiculturalism and towards cultural assimilation (Husband and Alam, 2011).

Earlier in this chapter, we discussed how some scholars viewed whiteness as being invisible in the different iterations of multiculturalism. The white working class was almost a non-group compared to the visibility of minority communities and the importance of addressing racism following a number of interventions, including the Scarman

(1981), Macpherson (Home Office, 1999) and Parekh (2000) Reports. This should have changed following the 2001 riots, and the advent of community cohesion, because white working-class communities were not ambivalent bystanders, but actively took part in the disturbances. However, in the community cohesion reports (Clarke, 2001; Home Office, 2001; Ouseley, 2001; Ritchie, 2001), as well as the CIC (2007) publication, white working-class communities were represented as angry, as resentful and as blaming the government and Asians for their predicament (Ouseley, 2001).

The CIC report has fewer than five references to the white working class. Their absence may seem puzzling because they are part of the story of the 2001 riots. Yet, following the attacks of 11 September 2001 and 7 July 2005, Britain was gripped not by community cohesion, but a fear of violent extremism that fixated on British Muslims (Husband and Alam, 2011). The London bombings of 7 July 2005 created the spectre of 'home-grown terrorists'. The assumption was that British Muslims who were born or raised in the country had become so detached that they could indiscriminately kill their follow Britons. In this context, community cohesion, based as it was on cultural self-segregation and a loss of common identity, became a perfect foil for the anti-terrorist policies geared towards addressing violent extremism known as Prevent (Kundnani, 2007). The thinking was that not only had multiculturalism become the cause of segregation between communities (Phillips, 2005), but it had implicitly led to a situation where violent extremism was given intellectual space to attack Britain. The transformation of the multiculturalism and anti-racism of 2000 to a position in 2005 that focused on Muslims as problematic left some incredulous:

> But here we need to enquire how it is that a demographic reality which indicates that Britain is de facto an implacably multi-ethnic society ... becomes translated into a heavily politicised discourse in which multiculturalism as a principle and practice of managing diversity has become vilified. (Husband and Alam, 2011: 78)

Community cohesion, and the agenda of preventing violent extremism, moved the focus of problematic communities from the white working class to British Muslims. Debates about cultural difference were loaded on to the premise that this group should be doing much more to adopt British values. Returning to the acculturation that dominated many sociological perspectives of the 1960s (eg Patterson, 1965) the dismantling of multiculturalism was led by voices previously associated with the Left. Goodhart (2004) suggested that multiculturalism and high levels of immigration were placing a strain on British solidarity and the redistributive welfare state. In taking this position, he frames some people who are different (eg Muslims, immigrants and asylum seekers) as being part of the 'stranger' problem: 'We feel more comfortable with, and are readier to share with and sacrifice for, those with whom we have shared histories and similar values. To put it bluntly most of us prefer our own kind' (Goodhart, 2004).

By blaming immigrants and Muslims for diluting identity and trust, neo-nationalism became de rigueur, finding support across the political spectrum (Kundnani, 2007). The retreat from multiculturalism, which was being replaced by a culturally defined racialised agenda, enabled white working-class communities to find a voice under the banner of a newly, if ill-defined, British identity. Community cohesion and the new discourse was ethnicised and essentialised (Ratcliffe, 2013). In this context, whiteness allowed the white working class to be seen as part of the nation-state that had previously excluded them.

The contention was that the diminished influence of multiculturalism, and its replacement by community cohesion, enabled the white working class to gain an accepted identity, albeit one that pitted them against the threat of Muslims and immigrants. In this way, they became and are part of the majority norms. However, this is not an explicit recognition of the white working class by policymakers, but rather a smothering of whiteness against common threats.

In 2009, the terms of reference to white working-class communities changed with Labour's announcement of the Connecting Communities programme (DCLG, 2009). This was a £12 million government initiative targeted at more than 160 neighbourhoods across the country that were badly hit by the 2007 recession. The areas varied in size and location but they shared three themes in common: first, a decline in manufacturing that impacted on jobs within white communities; second, increased immigration, perceptions of neighbourhood change and competition for jobs; and, third, problems with crime and general anti-social behaviour. At its core, Connecting Communities focused attention on the needs of white working-class communities and on preventing the rise of support for far Right organisations such as the BNP. Being supported by taxpayers' money, the programme could not state too explicitly the threat of an extremist party. Nevertheless, John Denham, the minister responsible for Connecting Communities, later admitted his concern with the rise of the BNP in an interview with the anti-fascist magazine *Searchlight*:

> Very crudely, I think you always have to be clear in your
> mind when you are talking about draining the pool in
> which extremism can take root, and when you are trying to
> tackle hard-core extremists. In Connecting Communities,
> we were not trying to take on the BNP, indeed, it was a
> state funded activity and to do that would have been quite
> illegal. But it was about trying to work in communities
> where the propensity to be open to far right extremism was
> there. And that, we said, began by giving people a voice.
> (*Searchlight*, 2013)

Connecting Communities could be viewed as a programmatic device
for government to recognise and listen to the concerns of white
working-class communities, as well as to counter the threat to Labour
from far Right parties. Perhaps this was recognition that both whiteness
and class had been too easily erased from the New Labour landscape
and there was a need for the party to reconnect to its traditional core
support. Before Connecting Communities, and, indeed, community
cohesion, the two major interventions on race relations by the Labour
government had been Parekh and Macpherson. In different ways, both
reports were focused on promoting multiculturalism and addressing
racism. Whiteness was either problematic or muted and viewed as a
barrier in the evolution of a modern Britain because it was associated
with outmoded values and racial discrimination. In addition, class had
faded from the fore because winning national elections was predicated
on the 'marketplace' of the middle ground (Cruddas, 2006). White
working-class voters were seemingly 'up for grabs' and the BNP
manoeuvred to win them with the slogan 'We're the Labour Party
your parents voted for' (see Trilling, 2012). The BNP partly succeeded
at the 2006 local elections when its vote doubled and it became the
opposition party in the London Borough of Barking and Dagenham.[5]

The government recognised that policies, including community
cohesion, had been overly concerned with minority and, especially,
Muslim communities in Britain at the expense of other groups,
particularly the white working class. Again, Denham, this time in a 1
December 2009 speech to the Trade Union Congress, suggested that
inequality need not be about race alone:

> We can only challenge racism and race inequality effectively
> as part of a strategy that tackles all forms of inequality and
> disadvantage. This must include poorer white working
> class communities, as well as disadvantaged minority ethnic

communities. Agencies which have been blind to these issues, or thought their only remit was to address minority issues, must re-assess the way they work. (*Daily Telegraph*, 2009)

The association of the white working class with the far Right has a long history (Goodwin, 2009; Trilling, 2012). However, it has been argued that the threat of the BNP at local and national elections was overplayed. Much of the extended support was located not necessarily in traditional working-class neighbourhoods, but in semi-skilled areas next to diverse constituencies (Eatwell and Goodwin, 2009). In creating policy space for the white working class, there is a risk that they become framed only as a reified group, unconditionally supportive of the BNP. This is not the case. White working-class communities engage with minority communities in the same neighbourhoods, workplaces and schools. Recent research has shown that while language may be racialised, there is a wide range of political views, including criticism of the far Right (National Community Forum, 2009; Beider, 2011, 2014).

Disappointingly, Connecting Communities was launched in 2009, almost 13 years after the Labour government was elected in 1997. There was insufficient time to consider the impact of the programme. After the defeat of Labour in the 2010 general election, the new Conservative–Liberal Democrat Coalition decided to abandon Connecting Communities, and much of the infrastructure that had been created to support community cohesion, as part of the package of measures to reduce public spending following the 2007/08 financial crash. Connecting Communities, and the focus on white working-class communities, has not been replaced in the new government framework, which is embodied in *Creating the conditions for integration* (DCLG, 2012). On balance, the Labour policy approach to white working-class communities was too little and too late. Connecting Communities was merely an appendage to the much more embedded policies of community cohesion but it did mark a change whereby the white working class became visible policy actors. This has become even more important given the success of UKIP after the 2014 local and European elections.

The Conservative–Liberal Democrat Coalition government continued with the approach of New Labour by moving away from multiculturalism. The strategy, showcased in *Creating the conditions for integration*, emphasises the importance of minorities assimilating to British culture and norms. In contrast to the New Labour approach on community cohesion, integration was not necessarily the government's responsibility, but should be locally delivered by people and civic organisations working with the state.

The white working class may be viewed as making a political comeback because of the retreat of multiculturalism and a new focus, albeit belated, in programmes such as Connecting Communities. They were reintegrated into the fold after being isolated as part of the invisible majority. An exception to this trend is the poor educational performance and disappointing outcomes of white working-class boys at school. Returning to some of the cultural frameworks that had been popularised by ideologues such as Murray (1996), this group have been described as an 'educational underclass' by the right-wing think tank Centre for Social Justice. Putting forward evidence that showed that white working-class boys were now the poorest performing students in secondary schools, their report went on to suggest 'that despite much money and effort white working-class boys are in danger of becoming an educational underclass. They are falling further behind other disadvantaged groups and they lag far behind the majority of pupils' (Centre for Social Justice, 2013).

This was again the theme of the House of Commons Education Select Committee report which showed that white boys on free school meals were performing worse compared with minority groups with a similar background. Some called to give evidence to the Select Committee suggested that this was because white working-class communities have low aspirations, for example: 'White working class culture is characterized by low aspirations and negative attitudes towards education' (House of Commons Education Select Committee, 2014). The discussion related to white working-class boys and their school performance almost seems a return to the visible 'dirty whiteness' based on pathologies and culture. These cultural frames regarding poor, white working-class boys suggest that this group are backward, in opposition to societal norms and problematic in their attitude towards education.

Some have questioned the 'master narrative' of the fall of multiculturalism (Kymlicka, 2012). It appears that multicultural policies, such as supporting minority children in education and addressing access to jobs, continue to be implemented (Madood, 2007; Kymlicka, 2012). However, it would also be disingenuous to say that there has not been a decline in the concept. Multiculturalism has been under sustained attack (Back et al, 2002; Kundnani, 2002; Cheong et al, 2007; Ratcliffe, 2013). It has been viewed by the British government as the reason why some communities are leading 'parallel lives' (Home Office, 2001). Alongside this debate, multiculturalism and increased levels of diversity were seen as eroding trust in institutions, as well as compromising a sense of national identity (Goodhart, 2004; Putnam, 2007).

The decline of multiculturalism, its replacement with cohesion and integration, and the focus on British Muslims has meant that the position of the white working class has shifted. Some initially suggested that white working-class communities were excluded by multiculturalism during the first New Labour government (Haylett, 2001). In short, the white working class were seen as problematic in building a new and diverse country fit for the 21st century because they displayed attitudes on race that were dated and backward. During this period from 1997 to 2000, the seminal Macpherson Report (Home Office,1999) could be viewed as the zenith of anti-racism in Britain (see Bourne, 2001). It was this historical moment that the white working class, and to a lesser extent, the ethnicity of those suspected of the murder of Stephen Lawrence, zoomed into sharp focus. They were white working-class trash from a dysfunctional and 'dangerous' council estate in a depressing part of South-East London (Neal, 2003). Here was the unedifying 'dirty whiteness' out of step with societal norms and the '*quiet dignity*' of the Lawrence family. The high point of post-1945 race relations in Britain was announced alongside the low point of white working-class habitats such as the Brooke Estate, which was home to some of the murder suspects. The two sides of Britain were assessed and the consensus was that a modern multicultural country was preferable to the alternative embodied by the people who occupied isolated white working-class estates.

It was only after 11 September 2001, and the emergence of community cohesion, that the white element of the white working class became part of the construct of British identity, which also marked Muslims as a problematic other. It was almost as if the retreat of multiculturalism washed away 'dirty whiteness' and while not revealing a clean and rehabilitated white working class, nevertheless removed some of the grit that had been linked to it from the discussions of the Macpherson Report. Now, the most dysfunctional group was not white working-class communities, but British Muslims.

A view seems to have formed in some of the academic and policy discussion that white working-class communities are marginalised and displaced by multiculturalism. Viewing the discussion through this lens shows the white working class as challenging the 'norms' associated with a modern society, as being out of date and obsolete, and as losing out in the competition for scarce public resources (Haylett, 2001; Hewitt, 2005; Dench et al, 2006). It is almost as if multiculturalism washes over and erases any sense of whiteness and the concept becomes a matter simply for minority communities to address. In this context, the ebbing tide of multiculturalism should be viewed as enabling whiteness to be revealed once again. Certainly, whiteness has become a core component of British identity. Conversely, apart from the short-lived Connecting Communities programme, the white working class has continued to be mocked and reified in policy debates and in the mass media (Sveinsson, 2009). Indeed, it could be argued that the white working class only started a political comeback in 2014. The push came from UKIP, once a fringe party that David Cameron described as being composed of *'fruitcakes, loonies and closet racists'*.[6]

'White backlash' and the left behind

The roots of a 'white backlash' were based in multiculturalism, with the perception that preferential treatment was being given to minority communities by the state. This zero-sum scenario resulted in white working-class communities losing out in the scramble for limited public benefits, such as housing, education and employment (see Hewitt, 2005; Rhodes, 2010). Concern about not being able to access social housing and jobs has been discussed in recent studies based on the experiences of white working-class communities in Britain, as well as a number of European cities, but it is debatable whether it could be viewed as a 'backlash' (National Community Forum, 2009; Pearce and Milne, 2010; Beider, 2011; OSF, 2014). Whether it is a concern, resentment or, indeed, a 'backlash, the perception of migrants and minorities receiving preferential treatment cannot be identified as a recent phenomenon; rather, it has deep roots going back to at least the 1960s (Rhodes, 2010).

The interventions of Enoch Powell, such as the 'speech' delivered in Birmingham in 1968, conveyed Britain as a country convulsed in racial conflict, with white opinion being ridiculed and supplanted by an increasing and unruly minority presence. Powell presented white working-class communities as being the victims of multiculturalism, being displaced in neighbourhoods by the marching tide of immigration and not being considered in policies to address racism in the workplace and in schools. This proposition continued with Margaret Thatcher's Conservative government, first elected in 1979, as it developed an approach that combined a patriotic nationalism spurred on by the Falklands conflict, as well as an attack on the anti-racist and multicultural policies implemented by left-wing Labour councils (Gilroy, 2005). However, 'white backlash' is not just a creation of Powellism and Thatcherism.

As noted, New Labour's interventions, such as community cohesion and preventing violent extremism, helped to ethnicise the public policy agenda (Ratcliffe, 2013). Immigrants and Muslims were framed as being a threat to jobs and security, which fed into a narrative on the decline of Britain as an imperial nation and its vulnerability to a new 'enemy within'. Unsurprisingly, this account, combined with the view that multiculturalism favoured everyone apart from white working-class communities, gained currency, as did resentment by the white working class for what it perceived as being lost (Hewitt, 2005; Kundnani, 2007; Rhodes, 2010). Based on his research with white working-class communities in East London, Hewitt (2005: 5) summarised white backlash in the following terms: 'White backlash ... to official policies aimed at providing equal rights, opportunities, and protection under the law'. Similarly, senior Labour politicians were articulating sentiments that seemed to embolden the 'white backlash' agenda:

> We have norms of acceptability and those who come into our home – for that is what it is – should accept those norms just as we would have to do if we went elsewhere. (David Blunkett MP, former Home Secretary, discussing the Inquiry report on the 2001 disturbances, quoted in BBC Online, 2001)

> We should look at policies where the legitimate sense of entitlement felt by the indigenous family overrides the legitimate need demonstrated by the new migrants. We should also look at drawing up different rules based on, for instance, length of residence, citizenship or national insurance contributions which carry more weight in a transparent points system used to decide who is entitled to access social housing. (Margaret Hodge MP, Barking, on addressing the impact of immigration and allaying the fears of white working-class communities, quoted in *The Guardian*, 2007)

> As we set out on the next stage of our journey this is our vision: Britain leading the global economy ... drawing on the talents of all to create British jobs for British workers. (Gordon Brown, former Prime Minister, giving his first speech to the Labour Party Conference, quoted in BBC Online, 2007)

These three statements speak to the racialised politics and positions that were formerly adopted by neo-fascist organisations such as the National Front and British Movement. Blunkett's emphasis on 'norms' and acceptability suggested that immigrants and minority communities were the equivalent to guest workers; Hodge's move to link access to social housing to the 'legitimate sense of entitlement felt by the indigenous family' put white working-class families at the head of the waiting list before the presumably illegitimate concerns of 'non-indigenous' families; Brown took a slogan from the National Front in the 1970s and put it into a New Labour context. This explicit and aggressive language racialised the political debate and was at odds with the energetic commitment to anti-racism embodied in the Macpherson findings in 1999. The could be viewed as a response to the 'backlash' politics that led to increasing support for the racist BNP and later to the ultra-nationalism of UKIP. The former secured 564,331 votes at the 2010 general election (see Trilling, 2014) and the latter, after coming second at the 2009 European elections with 2,498,226 votes (see BBC News, 2009, went one better in winning the 2014 European elections.

'White backlash', white resentment and white lack of voice have all been put forward as important reasons for the rise of UKIP, which will be discussed in Chapter Five when we consider the breakthrough and success of the Tea Party as a political movement in the US, as well as other populist right-wing movements across Europe. For now, the popularity of UKIP has been allied with renewed interest from the white working class in politics. This is explained by Ford and Goodwin (2014: 257) in a passage from their book *Revolt of the Right: Explaining the support for the radical Right*:

> UKIP's revolt is a working class phenomenon. Its support is concentrated among older, blue-collar workers, with little education and few skills: a group who have been 'left behind' by the economic and social transformation of Britain in recent decades, and pushed to the margin as the main parties have converged on the centre ground. UKIP is not a second home for disgruntled Tories in the shires: they are the first home for angry and disaffected working-class Britons of all political backgrounds, who have lost faith in a political system that ceased to represent them long ago.

The disconnection of the white working class from mainstream politics has been put forward by studies based in different locations (eg OSF, 2014). Lack of voice, discontent and frustration became recurring themes in the media in the run-up to and aftermath of the 2014 elections. For example, Chris Blackhurst (2014), writing in *The Independent*, puts forward a view that UKIP is '*Britain's most working-class party*' and he goes on to explain the reasons for its increased levels of support. These have now become a context for the mantra of the '*left behind working class*', which struggles with no prospect for employment while the government apparently supports '*wave after wave of immigrants*'. Alongside economic disconnection is the mockery from the media and political establishment about how they conduct their lives, about their cultural tastes, or lack thereof, and unhealthy eating habits. White working-class alienation is exacerbated by what it sees as the transformation of the Labour Party from a working-class to a middle-class organisation, represented by the type of person who studied at elite universities, worked as a political researcher and was then selected as a Labour candidate. Finally, there is the sense that the political establishment is represented by leaders who have the same background and speak in a similar language, which is at odds with working-class mores.

The problem for the Labour Party in losing a connection with the white working class was explored by *The Huffington Post* (2014). Much of the discussion was about losing the trust of this group, about disconnection and an undefined sense of resentment. Analysing the success of UKIP and the implications for the British Left, Nick Cohen (2014), writing in *The Guardian*, suggests that the disengagement is partly the result of political correctness and the 'policy-speak' spouted by a detached political class. The success of UKIP in attracting white working-class votes prompted six Labour MPs to write an open letter to *The Guardian* (2014). Dripping with backlash rhetoric, the letter framed the problems of immigration in terms of competition for jobs, housing, schools and even transport infrastructure. In doing so, the MPs contrasted these problems with the benefits from the inflow of migrants accruing to the middle class and businesses that take advantage of cheap foreign labour in order to support childcare or increase their profits. The letter concluded by calling for restrictions to be imposed on European immigration to relieve 'pressures' on the country. Thus, white working-class backlash against the impact of multiculturalism found a voice in UKIP. At its core, UKIP's appeal is the view that some people have been 'left behind', who are now taking retribution against the political class by voting for an insurgent party (see Ford and Goodwin, 2014). After its success at the 2014 European elections, this strategy gained credibility when UKIP targeted constituencies such as

Rotherham, Great Grimsby and Thurrock, all of which have a high proportion of working-class voters, in the 2015 general election.

The argument of the political exclusion of the white working class and its new home in organisations such as UKIP appears compelling. However, there have been a number of criticisms to this viewpoint. Rhodes (2011) suggests that it is too easy to reify the support for UKIP and the BNP as the preserve of an angry, white working class. Often, the white working class are portrayed as either in the vanguard of the Right, left behind or voiceless, which precludes perspectives that deviate from these views. As we have discussed, recent studies have shown that the reality may be different for white working-class communities, with opinions ranging from being fatalistic to embracing multiculturalism (Beider, 2011, 2014; Garner, 2011). The variation in viewpoints, and particularly those that demonstrate a progressive assessment of the issue of race, immigration and change, suggests that a more refined explanation is required.

A related issue is that white working-class voters who previously supported Labour, or did not turn out at the ballot box at all, are now prepared to switch to UKIP. Yet the evidence from polling suggests that UKIP support tends to come from middle-class Conservatives rather than working-class Labour supporters. For example, data after the 2014 local elections found that 20% of UKIP votes were drawn from former Conservatives compared to 10% from Labour.[7] However, the importance of social class is revealed and shows that the middle class are likely to be divided in terms of immigration restrictions while the working class want tougher and more immediate controls. Against this background, there is also evidence which demonstrates that working-class voters want more immediate and stricter controls on immigration than their middle-class counterparts (see Ipsos Mori, 2014). Rather than taking the view that a resentful and disconnected working class are supporting UKIP, this electorate is fractured and fluid. The popularity of UKIP in 2014, as well as the BNP in 2009, shows the importance of listening, engaging and challenging the white working class and other voters about their views on immigration. The facts are that an ultra-nationalist party won the 2014 European elections against the 'perfect storm' of a faltering economy, continued distrust in the political class and a strongly Euro-sceptical electorate. The extent to which 'backlash' politics may continue to impact on national narratives remains to be seen but this has not stopped rethinking on immigration and identity in the Labour Party – the traditional political organisation that represents the needs of the working class.

Labour is turning blue

Concern about meeting the needs of the white working class, coupled with the impact of immigration, preceded the breakthrough 2014 election for UKIP. Although New Labour has been considered as advocating a modernising endorsement of multiculturalism (Haylett, 2001), it also presided over a political narrative that associated ethnic difference with challenging the cohesiveness of British identity (Goodhart, 2004) and tended to label Muslims as a security threat (Blunkett, 2002). Policies of community cohesion (communities who were different coming together in shared values and places) and preventing violent extremism (marking out communities for special scrutiny and seeding mistrust) were contradictory in conception and practice. After the Macpherson and Parekh Reports, the Labour government moved towards a much harsher view of the merits of multiculturalism. This gained momentum through a decision to allow the free movement of workers into Britain following the 2004 expansion of the European Union. Immigration, as well as asylum and integration, became key political issues when it is estimated that a net 1.8 million migrants arrived in Britain between 1997 and 2008 (Migration Policy Institute, 2009).

There was much introspection within the Labour Party after the 2010 election defeat. Apart from the numbing loss after 13 years in power, there were some MPs who thought that immigration was partly to blame for the 5 million voters who had ceased to support Labour. In short, working-class communities felt disconnected from political parties on this issue. This was exemplified by the exchange between then Prime Minister Gordon Brown and Rochdale pensioner Gillian Duffy during the 2010 election campaign. Here was a voter who apparently exemplified the white working class – hard-working, giving 30 years of service to Rochdale Council, a lifelong Labour voter but concerned about the scale of immigration (see BBC, 2010). After listening to her concerns, and, indeed, challenging some of her ideas on immigration, Brown later referred to Duffy as '*some bigoted woman*' while being unknowingly recorded. This vignette led to a revisiting of Labour's immigration policy after the 2010 defeat. Following Brown's resignation, the former Labour Health Secretary Andy Burnham pitched himself into the leadership contest under the auspices of developing an honest debate on immigration. He was quoted as stating:

> We were in denial. We were behind the issue all the time and myths were allowed to develop. There's still ambivalence

among some in Labour about discussing immigration. I've been accused of dog-whistle politics for doing so. But it was the biggest doorstep issue in constituencies where Labour lost. People aren't racist, but they say it has increased tension, stopped them getting access to housing and lowered their wages. (Quoted in *The Independent*, 2010)

In a similar vein, Ed Balls, the former Education Secretary in the previous Labour government, identified with concerns about the impact of immigration on working-class communities but prefaced this with acknowledgement that the British economy required immigrants to support its expansion:

There have been real economic gains from the arrival of young, hard-working migrants from Eastern Europe over the past six years. But there has also been a direct impact on the wages, terms and conditions of too many people across our country – in communities ill-prepared to deal with the reality of globalisation, including the one I represent. (Quoted in *The Observer*, 2010)

Labour started recalibrating policy on immigration because it wanted to reconnect with its working-class base. Following the election of Ed Miliband as Leader, the party sought to be viewed as not pandering to minorities, while support to the white working class, or 'hard-working families', became an important political objective. This was augmented by the emergence of *Blue Labour*, a group founded by Labour strategists in the wake of the 2010 defeat (for an exploration of Blue Labour, see Glasman et al, 2011). Rejecting the neoliberal and market approach of New Labour, this new thinking urgently sought to connect with working-class voters through a mix of local democratic engagement and socially conservative views on the European Union, criminal justice and, importantly, immigration. The Blue Labour raison d'être affirms the importance of community, solidarity and mutualism, which others have described as '*family, faith and flag*'.

As we have seen, concerns about immigration, as well as the need to connect to the white working class, follows a strong tradition within the Labour Party. This was emphasised by former Housing Minister Richard Crossman (1991) in his *Diaries* when serving in the Labour government from 1964 to 1970. He referred to immigration as the 'greatest potential vote-loser if we are seen to be permitting a flood of immigrants to come in and blight the central areas in all our cities' (Crossman, 1991: 73). These sentiments did not disappear in the first decade of the 21st century. The rhetoric was increased, with interventions by the leading architect of Blue Labour, Maurice Glasman, whose contributions pointed to the adverse impact of immigration on neighbourhoods. He suggested that multiculturalism was problematic to community solidarity while immigration under New Labour had been damaging to working-class communities:

> But it is immigration and multi-culturalism which has become the big monster that we don't like to talk about ... there was no public discussion of immigration and its benefits. There was no election that was fought on that basis. Labour lied to people about the extent of immigration and the extent of illegal immigration and there has been a massive rupture of trust. (Progress, 2011)

This feeds into the tropes of working-class abandonment, disconnection and having a multicultural society imposed against its wishes. In addition, Blue Labour invokes an imagery of a better and whiter Britain in some idealised, distant past. In this way, it has alarming similarities with parties such as UKIP and the BNP, and, indeed, Glasman called for a dialogue between Labour and supporters of the racist and violent English Defence League, viewing them as an example of the angry and disillusioned voters that needed to be engaged.

The Blue Labour project appears to resonate even louder given the success of UKIP at the 2014 elections. However, it seems counterproductive and short-sighted to beat the anti-immigration drum on behalf of white working-class voters while promoting a type of social conservatism that demonises a section of minority communities when common cause ought to be forged. The working class need not be lionised as the model of social solidarity in some modern reworking of the East End of the 1950s (see Dench et al, 2006), nor should it be seen as having sole ownership of racist perspectives on multiculturalism and change. One of the challenges of the debate related to the white working class and multiculturalism is to refrain from taking positions at the extremes of the continuum and to work towards the points in between, which is often where reality lies.

Hanley has pointed to the dangers of homogenising white working-class identity by citing community solidarity in a bid to protect them from needing to change attitudes of difference, immigration and gender. She offers pithy and telling commentary on working-class exclusion and racism:

Anyone who believes that racist sentiment among working-class people was non-existent until the most recent wave of immigration must remind themselves of the dockworkers' marches in support of Enoch Powell, of support for the British Union of Fascists in the 1930s and for the National Front in the 70s. It's a form of dirty protest with a long history, and which, alas, has yet to die. (Hanley, 2011)

The white working class has long included factions that have been antagonistic to the issues of immigration and social change. To the list of Powellism and the National Front can be added: the 1958 Notting Hill riots between white working-class communities and newly arrived Caribbean migrants; the shock of the Conservatives winning a seat at the 1964 general election in the working-class constituency of Smethwick in the West Midlands; the anti-immigration campaign that endorsed the slogan 'If you want a nigger for a neighbour, vote Labour'; and, of course, the nationalist and racialised campaign at the 2014 European elections that led to the UKIP victory. The Blue Labour approach is not new. It repeats a hackneyed and racist narrative that has pocked the approach of the Labour Party to these issues in the post-1945 period.

Multiculturalism and community solidarity need not be mutually exclusive. Yet, in politics and policy, they are because increased levels of difference are too readily viewed as a threat to the white working class. In this way, the dominant framework becomes a community under siege because of immigration and multiculturalism, pitted against established and emerging minority communities, and longing for a past that was brimming with social capital. The white working class are reified as victims because of a loss of identity and are viewed as perpetrators because they are unwilling to change. Crude reductionism of this kind gives rise to a social construct that forces an identity on white working-class communities framed singly and above all else by immigration, a stance that becomes difficult to shed.

Conclusion: Multiculturalism, the white working class and the new racism

Given that the topic of multiculturalism has occupied so much attention among scholars, politicians and policymakers not just in Britain but around the world, it seems surprising that its meaning has proven so elusive. However, just like the white working class, multiculturalism has become a social construct that is shaped in many different ways to meet political objectives. The rise of multiculturalism has been associated with a corresponding reduction in the voice of white working-class communities. In short, multiculturalism symbolised the rise of identity politics in the 1970s, 1980s and 1990s and gave prominence to minority communities at the expense of white communities. Indeed, some have suggested that the simmering resentment from white working-class communities was based on the perception of preferential treatment given by the government to minorities and newly arrived immigrants. White working-class communities object not simply regarding identity (whiteness was excluded from the multiculturalism project), but also concerning the day-to-day competition for public resources, including social housing, education, social services and jobs. It follows that the rise of racist and ultra-nationalist political parties such as the BNP and UKIP has been based on the 'white backlash' against multiculturalism, which seemed to suppress white identity and exclude white working-class communities.

Reporting the decline, or even the death, of multiculturalism may be over-exaggerated as some key tenets still exist in public policy. Yet, there is little doubt that there has been a distancing from the type of multiculturalism that featured so prominently in the Parekh and Macpherson Reports of 2000 and 1999. After 2001, multiculturalism was variously eroded, undermined and vilified. In the framework of community cohesion and preventing violent extremism from 2001, and later the hard-edged integration policies introduced by the Conservative–Liberal Democrat Coalition after 2010, multiculturalism became something not to be celebrated, but to castigate. It was blamed for racial segregation, resentment and conflict between different communities and, by association, creating an environment that supported a *'clash of cultures'*.

Our analysis suggests that in the rise and decline of multiculturalism, the white working class were either ignored or seen as backward because of their attributed opposition to celebrating difference. A theme developed that multiculturalism was part of a modernisation project for Britain in the 21st century and that the white working class were viewed as being resistant to the social and cultural change so readily accepted by middle-class peers. The former were viewed as outliers, problematic and racist. As multiculturalism has ebbed and a new period of racialised discourse has been ushered in, with a focus on national identity, social norms and the threats from new immigrants and British Muslims, the definition of the white in white working class has been reconstituted as the preferred norm.

Defining the class component of the white working class continues to be a concern for the government and media, which sees it as being associated with problematic behaviour. However, as multiculturalism faded, the concept of class was also revived and came into sharp view because of increased levels of support for the BNP, as evidenced by two members of the European Parliament being elected in 2009, as well as election breakthroughs in Barking in London that focused the attention of policymakers on the white working class as an entity. Connecting Communities, introduced in the dying days of New Labour, was an attempt to challenge the growing levels of support for the racist Right. In this way, the white working class was rehabilitated and found its voice with the dismantling of multiculturalism but only in a reified form: as being enthralled to the extreme Right, resentful and losing out to minorities in a playing out of a micro-clash of civilisations. The success of UKIP in 2014 continued to frame the white working class as being 'left behind' and concerned with societal change and high levels of immigration.

Rather than pointing to the significant scale of deindustrialisation, growing levels of insecurity and political disconnection as the causes of a loss of political support to the BNP and UKIP, it is argued that the white working class have become the unwitting victims of multiculturalism. The Left focus unhelpfully on culture rather than class, while the Right continue the siren calls of a loss of identity. This rationale of identity loss and lack of representation has been distilled by Blue Labour, which advocates a return to a mythical past of white working-class solidarity, devoid of the distractions of multiculturalism or, indeed, immigration. However, in attacking multiculturalism, both Left and Right are guilty of endorsing a new type of racism that exonerates racialised discourse and only sees the white working class through the lens of social conservatism and immigration. Both are wrong in principle and reality. The lived experiences of white working-class communities do reveal racism but also progressive attitudes towards multiculturalism. Alternatively, they are no different from many groups in society and need not be condemned or lionised to retrofit defunct political prescriptions from discredited representatives.

Notes

[1] See *The Guardian*, available at: http://www.theguardian.com/politics/2012/oct/02/ed-miliband

[2] See *The Guardian*, available at: http://www.theguardian.com/world/2010/oct/17/angela-merkel-germany-multiculturalism-failures

[3] The comment was made in a TV debate on French Network TV, see: http://www.dailymail.co.uk/news/article-1355961/Nicolas-Sarkozy-joins-David-Cameron-Angela-Merkel-view-multiculturalism-failed.html

[4] The main protagonists who were in conflict were white working-class communities and Asian communities, the latter being largely of Pakistani descent.

[5] See: http://news.bbc.co.uk/1/hi/uk_politics/4974870.stm

[6] This was stated in an interview on LBC Radio in 2006, see: http://www.independent.co.uk/news/uk/politics/ukip-are-closet-racists-says-cameron-472769.html

[7] See *The Guardian*, available at: http://www.theguardian.com/politics/2014/may/24/more-than-half-ukip-voters-disenchanted-tories-ashcroft-poll

THREE

White, working-class and racist?

Introduction

A popular theme in defining white working-class communities is that they have been in the vanguard of racism. This is usually linked to the perceived adverse impact of immigration in a number of areas, including national identity, public benefits (such as welfare or subsidised housing) and competition for meaningful employment. The narrative surrounding immigration has been fuelled further by the national interventions of politicians who have championed the slogan '*British jobs for British workers*' or who have decried the failure of '*state multiculturalism*' in an attempt to protect the white working class from the excesses of multiculturalism and to gain short-term political dividends for themselves.

This chapter will consider the cultural representation of white working-class communities with reference to their portrayal in film and television, which are two of the most accessible forms of consumer culture. They shape and challenge our interpretation of communities and individuals ,as well as places and neighbourhoods. In addition, we will also explore the representation of white working-class communities with regards to issues of race and multiculturalism within the musical subcultures known as punk, Oi! and ska. Charting the cultural representation of white working-class communities against the frame of social change supports a much more rounded picture than is gained from policy responses alone. These communities are variously viewed as being both 'hero' and 'zero' with regards to multiculturalism. This can be seen in two examples, both of which have been framed, in part, as popular white working-class interventions on multiculturalism and change. These are the 1958 Race Riots in Notting Hill, where their involvement is viewed in negative racial terms, and the rise of 2 Tone in the city of Coventry, which was viewed locally as a union of diverse elements of the working class, merging to celebrate difference. These two events show how the pathology of whiteness and class have been interpreted differently.

At the outset the focus will be on the portrayal of the white working class in film and television, with a concentration on the social realism that emerged in the late 1950s. We will then turn to the iconic, but controversial, *Till Death Us Do Part*, a television show based on overt racialised discussions of immigration and social change that depicted the working class in a caricatured way as being racist and reactionary. In cinema, at least, the representation was multifaceted and framed against a rapidly changing society.

Representing a 'heroic working class'

Cinema has been an effective way of communicating changing cultural norms to a mass audience. In the post-1945 period, Britain was recovering from damage suffered during the Second World War. Rationing – restrictions on the supply of goods to the public – was introduced in 1940 and only ended in 1954. This was a period of reconstruction. Fittingly, many of the films during the 1950s reflected the importance of class unity (Hanley, 2011). The Labour Party had secured victory at the 1945 general election in a landmark event where the electorate voted for a new Britain based on a more egalitarian society characterised as implementing a welfare state. This included government-financed universal health care, unemployment insurance and investment in education, all of which were designed to bolster the population during economic depression and the conflict that had marred the first 50 years of the 20th century.

Yet, the political and economic ascendency of the working class was not publicly portrayed. Cinema oscillated between two different positions. The first was one that depicted the people of Britain as coming together during the war, with films such as *The Bridge Over the River Kwai* (1957). Emphasis was placed on class cooperation rather than conflict so that a common enemy (in this case, the Japanese army) could be defeated. The dual themes of class unity and preserving the British way of life can be seen in a number of films that focus on Britain's success during the Second World War, including *The Dam Busters* (1953) and *The Cockleshell Heroes* (1957). Members of the working class are framed as non-antagonistic combatants, seen and treated as ordinary 'Tommies' who take their orders from an officer class (Rattigan, 1994). Neutralising class conflict by an evocation of the people's war suggests that the working class were not ridiculed or pathologised as in later depictions, but they still had no voice. In essence, they were depicted as loyal and resilient subjects who knew their position in a stratified society. In the second position, the working class were framed as comedic characters in a series of films such as *Passport to Pimlico* (1949). One of the key protagonists is a greengrocer,

Arthur Pemberton, who wants to transform a bomb-damaged crater into a lido for the then working-class district of Pimlico. Pemberton speaks in authentic cockney twang rather than the received English spoken by officers in war films, as noted earlier. Although *Pimlico* creates comedic working-class characters, the film also suggests the importance of class cooperation between the different groups portrayed in the film. The objective of creating the lido is seen as a benefit for the community rather than a class or individual. In short, *Passport to Pimlico*, by putting forward wartime themes such as the sense of solidarity, helped to put on hold the issues of working-class rights in post-war Britain.

Representation of working-class communities in the post-1945 period was not restricted to popular films. Documentaries focusing on different aspects of working-class life presented this group in a different and realistic way rather than being restricted to being comedic or subordinates. This genre became known as Free Cinema because filmmakers wanted to be free from the studio system and make independent and realistic documentaries of Britain rather than in the idealised format portrayed by some films. Moreover, leading Free Cinema advocates aspired to create a space for working-class communities who had not been featured in a rounded form in cinema. Productions such as *O Dreamland* (1953) focused on the funfair (Dreamland) and showed working-class communities as individuals enjoying leisure time. Another example of cinematic realism can be seen in *We are the Lambeth Boys* (1959). The subjects are a group of young men who are members of a youth club in Kennington, South London. The documentary presents working-class lives without caricature or ridicule and could be viewed as the beginning of a realist approach to these communities.

The radical emergence of the working class in cinema is associated with British New Wave from 1959 to 1963. This period is noted for its social realism and a focus on the lived experiences of people, communities and places that had been marginally represented in cinema and media prior to this. A series of films such as *Room at the Top* (1958), *Saturday Night and Sunday Morning* (1960), *A Taste of Honey* (1961), *The Loneliness of the Long Distance Runner* (1962) and *This Sporting Life* (1963) shared a common theme by representing the lives of working-class communities as multifaceted, with gritty portrayals of divisions in the workplace and antagonism and conflict in society (Hill, 1986; Lay, 2002). The genre suggests an authenticity and realism in characterisation that was missing from earlier interpretations (Lacey, 1995).

In many of the films, an individual, usually young and male, was cast as the working-class anti-hero. For example, Arthur Seaton is the main character in *Saturday Night and Sunday Morning* and the film charts his life against the landscape of factory work, the terraced home he shares with his parents and, above all, the complicated personal relationships he holds with family and lovers based in and around Nottingham in the East Midlands. Arthur is neither comedic nor compliant, but a charismatic, sardonic and anti-authoritarian character. The opening credits of the film give way to the first scene showing the factory floor with Arthur undertaking hard, manual labour and given his weekly pay packet by the foreman. His opening comments are uncompromising and set the tone for the film:

> Nine hundred and fifty four, nine hundred and fifty bloody five. Another few more and that's the lot for a Friday. I'll have a fag in a bit, no use working every minute God sends. I could get through in half the time if I went like a bull, but they'd only slash my wages so they can get stuffed!... What I'm out for is a good time – all the rest is propaganda!

Saturday Night and Sunday Morning is a landmark film because it provides a multidimensional portrayal of working-class communities. They are not characters to be made fun of or demonised as being lazy or welfare-dependent. They are engines for social change in an increasingly affluent post-war Britain. Arthur has little respect for his employers ('... they can get stuffed!') and lives for the weekend of socialising. In contrast with earlier superficial depictions of working-class communities, his character is revealed at different levels by, for example, a complicated personal life, splitting his time between two lovers, one of whom is married to a co-worker and becomes pregnant with their child. He also has a difficult relationship with his father, who comes across as conforming to rules and structures in sharp contrast to his son.

British New Wave cinema attempted to move the location of filmic representation to places and people that had been ignored or silent. This genre of films constructed nuanced depictions of working-class lives. This was social realism writ large and the characters, albeit flawed, appeared on screen as resilient and charismatic. The diverse representation of working-class characters also had political consequences. People like Arthur Seaton rejected the narrow conformism and hierarchy in the workplace and domestic settings. He is the quintessential outsider who questions and challenges dominant norms. Yet, neither did these new representations embrace traditional institutions such as the Labour Party or trade unions. Rather, the story in films such as *Saturday Night and Sunday Morning* is of individual rebellion against society and institutions. The framing of the working class as an easily mobilised group of class warriors is generally rejected. This is summarised by Bentley when considering the novels on which many of the New Wave films were based:

> Arthur ultimately rejects collective action in favour of anarchic individualism ... rebellion is articulated as a personal attitude and release against the harshness and constraints of society ... represents a 'post-Marxist' discourse that is concerned to reject the notion of working class as a mass homogenized group with identical beliefs and aspirations ... celebrate the anarchic and unstructured spirit of resistance against dominant society. (Bentley, 2007: 201)

British social realism showed working-class communities as largely white. There was little, if any, reference to issues of race and immigration even though these were important political issues at the time. The economic boom created demand for cheap labour and stimulated immigration from the former British colonies in the Caribbean and the Indian subcontinent. This led to increased political anxiety based on concerns about assimilation and integration (Joshi and Carter, 1984). The 1958 Notting Hill riots, which were marked by violent incidents between Caribbean migrants and white working-class 'Teddy Boys', merely underlined the political combustibility of race, class and immigration (Bourne and Sivanandan, 1980). Yet, these issues are absent in British New Wave films, except for a fleeting but positive reference to a black co-worker by Arthur Seaton in the opening of *Saturday Night and Sunday Morning*. Seen critically, the disjuncture between the impact of immigration and growing ethnic diversity and its lack of voice in British New Wave perhaps demonstrates that class rather than race was easier to represent.

A Taste of Honey (1961) was an exception. The central premise of the film was a short-lived relationship between Jo (a working-class teenager who lives with her mother, Helen, in Salford) and Jimmy (a black sailor), which led to an unwanted pregnancy. The film also explores the dysfunctional relationship between Jo and her wayward mother and the more empathetic support provided by her gay male friend, Geoffrey. By putting forward the proposition that white working-class people were going to have relationships with minority communities, *A Taste of Honey* challenged a deep sexual taboo of interracial relationships that continued long after it was screened. The film demonstrated the reality of multiculturalism and the lived experience in Britain. That is to say, white working-class communities and neighbourhoods, especially those located in major conurbations such as Greater Manchester, Birmingham and London, were ethnically diverse and places where people needed to, and did, interact with each other. Rather than rejecting difference, they consumed multiculturalism as part of the changing face of cities during the post-war period.

The transition of white working-class communities from being compliant, or hidden, to a status that is antagonistic and visible was a radical theme in British cinema. Moreover, working-class communities in films such as *Saturday Night and Sunday Morning* are seen as multifaceted, with personal and political lives that challenge prevailing societal norms. It may be too far-flung to suggest that their portrayal was 'heroic', but these groups were seen as having an important contribution in building a modern country as Britain emerged from the deprivations of the Second World War. This is worth noting given the transformation of working-class communities to being problematic and part of the 'chav' culture little more than three decades later. In short, they went from hero to zero. The slowdown of the British economy in the 1970s and the loss of jobs in industries such as coal-mining, steel and shipbuilding had a devastating impact on neighbourhoods but also on how working-class communities were portrayed.

The themes of white working-class culture, multiculturalism and change are discussed in later films directed by Shane Meadows, specifically *This is England* (2006). Set in 1983 in the aftermath of the Falklands conflict, which took place the year before, and in the midst of an urban landscape blighted by economic recession, the film explores identity and race by telling the story of a fatherless 12-year-old, Shaun, and his affiliation with a group of skinheads. They are shown as a mixed gang both in terms of gender and, importantly, ethnicity. After Shaun joins the group, he is looked after by the leader, 'Woody', who is depicted as being warm and empathetic. Another member who is equally welcoming is 'Milky', a black skinhead. In the first part of *This is England*, white working-class identity is seen through the prism of the skinhead group, as well as an extended network of familial relationships that is inclusive and diverse. This is not simply because Milky is an important and accepted member of the group, but because of frequent references to fashion and reggae that replicate the Jamaican 'Rude Boy' style.

Everyday nods to multiculturalism help to frame the narrative as the group listen to music, attend parties and generally hang out with each other. Woody's skinhead gang, largely unemployed or at school, with little prospect of finding a job in 1980s' Britain, consume the normalcy of difference and see it as an important part of their lives. This is an important point given the way that white working-class communities are represented in the media as being resistant to social change and concerned about the scale and impact of immigration (see Sveinsson, 2009; Ford and Goodwin, 2014). The film *This is England*, together with earlier New Wave contributions such as *A Taste of Honey*, discusses multiculturalism as part of the social realism of white working-class communities. They are friends, family members and lovers, as well as sharing the same neighbourhoods, towns and cities. This is quite a distance from the government framing of the white working class as living '*parallel lives*', not only segregated, but antagonistic towards minority communities (Home Office, 2001). With the caveat that films are, of course, dramatic representations of social issues, there is a gap with the grassroots reality of multiculturalism, which could be better addressed by government policy.

This is not to say that the white working class need to be eulogised as being anti-racist. Indeed, *This is England* depicts another and murkier side of racism and racist violence. Much of this happens when the character 'Combo' is introduced midway through the film as someone who has just been released from prison. He was formerly part of the group and Woody's friend. However, while still a skinhead, Combo takes a hostile and vitriolic view of multiculturalism. Immigration is seen as the root cause of many problems afflicting Britain, ranging from the unemployment of the white working class, imperial decline and a growing dependency on welfare. This tirade is best encapsulated in a scene at Combo's flat in the presence of the wider group. Standing, with others seated, Combo delivers a blistering speech infused with racist hatred and vilification:

> Two thousand years, this little tiny fucking island has been raped and pillaged by people who have come here and wanted a piece of it. Two fucking world wars, men have laid down their lives for this. For this, and for what? So we can stick our fucking flag in the ground and say, 'Yeah, this is England, and this is England [points at his heart], and this is England [points at his head].' And for what? So we can just open the fucking floodgates and let them all come in?

And say, 'Yeah, come on, come in.' Get off your ship. Did you have a safe journey?

'Was it hard? Here y'are, here's a corner, why don't you build a shop? Better still, why don't you build a shop and then build a church? Follow your own fucking religions. Do what you want.' When the single fucking parents out there, who can't get a fucking flat and they're being given to these.... And I'm gonna say it, cos you're gonna have to fucking hear it. We're giving the flats to these fucking Pakis. Right? Who've got 50 and 60 in a fucking flat on their own. Right? We're giving that to them. There's three and a half million unemployed out there. Three and a half million of us, who can't get fucking work. Cos they're taking them all. Cos it's fucking cheap labour. Cheap and easy labour. Fucking cheap and easy, which makes us cheap and easy. Three and a half fucking million! It's not a joke. It's not a fucking joke.

This lengthy quote encapsulates the 'common sense' and often depicted narrative associated with white working-class communities on the issues of immigration and multiculturalism. The references to 'this tiny little island … world wars … men have laid down their lives' speaks to a small and proud country that has been trashed by immigrants. The clear disgust is made even worse because of the personal sacrifices and losses in world wars, as seen in 'men have laid down their lives'. The inference being that the nation-state, heritage and legacy have been compromised by uncontrolled immigration ('open the fucking floodgates'). Combo's speech continues apace from the desecration of national identity to the manner in which the state unfairly supports immigrants once they are in the country – 'Here y'are, here's a corner, why don't you build a shop? Better still, why don't you build a shop and then build a church? Follow your own fucking religions. Do what you want'. The concluding elements of the speech are focused on competition in housing and job markets that disadvantage white working-class communities. Combo advances the view that white parents are losing out to larger immigrant families who are jumping the queue for social housing. Referencing '50 or 60 in a flat' emphasises the 'otherness' of immigrants who hold values markedly different to established communities. The final section of the quote is fixed on white working-class communities and how they are losing out to immigrants because of 'cheap and easy labour'. In addition to an increase in competition for jobs, there is also a view that uncontrolled immigration is depressing wages for those jobs that can be obtained.

The concerns expressed by Combo may be brutal and stripped-down racist invective set in the political landscape of the 1980s, post-Falklands and in the midst of deindustrialisation. Yet, the sentiments are familiar to much more recent debates on immigration. For example, both Labour (community cohesion) and the Conservative–Liberal Democrat Coalition (integration) expressed concerns about the adverse cultural impact on British identity of a mass immigration that threatens rather than adds (Kundnani, 2002; Beider, 2014). Successive governments have put into place policies that were designed to allay the fears of white working-class communities regarding the pace of change. Citizenship tests, English-language proficiency, proscribing welfare benefits, instructing employers to recruit locally and limiting access to social housing are all attempts to address popular concerns. In the campaign for the 2014 local and European elections, Nigel Farage, the leader of the ultra-nationalist and ultimately victorious United Kingdom Independence Party (UKIP), intervened in debates about identity, legacy and heritage. He suggested that Britain had changed beyond recognition because of immigration. To make the point, Farage claimed that he felt uncomfortable in a train carriage because very few people were speaking English (*The Daily Telegraph*, 2014). Being under siege, loss of identity, hankering for an idealised past are common tropes that continue to shape the policy debate on immigration and race in Britain. Racist commentary is not simply the preserve of the white working class, but extends to different socio-economic groups and is often voiced by political representatives.

This is England reveals two opposing perspectives on white working-class culture. Multiculturalism is embraced by Woody and rejected by Combo. After Combo's speech, the gang is disbanded, with Shaun and others following the path towards overt and violent racism. Members are shown attacking a shop that is owned by Mr Sandhu, who is presented as being a submissive Asian victim. Combo also takes the group to a National Front meeting held in the back of a public house to hear a more refined but menacing message by a spokesperson on the threat of immigration. The audience is not simply composed of people like Combo, but young and old, as well as those working in offices or on the land. Presented as a cross-section of society, the scene suggests that the appeal of the National Front and the racist messages of cultural loss and political disconnection have broad support. Ultimately, Shaun decides that he does not want to follow the path of Combo towards racism and violence. He realises that nationalism and patriotism are political cul-de-sacs, which led to his father having to fight and lose his life in the Falklands. The film closes with Shaun throwing the English flag into the sea, which could be interpreted as a rejection of narrow identity.

Representing the white working class in its different forms and within the context of economic decline and multiculturalism is challenging. As individuals, Woody and Combo show two stylised versions of white working-class male identity. In reality, *This is England* helps to demonstrate that class identity and ethnicity cannot be reduced to a simple narrative, but are part of a continuum that is influenced by many different factors. The benefit of this film and other social realism contributions is that they put forward a multidimensional aspect to the white working class that embraces the fluid rather than the fixed identity.

The gritty portrayal of working-class communities in British New Wave continued with films such as *Kes* (1969), *Secrets and Lies* (1996) and *Nil by Mouth* (1997), which discussed themes of loss, violence and family relationships. It is important not to over-glamorise white working-class communities in the same way that later representations demonise the subject. It could be argued that on difference and change, the sometimes contradictory positions adopted during *This is England* merely reflect the fragmented nature of political discourse and society more generally.

Working-class representation in film has been shown to be largely positive and multilayered. Yet, this group soon descended into being categorised as being either unreconstructed racists or caricatured as being unremittingly stupid.

Increased affluence and access to consumer goods in post-war Britain changed the landscape of the average household. Among these, television was seen as not only desirable, but also an important way to be entertained and to receive information. By 1965, almost 90% of households had a TV (Childs, 2006: 71). As a medium for the discussion of political issues and representation of shifting cultural mores, television had few equals in the age of mass media. Two different programmes shown by the BBC substantiate this perspective. The first, *Till Death Us Do Part*, was a comedy that openly used uncouth and racist language on prime-time television to discuss social change and immigration in society. The second, *The White Season*, was a documentary series that showcased white working-class communities in different parts of the country as they tried to make sense of a changing England. These two examples are very different. *Till Death* was first shown in 1965 and ran in two phases until 1975, while the *White Season* first aired in

2008; the former used comedy to raise important and sensitive issues, while the latter deployed documentary and real-life characters to frame discussion. Both generated much discussion and debate, not to mention controversy, as to how they represented white working-class communities regarding multiculturalism and immigration.

Till Death Us Do Part (1965) showcased a working-class household based in the East End of London during the 1960s. The main character, and family patriarch, was Alf Garnett. In the show, he vents extreme opinions on the permissive society, feminism and, importantly, immigration against the context of the decline of Britain as an imperial power. This puts him in opposition to his daughter Rita and son-in-law Mike, who are presented in the programme as being much more progressive. The show proved hugely popular with viewers, being watched by up to 7 million people during its first airing between 1965 and 1968, reaching a peak of up to 9 million in its second showing between 1972 and 1975 (Bebber, 2014).

The crude racist discourse during *Till Death* was unrelenting, with an increased blame of immigration as symptomatic of the disintegration of Britain. Former colonial subjects, who Alf considered as biologically inferior, were now establishing communities in *his* white working-class neighbourhood. Given that the show presented minorities as outsiders, or the dangerous 'other', the cherished institutions that underpinned working-class culture – council housing, the pub and football – were all under threat from difference and diversity. *Till Death* claimed that it was offering a social realism framed on a range of topics, including race relations, from the viewpoint of a white working-class household. However, this has been disputed. Hall (1995) suggested that the terms of reference between different characters were weighted in favour of Alf. He was the chief protagonist and shaped much of the narrative and flow of the shows. More than this, the programme challenged the very legitimacy of minorities to live in Britain, a claim that was being promoted by the neo-Nazi organisation National Front. Malik (2002) states that Alf's strength of character and centrality, together with an absence of a black presence to counter his narrative, results in the show's depiction of racism as a legitimate response to such social concerns.

Countering the view that the show created a space for racism to be promoted, its creator and chief writer, Johnny Speight, put forward the view that the concerns of white working-class communities needed to be heard. Further, *Till Death* was about intergenerational concerns rather than simply dissecting race relations (Bebber, 2014). It could be claimed that it was important to create a space in a comedic show to discuss matters that were being played out in society. There were a number of high-profile interventions into race relations, including Enoch Powell's 'River of Blood' speech and the passing of the Commonwealth Immigrants Act, both in 1968, as well as the influx of Kenyan and Ugandan Asian immigrants in the late 1960s and early 1970s (Solomos, 2003), the inference being that *Till Death* was social realism in action and mirrored debates that were taking place in Britain and being reported on by the media. In a prescient comment given the rise of UKIP in 2014, and on the basis that it was speaking on behalf of ordinary Britons about the impact of immigration, Speight stated that his objective was 'to give a voice to the working classes on the issue of immigration, in opposition to what he perceived as the dominance of liberal elites in setting racial attitudes and immigration policies' (Bebber, 2014: 258).

While the character of Alf in *Till Death* may have been viewed as outlandish and grotesque in his racist commentary, it appeared to reflect popular concerns felt by the socio-economic group that he was seeking to represent. The programme created a space for the volume to be turned up rather than down on immigration. It should also be noted that the print media were, and continue to be, largely in favour of restrictive measures on immigration (Hall et al, 1998). The rhetoric, supported by the unprecedented levels of airtime on television and anti-immigrant stories in the newspapers, played to common-sense fears about the impact of multiculturalism on the British way of life. In short, a cultural battle was taking place to maintain and keep a white identity (see Ford and Goodwin, 2014).

It could be said that the legacy of *Till Death* was to present an extreme characterisation of a working-class intergenerational family within the context of Britain's place in the world, its changing demographics and its acceptable societal norms. In challenging and ridiculing Alf, his daughter and son-in-law showed the absurdity of the positions that he took on immigration and race. By focusing on the sharp divisions in the family, *Till Death* may be viewed as showing the range of views on the white working-class spectrum. Despite this, and the contention from its makers that *Till Death* was simply reflecting societal concerns, the spewing of unreconstructed racism on prime-time television legitimised this type of discussion on the minority presence in Britain that continues to the current day.

The BBC commissioned and continued to support *Till Death* despite the furore caused by the racist language used in the series. It justified the decision on the basis that there were low levels of white working-class representation on TV and that it needed to create a voice for this group. Some 40 years later, the BBC featured *The White Season* (2007), a series of programmes that focused on white working-class anxieties about immigration and social change. In the press pack accompanying the series, the rationale and framing of the programmes is clear:

> The White Season features a series of films that shine the spotlight on the white working class in Britain today. It examines why some feel increasingly marginalised ... [and] explores reasons behind the rise in popularity of the far-right in politics ... the films explore the complex mix of feelings ... [that] lead some people to feel under siege and their very sense of self is being brought into question. (BBC, 2007)

The season was largely comprised of a series of documentaries that looked at the reactions and responses of white working-class communities to the presence of minority communities. The commissioning editor, Richard Klein, justified the topic on the basis that the views of the white working class had been marginalised. Writing in the right-wing *The Daily Mail*, Klein seems to link the lack of voice with the presence of minorities and the impact of multiculturalism:

> these BBC films demonstrate, the white working class claim that they are the ones who suffer from the changes: losing their jobs, seeing their wages undercut, watching their local services under increasing strain ... a deep sense of resentment ... in part as a consequence of multiculturalism ... in the modern world's rush to embrace diversity and globalisation, we cannot afford to ignore the voices of any section of society which feels bewildered by the pace of change. (*The Daily Mail*, 2008)

The premise of the press release and Klein's article is troubling. In attempting to give a voice to an embattled group, the parameters appear to have been drawn to deliver a decidedly one-sided and partial perspective. The programmes cast the white working class as victims of globalisation, employers, local government, immigrants and, of course, multiculturalism. The message is that they are unable to cope with social change. Instead, they opt for a default response, showing support for parties like the British National Party (BNP). The narrative offers a rigid framing of race and immigration, misses commonalities with minority groups and diminishes the importance of the collapse of manufacturing during the recessions of 1981 and 2008.

In each episode the inference is that the white working class are 'under siege' and resentful of change. For example, in *Last Orders* the focus is on Wibsey Working Men's Club, which is based in Bradford. A number of members, largely older white men, are interviewed on their views. In the course of the programme, they variously complain about being let down by a Labour Party that used to represent their interests, the unsettling prospect of a growing and encroaching Asian community, and the lack of support given to them by Bradford Council. Their views, studded with racist language, are left unchallenged. Instead, the scene established is a decrepit Working Men's Club and Wibsey being under threat by immigrants as the protagonists hanker for an idealised past. In this sense, *Last Orders* seemed to be a continuation of some of the themes from *Till Death*. Like Alf, they railed against social change, were resentful of the perceived favourable treatment given to immigrants and implied that they had a superior and stronger claim to being British than other Britons who were not 'indigenous'.

The White Season also featured *All White in Barking*, *The Poles are Coming* and *Rivers of Blood*, all of which were framed by the premise that immigration and multiculturalism created challenges for white working-class identity and neighbourhood cohesion. The supposition that immigration leads to the erosion of white working-class survival courses through the programme. In turn, different immigrant communities are set up as in adversarial combat against low-income white people, who are invariably viewed as the losers. Lawler (2012) suggested that *The White Season* only served to represent white working-class communities as being rooted in the past and being part of 'anachronistic space'. Rhodes (2010) comments that the programmes repeated the politics of resentment debates that seem to have isolated white working-class communities and depicted them as being problematic to a modern, multicultural Britain (see also Haylett, 2001). *The White Season* constructed a simplistic picture of the white working class as racist and largely male. The resultant representation of white working-class identities is akin to modern-day Alfs from *Till Death*.

The assumption that the white working class is voiceless on issues of immigration and race should be challenged. Representation through the medium of cinema and especially television has been significant. The social realism of British New Wave cinema presented a multifaceted and progressive picture of working-class lives that was missing from earlier productions, and the presence of newly arrived immigrants featured in some of the films. There was more coverage on television. In both examples discussed here, white working-class opinion, or, more accurately, a conservative section of it, was allowed a voice to promote views on immigration and race that negatively fuelled rather than educated the country on the impact of multiculturalism. It can be argued that whiteness is not hidden, but present in the everyday.

Earlier, we discussed how the white working class have been framed as racist. We also showed the influence of film and television in both reinforcing and challenging commonly held stereotypes. It is not only in drama and documentary work that white working-class communities have become typecast as the antagonistic and racist battering ram against immigrants.

Government interventions to legislate on even more restrictive immigration controls has often been justified as responding to popular concerns (Small and Solomos, 2006; Tomlinson, 2013). In some cases, the white working class is viewed as being in direct conflict with newly arrived immigrants or the implications of multiculturalism. For example, the 2001 riots involved British-Asian and white working-class communities in Burnley, Oldham and Bradford, where the latter were seen as being concerned about the supposedly favourable treatment given to minorities by local government in contrast to the lack of investment and support in white working-class neighbourhoods (Home Office, 2001). The theme of a micro-clash of civilisations is repeated in local and national narratives (Rex and Tomlinson, 1979; Ford and Goodwin, 2014).

The role of the white working class as active and racist participants may be illustrated by three momentous events that shaped the discussion and policy responses in race relations in Britain: the 1958 Notting Hill race riots, the 1964 Smethwick election and the 1969 'Rivers of Blood' speech made by Enoch Powell.

Today, Notting Hill is viewed as one of the most sought-after neighbourhoods in London. It is a diverse place in a global city that has become known for celebrating cultural difference through the Carnival that takes place each year during August Bank Holiday weekend. Its current depiction as a desirable, ethnically diverse and harmonious community has not always been the case. Back in the post-war period, the contrast could not have been sharper. The area was a warren of poor-quality private-sector housing maintained by slum landlords such as Peter Rachman, whose actions – Rachmanism – became synonymous with poor-quality housing, minimal housing rights and threats of violence in order to ensure that tenants either moved out or paid their rent despite the deplorable conditions. The availability of cheap housing made Notting Hill a popular choice for migrants, especially from the Caribbean, who as colonial subjects, and in accordance with the Nationality Act 1948, had free movement to the UK in order to seek work in a fast-growing economy (Joshi and Carter, 1984; Solomos, 2003).

Alongside the growing presence of immigrant communities in Notting Hill was the established white working-class neighbourhood of Notting Dale, which had a reputation throughout London as '*hell on earth*' (cited in McLeod, 2004). In his book on the 1958 riots, Pilkington (1988: 83) described Notting Dale as a 'settled and closed community, virulently hostile to "foreigners"'. Mike and Trevor Phillips provide another description of the neighbourhood, which had become home to:

> a large population of internal migrants, gypsies and Irish ... packed into a honeycomb of rooms with communal kitchens, toilets and no bathrooms. It had depressed English families who had lived through the war years then watched the rush to the suburbs pass them by while they were trapped in low income jobs and rotten housing. It had a raft of dodgy pubs and poor street lighting. It had gang fighting, illegal drinking clubs, gambling and prostitution. (Phillips and Philips, 1998: 171)

The picture of 1950s' Notting Dale was of a closed and insular white working-class community, under threat from a growing immigrant population. Resentment was multifaceted and included competition for jobs, housing and services, but also the more visceral and personal issue of an increase in relationships between white women and black men (Pilkington, 1988). Increased colonial immigration into the UK, and places like Notting Hill, had also generated fascist political mobilisation (Bourne and Sivanandan, 1980; Pilkington, 1988). Both Oswald Moseley's Union Movement and Colin Jordan's White Defence League were based in the area. Indeed, they had a local following, meetings were well-attended and racist propaganda was circulated through the Defence League's newsletter, *Black and White News*, which displayed lurid headlines such as 'Black gets white girl' and 'Negroes lead in VD' (Olden, 2008; Moore, 2013).

Given the portents, and the increasingly fractious political debate on the impact of immigration (Joshi and Carter, 1984), there was little surprise when rioting broke out between white youths and the Caribbean community from 29 August to 5 September 1958 (Pilkington, 1988; Olden, 2008). The origin appeared to be an argument between a black man and his white wife, which instigated a fight between groups of white and black men. This was on Friday 29 August, the start of the British Bank Holiday weekend. On the following day, and then sporadically until 5 September, serious disturbances occurred in Notting Hill, Paddington and Shepherds Bush before a combination of poor weather and policing led to a cessation of the violence. In total, 108 people were arrested and charged with offences that included grievous bodily harm, rioting and possessing weapons. Of these, 78 were white and 36 were black (Travis, 2002). Later, inspection of internal police reports confirmed that the perpetrators were mainly white working-class youths who indiscriminately attacked Caribbean migrants. In the midst of the rioting, *The Daily Mail* called for stronger controls on colonial immigration with the headline 'Should we keep them coming in?' (Olden, 2008). Sentiments expressed by white youths included 'We'll kill the black bastards' and 'Down with the niggers' (Olden, 2008), the consensus being that the riots were started by large groups of white working-class youths from Notting Dale:

> the disturbances were triggered by 300–400 strong 'Keep Britain White' mobs, many of them Teddy boys armed with iron bars, butcher's knives and weighted leather belts, who went 'nigger hunting' among the West Indian residents of Notting Hill and Notting Dale. (Travis, 2002)

The linkage of Notting Dale and its white working-class population as being in the forefront of the attacks is one of the key narratives of the 1958 riots. Some have suggested that the violence was viewed as a tactic to keep black immigrants from settling in Notting Dale (Pilkington, 1988; Moore, 2013). Others have claimed that residents, many from Irish and Traveller backgrounds, reformatted this as an explicit urban identity framed on Englishness in order to differentiate themselves from newly arrived migrants. In doing so, whiteness could be viewed as being an important marker that needed to be shielded in the wider context of Britain's fading role as an imperial power alongside the reality of colonial immigration to the country. In a sense, the response of white working-class residents participating in the Notting Hill riots has been seen as a '*re-racialisation of Englishness*' during a period of societal change (Featherstone, 2009: 109).

It was not only the class and neighbourhood of Notting Dale that was perceived to be generally problematic, but young people, and especially 'Teddy Boys' or 'Teds'. This group has been described as a teenage subculture that emerged during the 1950s in working-class areas of London. Replicating the extravagant style of Edwardian '*dandies*', with long jackets, narrow trousers and hair made into a high quiff, the 'Teds' became a popular phenomenon in austere post-war London (Clarke, 1998a). This was exacerbated after screenings of the film *Blackboard Jungle* (1955), which was based on a teacher addressing challenging behaviour in an inner-city school, which resulted in violent incidents, with 'Teds' being identified as ring leaders. In short, by 1958, this subculture had been characterised as being violent, delinquent, anti-authoritarian and almost always the white lumpen proletariat. The reports of the 1958 riots state that 'Teds' from Notting Dale and elsewhere from London were the cause of the racist violence (Olden, 2008; Travis, 2002). This conflation of youth, white working-class identity and racism has been viewed as part of a '*moral panic*' at times of crisis (Hall et al, 1998). As we shall see later, there are similarities with the skinhead movement in the 1970s, which, again, could be viewed as a period of economic and social change in Britain.

The 1958 Notting Hill riots were the most serious violent outbreak in Britain since 1945. A number of factors came together that mark the riots as important moments in the discussion of multiculturalism and change: the protagonists were newly arrived immigrants; they inhabited white working-class communities; and the disturbances took place in the context of fascist activity locally and the demise of the British Empire abroad. Notting Dale and its residents are described as being closed, resistant to change and the main instigators of the racist attacks on immigrants. This narrative reduces them to a lumpen proletariat, or, as we discussed in Chapter One, an example of 'dirty whiteness', that is, akin to being viewed as abnormal, deviant and against societal norms. In the aftermath of the riots, Notting Dale was cleared as part of the 1960s' urban renewal. 'Teds' became less popular after their association with racism and violence, and the Notting Hill Carnival, as the quintessential celebration of multiculturalism, was born. The changes since 1958 are summed up by a resident of Notting Dale, now in her 80s, who remarked: 'Black and white didn't mix back then.... Now they're our strongest allies. I've got a black son-in-law and he's everything a husband and father should be' (Olden, 2008).

Only a decade later, in 1968, the white working class were again invoked as victims in the debates on immigration and multiculturalism. Enoch Powell, then a leading Conservative politician and member of Edward Heath's 'shadow cabinet', addressed the West Midlands Conservative Association at the Midland Hotel in Birmingham on 20 April 1968 in what has since been dubbed the 'Rivers of Blood' speech (Schofield, 2013; Wellings, 2013). The actual speech, and the subsequent emergence of a Conservative thinking known as Powellism, has been extensively covered (Foot, 1969; Heffer, 1999).

How did the response to 'Rivers of Blood' become associated with the white working class? The speech was made during an important historical period. Ten years after the Notting Hill riots, the right of colonial immigrants to free entry had been gradually stripped away by the passing of legislation starting with the Commonwealth Immigrants Act 1962 (Solomos, 2003). At the 1964 general election, the Labour Party's spokesperson on foreign affairs, Patrick Gordon Walker, lost his contest in the working-class seat of Smethwick to his Conservative opponent, who endorsed the sentiment 'If you want a nigger for your neighbour, vote Labour' (Foot, 1969). Labour won the election but was aware of the agency of immigration in mobilising popular support. Confronted by the challenge of addressing racism among some sections of its own working class, and in the country as a whole, the new government buckled and introduced further measures to restrict immigration from the Caribbean and the Indian subcontinent in a blatant abdication of principle in favour of perceived political pragmatism (see Crossman, 1991).

Powell intervened in a climate that was already racialised (Tomlinson, 2013). His speech magnified immigration as a problem by illustrating the cases of two people who came to see him at his MP surgery in his Wolverhampton constituency. The language he used conveyed the sense that these were '*ordinary*' white people who had worked hard and played fair only to have immigrants threaten their identity and existence. One of these was 'a middle-aged, quite ordinary working man employed in one of our nationalised industries' (for the full text of the speech, see *The Daily Telegraph*, 2007). Powell continues the exchange with this 'ordinary working man', who states that he wants to leave the country because the government was giving too much support to immigrants. Claiming that the situation will deteriorate, the anonymous constituent declares in a famous passage from the speech 'In this country in 15 or 20 years' time the black man will have the whip hand over the white man' (*The Daily Telegraph*, 2007). Powell concludes by agreeing with this bleak scenario and prophesises conflict rather than accommodation in British multiculturalism: 'As I look ahead, I am filled with foreboding; like the Roman, I seem to see "the River Tiber foaming with much blood"' (*The Daily Telegraph*, 2007).

The reaction to 'Rivers of Blood' may be viewed in terms of an institutional and populist perspective. Powell was sacked by the Conservative Party leader, Edward Heath, and treated with opprobrium by the majority of his peers at Westminster. In contrast, the popular reaction has been framed as being supportive, with opinion polls indicating a majority of those interviewed agreed with the sentiments contained in 'Rivers of Blood'. Famously, Smithfield Meat Porters and Tilbury Dockers marched to the Houses of Parliament in support of Powell with placards stating 'Back Britain, not Black Britain' (Heffer, 1999). There was also backing from other workers, including Immigration Officers at Heathrow Airport (Schofield, 2013). Those opposing maintained that some leaders of the pro-Powell Dockers had links with extreme right-wing organisations (*The Guardian*, 1999) and there were many workers who were anti-Powell and strongly opposed their fellow Dockers who marched to the Houses of Parliament (Wellings, 2013).

Different representations of white working-class identities have been discussed using the frames of TV programmes in the 1960s and cinema in the 2000s, linking into political narratives between historical periods that show continuity rather than change. In the context of an increasingly racialised political environment, which had been marked by restrictive immigration measures, a conflation between race and immigration, and generally negative coverage in the print media, it is little surprise that white working-class communities have been framed as the 'victims', unwitting or otherwise, of difference and multiculturalism. Characterisations such as Alf Garnett in *Till Death* and Combo in *This is England* represented a turbocharged stereotype of a white working-class male bigot. This is further embedded by the popular reactions to immigration, such as the 1958 Notting Hill riots or the sight of workers marching on the Houses of Parliament in support of a racist speech. Seen in this light, the white working class appear to have confirmed the view that they are racist and resistant to change. However, the politics of race and immigration needs to be factored into the analysis. Historically, communities have been reified as in a zero-sum competition for scarce public resources and identity has been framed around the myth of whiteness rather than the reality of multiculturalism. More than this, Alf and Combo or Notting Hill and Powell are not the only markers of being white and working-class in the national debates on race. In the next section, we will discuss a place, time and cultural expression that demonstrate a different manifestation of whiteness, class and social change.

A different perspective on the white working class, multiculturalism and change

The depiction of the white working class as racist and resistant to change and diversity is deeply embedded into different types of academic and policy discourse in Britain. Indeed, the narrative discussed earlier regarding historic events such as the Notting Hill Riots, Smethwick, Powellism and the rise of UKIP seems to confirm this view. They are pitted against minority communities in an adversarial conflict for scarce resources within a framework of a micro-clash of civilisations. Addressing this reified framework is necessarily problematic because the '*everyday integration*', or the way in which different communities get on with their lives at home, school and work, does not lend itself to media scrutiny and headlines (Institute of Public Policy Research, 2012). Yet, white working-class communities share neighbourhoods, schools and workplaces with minority communities (Beider, 2011, 2014). In this context, government policies such as community cohesion (Home Office, 2001) and integration (DCLG, 2012) neither focus on white working-class communities nor have proven to be successful in meeting objectives on building common norms or values. Instead, it may be argued, they have placed communities in a traditional and well-versed role as being implacably opposed to each other.

In this section, we will propose a different view of period when it appeared that white working-class and minority communities emerged in common cause and celebration of multiculturalism, as well as mobilised against the far Right. The emergence of punk and 2 Tone created a platform for diverse communities to reshape identities based on multiculturalism, class identity and space. Both punk and reggae have been viewed as connecting and articulating the experiences of working-class culture and communities and forms of cultural resistance (Hall et al,1998). In this sense, articulation is about the communication of material conditions within a neighbourhood, city or nation, as well as linkage to a wider group or community (Negus, 2002). Earlier, the impact of film and television was discussed in presenting different types of working-class identities as moving from 'hero' in some of the social realism screenings to the 'zero' of Alf Garnett in *Till Death*. Taking this forward, an analysis of white working-class cultural identity shaped by important genres such as punk and ska helps to provide a variation from the default view that these communities are resistant to cultural diversity. In experiencing music and absorbing related styles, white working-class communities may be reframed as progressive and enlightened.

The roots of 2 Tone are embedded in the skinhead movement that emerged in the late 1960s and is associated with two different and apparently contradictory cultural forms. In his classic essay, Clarke (1998b) suggests that the skinhead genre was about recreating a sense of an idealised white working-class community that had come under pressure from a range of different sources, including post-1945 immigration and the loss of jobs. It was indicative of the wider trend of deindustrialisation and the need for communities to conform to societal norms, mediated by a disconnected government that had ceased to represent their needs and aspirations. Responding to the sense of loss and entitlement, this working-class subculture formed an organised community predicated on defending an idealised notion of community. As Clarke stated:

> the post war decline of the basis of that community had removed it as a real source of solidarity; the skinheads had to use an image of what that community was as the basis of their style. They were the 'dispossessed inheritors'; they received a tradition that had been deprived of its real social bases. The themes and imagery still persisted, but the reality was in a state of decline and disappearance. (Cited in Duncombe and Trembelay, 2011: 118)

The narrative that focuses on white skinheads and emphasises community 'loss', real or imagined, connects with recent political interventions on national identity and tropes about the '*left behind*'. This is not so much 'the country of long shadows on county grounds, warm beer, invincible green suburbs … old maids bicycling to Holy Communion through the morning mist',[1] but an altogether different urban space. In much of the political, and some of the academic, research on white working-class communities, there is an attempted recreation of an imagined country that white working-class communities could live in happily without the excesses of globalisation and the growing cultural insecurity of immigration. That Blue Labour shares the space with skinheads (as well as UKIP and the BNP) suggests an unholy alliance and a desire to regress to a time before equality legislation, when racism and sexism were given free rein, unencumbered by any sanction. This is recreating identity based on a monocultural myth rather than a multicultural reality. More relevant is the steady loss of working-class institutions such as unions, social clubs and public houses during the 1980s and beyond, a loss that is blamed on social change rather than political reforms. These reforms curtailed the power of organised labour and consumer market changes, both of which allowed supermarkets to undercut pubs in the pricing and selling of alcohol, subsequently leading to the decline of pubs.

Alongside the need to protect identity and place, the skinhead movement has been associated with promoting a white working-class identity linked to overt racism and support for extreme right-wing parties such as the National Front and British Movement (Brown, 2004). Sometimes, this has been bracketed with the rise of a music genre known as Oi! associated with late 1970s' and early 1980s' punk bands such as Sham 69. Interestingly, the identification with Oi! has been made not only by skinheads, but by a much wider landscape filled with working-class alienation and revolt, whether that be of government, education or the police. For example it was 'about real life, the concrete jungle, hating the Old Bill, on the dole, and about fighting back and having pride in your class and background' (cited in Worley, 2013: 1). As well as a revolt against 'smug politicians and greedy bosses ... [who had] destroyed whole communities and thrown an entire generation on the scrapheap' (Worley, 2013: 2).

An exploration of skinheads and Oi! enables the construction of a pathway to debates in 2014 following the success of UKIP. The late 1970s' derivative of skinhead culture was different from its first appearance in the late 1960s, which was described as a 'multicultural synthesis organised around fashion and music' (Brown, 2004). Moving away from the high-fashion statements and consumer culture of 'Swinging London', the first skinheads instead identified with the symbolism of rebellion embodied in 'rude boys', sharp-suited immigrants deriving fashion, music and anti-authoritarianism from urban centres in Kingston, Jamaica. Reggae was the means to build a bridge between white working-class communities from urban Britain and newly arrived Jamaican migrant communities. To this end, skinheads connected with Jamaican fashion and music through ska. The ironic fusing of two distinct and disconnected cultures is not lost on Hebdige:

> the unique and paradoxical manner in which this revival was accomplished ... not only by congregating on the all-white football terraces but through consorting with West Indians at the local youth clubs and on the street corners, by copying their mannerisms, adopting their curses, dancing to their music that the skinheads 'magically recovered' the lost sense of working-class community ... ironically, those values conventionally associated with white working-class

culture … 'the defensively organised collective' which had been eroded by time, by relative affluence and by the disruption of the physical environment in which they had been rooted, were rediscovered embedded in black West Indian culture.… The skinheads, then, resolved or at least reduced the tension between an experienced present (the mixed ghetto) and an imaginary past (the classic white slum) by initiating a dialogue which reconstituted each in terms of the other. (Hebdige, 1979: 56–57)

The imagery is germane to government preoccupations with both working-class loss and British Muslim threat. Many of the recent studies of white working-class communities, cohesion and integration are replete with commentary on the identity loss of anchors such as pubs, social clubs, traditional jobs and social housing. These losses have made it difficult for white working-class groups to remain cohesive (Hanley, 2007; Pearce and Milne, 2010; Beider, 2011; Garner, 2011). In contrast, British Muslim communities are viewed as building a sense of cohesion in terms of community organisations, mosques and shops, as well as political representation in local and national politics. The subtext is that this community has been supported by multiculturalism. Compared to the appropriation of cultural symbols such as reggae and patois from the British Caribbean experience, Muslims have been positioned by government and large sections of the media as a problematic 'enemy within', presenting a twin threat to security and identity (for an exposition of the 'stranger danger' perspective, see Goodhart, 2004). Hence, given the emphasis of cultural explanations to confirm the existence of 'parallel lives' in debates on cohesion, British Muslims have been racialised as a distinct 'other' with little in common with white working-class communities.

The empathy of the white working class in the late 1960s with Jamaican style, culture and music was some distance away from the later variant of skinhead culture that appeared as a part of the punk explosion in the late 1970s. Punk itself was linked with Britain's post-war decline, the fraying of the welfare state and economic and political crisis. To these macro-concerns, punk was a response to the bloated decadence of popular music, where the remoteness of performers, which was created by the vast physical space of the concert venues, as well as the contrasting lifestyle of the well-paid performers to their fan base, replicated the sense of alienation from government felt by voters (Hebdige, 1979; Savage, 2005).

In the midst of this, punk rock was claimed as a white working-class phenomenon against a backdrop of crumbling housing estates, mass unemployment, crime and misdeeds, setting it apart from the aforementioned middle-class rock that held sway (Savage; Worley, 2013). As Hebdige (1979) recounts, these class credentials were emphasised in punk at every opportunity. The leading bands that emerged in 1976, such as The Sex Pistols and The Clash, were the authentic voice of working-class alienation according to magazines such as *Sounds*, which stated that they were 'a mirror reflection of the kind of 1977 white working-class experiences that only seem like a cliché to those people who haven't had to live through them' (see Parsons, 1977); gigs were similar in experience to football terraces in terms of being with 'working-class kids with the guts to say "No" to being office, factory and dole fodder' (Burchill, 1977). In fact, The Sex Pistols and The Clash were composed of middle-class (Joe Strummer, Paul Simonon, from The Clash) as well as working-class members (Steve Jones, Paul Cook from The Sex Pistols; Mick Jones from The Clash) (Savage, 2005; Salewicz, 2006). The symbolism of punk was underscored by references to apparent 'working-class sensibilities', such as clothes made from basic and discarded materials including plastic, a commitment to an unrefined method of dancing known as the pogo, fanzines like *Sniffin Glue* that had production values littered with poor grammar and spelling mistakes and were held together with staples (Hebdige, 1979), and the readiness to swear in the media, which famously reached a climax when Steve Jones and Johnny Rotten were interviewed by Bill Grundy on *The Today Show* in 1976 (Savage, 2005).

Musically, punk referenced white working-class disconnection and alienation. For example, Sham 69, a band that came to prominence in 1978, shaped the Oi! skinhead movement through songs that authentically documented working-class life, as well as displayed a disdain for government and other class groups. Often, these were accompanied by football chants such as 'If the Kids are United', which spoke about the importance of all young people, irrespective of ethnicity, coming together to share common experiences, whereas 'Hey Little Rich Boy' asserts the pride of working-class identity and the dismissal of middle-class values and ethos. This type of storytelling through verse recounted the emergence of British social realism that was discussed earlier in this chapter. Bands like Sham 69 voiced white working-class lives without glamour or nostalgia. In these depictions, the ordinariness of going to the pub to meet friends and family, or to the bookies to place a bet on horse and greyhound racing, are recorded alongside more serious concerns, such as the problem of finding employment. Class was framed around these cultural symbols and the importance of spatial connection to a street, area or city. As stated by Worley, punk, and especially Oi!, was heavy with connections to local community, pride in your identity and being white working-class:

> Most obviously, Oi! expressed a class identity that was rooted in the politics of everyday life: in work, the weekend, the community, street, and home … best realized on Sham 69's That's Life (1978), which provided a twenty-four-hour snapshot of a working-class lad who gets up late, argues with his parents, gets sacked from work, wins on the horses, goes to the pub, meets a girl, has a fight, and wakes up with a hangover.… Oi! songs reverberated with the sound of concrete and steel … Oi! rarely moralized, concentrating instead on the documentation – sometimes serious, sometime humorous – of a life being lived. (Worley, 2013:24)

The Clash was arguably the most political of punk bands, with a focus not so much on the visceral concerns of whiteness, but on rebelliousness against authority and a pronounced anti-racism. To an extent, this was not surprising because, in contrast with bands such as Sham 69, The Clash was composed of individuals who came from a middle-class background and may have had difficulty in authenticating class and whiteness (Savage, 2005; Salewicz, 2006). Nevertheless, the music of The Clash did speak about the lack of prospects for working-class young people and the dangers of being exploited by big business. For example, 'Career Opportunities' focused on how the unemployed were being offered jobs that were low-paid, repetitive and with little or no prospect of career progression. In part, the sentiments of the song were a precursor to neoliberal policy narratives developed by Charles Murray (1996) and criticised by recent publications (see Hanley, 2007; Jones, 2011).

More importantly, The Clash created a platform to link punk, resistance and rebellion. By the late 1970s, the British economy was slowing down and this was accompanied by increased levels of labour unrest. Alongside the economic deterioration, there was concern about the impact of immigration on society. This had been highlighted by Smethwick and Powellism in the 1960s but the issue of immigration continued to occupy the concerns of politicians and the media (Crossman, 1991). The decision by the Ugandan government in 1974 to expel Asians led to an influx to Britain and was the forerunner of the 'swamping' comments made by Margaret Thatcher before she was elected prime minister in 1979 (Tomlinson, 2013). This racialised backdrop enabled some elements of punk to adopt anti-racism as part of rebellion. As in the case of the earlier skinheads, who were influenced by Jamaican ska, punk found common cause with minority communities. Reggae music, in particular, was championed by musicians such as Bob Marley and the Wailers, whose messages were filled with representing the needs of disadvantaged communities and fighting oppression and corruption, as well as racism. The common cause with punk was symbolised by the song 'Punky Reggae Party', where Bob Marley and the Wailers declared overlap and recognition between reggae bands such as The Clash, The Jam and Dr Feelgood. Reciprocating, The Clash recorded 'Police & Thieves' to a punk beat, after the song was originally recorded by Jamaican artist Junior Murvin, with the political message that police and criminals are both dangerous and were being used by a corrupt political system in Jamaica.[2] The version by The Clash simply changed the symbolism of Kingston, Jamaica to equate to the harassment of black communities by the police during the 1970s, as well as the subsequent inner-city riots that erupted in Brixton, Toxteth, Moss Side and Handsworth in 1981 (Benyon and Solomos, 1987).

In this context, the coupling of punk and reggae was as much political as musical and this distinction differentiated it from 1960s' ska. Punk implored white working-class communities to identify with resistance and rebellion, which was culturally espoused by black communities in music but also socially manifested on the streets of inner-city Britain. For example, The Clash's 'White Riot' was played out to the violent clashes between the police and black communities during the 1976 Notting Hill Carnival. The song was composed after band members Joe Strummer and Paul Simonon witnessed the riots and resistance of black communities to the police and racism (Duncombe and Tremblelay, 2011). The message of 'White Riot' was that there was a need for white working-class communities to replicate this form of active resistance in the midst of alienation, unemployment and disadvantage. In this context, collective violence was viewed as a legitimate method to get issues onto the political agenda and the lyrics of 'White Riot' demonstrated the inertia of the white working class, alongside the dynamism of minority communities:

> White riot – I wanna riot. White riot – a riot of my own....
> Black people gotta lot a problems, But they don't mind

throwing a brick; White people go to school; Where they teach you how to be thick…. All the power's in the hands; Of people rich enough to buy it; While we walk the street too chicken to even try it.

While suggesting that punk articulated the experience of white working-class anger and discontent with societal norms in the music of Oi! and Sham 69, and that a strong anti-racist message was promoted through The Clash, it would be naive to consider this as the sum total of the genre. Sabin (2011) counters that historians conveniently selected specific moments as critical to advancing the experiences of working-class angst and support for multiculturalism. These include support by punk bands through the Rock Against Racism campaign. He suggests that the reality was a multitude of factors, including ambiguity towards anti-racism, a level of support for the National Front, a fetish with Nazi symbols like the Swastika and its use on clothing and the appropriation of Third Reich terminology to name bands such as Joy Division and London SS. We have already noted that Oi! was adopted by white working-class skinheads and was supported by the National Front and British Movement (Worley, 2013).

In attempting to summarise the contributions of punk to the formation of white working-class identities and its intersection with multiculturalism, and before we consider the influence of 2 Tone, we note what appears to be a contradiction between the influence and embrace of minority culture (reggae, ska, style) and the language and symbolism of the far Right (racist, fascism). However, this is no different to the range of white working-class views on multiculturalism and social change highlighted by recent research. These alternate between celebrating difference and diversity at the local level to concerns about the impact on jobs and housing (National Community Forum, 2009; Garner, 2011; Beider, 2011). In this way, followers of punk are merely repeating contradictions between a national racialised framework and the local and lived reality of multiculturalism.

The roots of 2 Tone are based in reggae and punk. However, 2 Tone is associated with Coventry as a place. The city, located some 20 miles south-east of Birmingham, was industrialised in the 20th century, initially around aircraft manufacture. In the post-1945 period, and after the 1940 Blitz, when German air raids resulted in more than 500 deaths, Coventry became known as the 'British Detroit' because of the close agglomeration of car plants and associated industries. Brands such as Jaguar, British Leyland and Peugeot supported a skilled working-class labour force that became steadily affluent in the 1950s and 1960s. Indeed, workers in the city had among the highest standards of living in the country. The size of the population reflected the burgeoning economic confidence, with more than 335,000 people living in Coventry by 1961 compared to 69,000 in 1901 (Coventry City Council, 2008). During the 1950s alone, it was estimated that 23,000 migrants moved to the city, including people from different parts of Britain and those from former colonies in the Caribbean and Indian subcontinent (Coventry City Council, 2008). This was a place built on manufacturing, with 57% of employees based in the sector and many more in allied industries.

In 2007, the population of the city was estimated to be 306,700, which had grown by 1.3% since 2001 (Coventry City Council, 2009). This was largely the result of migration to Coventry, especially from the European Union (Coventry City Council, 2008). In terms of population breakdown, 74.8% of the city's population described themselves as white, 11.9% as Asian, 3.1% as black, 2.1% as 'mixed' and 2.4% as Chinese (Coventry City Council, 2008). Coventry, and the West Midlands, started to deindustrialise following the devaluation of Sterling in 1968, due to outdated production methods, exposure to international competition and increasing industrial strife. This accelerated throughout the following decade, when the government was forced to take over the ownership of major car manufacturers, such as British Leyland in 1975, in order to stave off bankruptcy and safeguard jobs. However, the Conservative victory at the 1979 general election heralded a shift from state intervention to market priorities, with less protection for industry, the reform of labour laws and reduced levels of public spending. Between 1979 and 1981, car production fell by 50% and manufacturing volume by 18%, and 20,000 people were being made redundant each week.[3] Manufacturing shrank from 57% (1976) to 44% (1986) and then 25% (1996) and 13% (2006) (see Coventry City Council, 2008). Unemployment increased sharply from 7.5% in 1976 to 16% in 1982 (Coventry City Council, 2008). Another way to consider the impact of deindustrialisation is by reviewing the change of the 'top 10' employers in the city. The statistics from 1976 showed that eight were based in manufacturing, including British Leyland, Chrysler-Talbot, Rolls Royce, Massey-Ferguson and Dunlop. These were all significant employers, with British Leyland alone employing more than 27,000 people. By 2007, there was only one manufacturing company – Jaguar Cars – in the top 10 employers, with 2,000 employees (Coventry City Council, 2008).

In 1981, the most serious violent disturbances since 1945 broke out across England. These were in disadvantaged urban neighbourhoods such as Brixton, Moss Side and Handsworth and involved black communities and the police (Benyon and Solomos, 1987). Coventry also experienced rioting but on a smaller scale. Nevertheless, the city was far from being a place of good race relations. In 1981, two racially motivated murders were committed within weeks of each other. In April, a college student, Satnam Singh Gill, was chased by a group of white skinheads in the city centre and stabbed to death; less than five weeks after this horrific incident, another Asian man, Amal Dharry, was murdered in the Earlsdon area of the city. In between, there were violent skirmishes between white and minority communities (Walters, 2012). Racial violence in Coventry seemed a long way from the 'City of Peace and Reconciliation' that symbolically reached out to cities across the world that had been ravaged by war and conflict. It was also a long way from being a peaceful or reconciled city, as confirmed by the Canon of Coventry Cathedral:

> Up until about 1960, Coventry had been a white, working class city.... They did not take kindly to the black and Asian communities moving in ... to opening up jobs. There was a lot of discrimination and the best jobs in Coventry were denied to the black community. (Kaczka-Valliere and Rigby, 2008: 591)

Against this backdrop of growing economic and racial crisis, 2 Tone was born. This was a fusion of the different musical subcultures of ska and reggae and formed a platform for both white and minority communities. Ska emerged initially in the late 1960s as a stripped-down version of 'mod culture', emphasising working-class identity and empathy with Jamaican culture; its later iteration during punk was much more fragmented, with some aspects of ska and skinhead culture associated with violent racism and support for the National Front. Reggae was popularised by migrant communities coming to cities like Coventry, and during the 1970s, it adopted a radical direction.

From the outset, 2 Tone both brought together and balanced these different traditions, rooted in working-class culture and taking place in a city that was in the grip of an unprecedented economic decline. The genre promoted black-and-white-chequered designs that, while branding an aesthetic, emphasised the importance of embracing multiculturalism and addressing racism. The stable of bands were comprised of a diverse group of musicians who largely came from local, working-class backgrounds. For example, The Specials, although started by Jerry Dammers whose father was the Deacon of Coventry Cathedral, had luminaries such as Neville Staples (ex-borstal boy and son of Jamaican migrants), Lynval Golding (brought up in Coventry and also son of Caribbean parents), Terry Hall (born in Coventry) and Roddie Byers (born in Coventry in the white working-class neighbourhood of Kersley). These musicians came together to form a group that pioneered a new form of music that made *"white working class men dance"* (Interview 1). Support for the bands was based in Coventry. While including students from the city's two universities, it also attracted white working-class people employed in factories and offices. The ska melody was deeply rhythmic but included politicised messages of economic collapse, racism and a depiction of urban life in Britain.

Songs like 'Ghost Town' had been written for Coventry but addressed the wider impact of deindustrialisation and rioting in the country during the summer of 1981. The economic success of the 1960s or 'boom days' of city were in the past, leaving young people with no apparent prospect of securing a meaningful job. The future was bleak and filled with the undercurrent of racist violence and social unrest. This is conveyed by lyrics that are a homily to the challenges confronting working-class communities in the 1980s:

> Do you remember the good old days before the ghost town? We danced and sang, and the music played in a de boomtown/ ... why the youth fight against themselves? Government leaving the youth on the shelf.... No job to be found in this country.

While 'Ghost Town' told the story of economic decline and deindustrialisation, other songs spoke to the issues of racism and violence. For example, 'Why?' was written following a racist attack on Lynval Golding in 1982 (2 Tone museum). It stated that racism was irrational and preached the gospel of multiculturalism:

> Why must we fight?/I have to defend myself/From attack last night/I know I am black/You know you are white/I'm proud of my black skin/And you are proud of your white, so.... We don't need no British Movement/Nor the Ku Klux Klan/Nor the National Front/It makes me an angry man/I just want to live in peace/

Talking to Pete Chambers, the curator of the 2 Tone museum in Coventry, gives an intriguing insight into the rise and importance of the genre and its relationship to the issues of class and identity. In the aftermath of Enoch Powell's 'River of Blood' speech in 1968, which, as noted earlier, took place in nearby Birmingham, there was a rise in visibility and electoral popularity of the neo-fascist National Front. As Chambers stated:

> "Back in the 1970s, there was lots of racism nationally, with the rise of National Front, and also Coventry, although generally I would say that people got on with each other. The working-class communities – white and black – shared the same workplaces, neighbourhoods and connected personally as neighbours or in social settings. I do remember the casual racism growing up in the home, amongst friends and in the factory that I worked after leaving school." (Interview)

The casual racism he heard on the shop floor was not confined to the white working class. Racism during the 1970s was pervasive and condoned (CCCS, 1982). The BBC continued to broadcast *Till Death* and the explicit racist outpourings from the principal character Alf Garnett at a time when 2 Tone, with its message of anti-racism, was being established. It was towards the end of the 1970s that Chambers and his friends first came across the music and multicultural message of 2 Tone, which made a lasting impression on him:

> "I heard the music on the factory floor with my white workmates and instantly connected with the music and then the lyrics. We had not heard music like this before and because The Specials were a Coventry band, it was like 'This is for me!'." (Interview)

Musically, 2 Tone came after punk and was considered more melodic. Chambers was clear that this music got white working-class men to get up and dance. Once they started to enjoy the cultural trappings of 2 Tone music, the telltale sharp suits and the checkerboard design, Chambers and his friends considered the lyrics. Chambers noted *"It was music for the head as well the feet; cerebral music if you like"*, but he knew The Specials were about promoting multiculturalism. This being said, the first 2 Tone gigs attracted an eclectic group of white working-class anti-racists, as well as supporters of the National Front, who, while enjoying the music, usually signed off the night with Sieg Heil salutes. Chambers remembers how the size of the fascist following dwindled, eventually stopped and was ultimately replaced by a multicultural throng. The early gigs took place in working-class neighbourhoods such as Stoke Heath and at venues such as The Binley Oak.

The interview with Pete Chambers gives a unique insight into the rise of 2 Tone and its working-class beginnings in a working-class city. This was an organic and grassroots movement that was not manufactured and emerged during a period of economic and social crisis in Britain. The music espoused the importance of difference and diversity and championed the values of working people and their coming together to fight racism. Chambers concluded the interview by restating the value of multiculturalism to the city and its people, as well as giving a warning about the rise of the BNP and UKIP at the 2009 and 2014 European elections, respectively: *"Multiculturalism is an essential and important life for working-class people in Coventry and* The Specials *were a key part of promulgation … more important now when the face of fascism wears a suit such as BNP and UKIP"* (interview).

Conclusion

This chapter has focused on how the white working class has been socially constructed and reconstructed as being problematic and celebrated in the post-war period, how they transitioned from 'hero' to 'zero', and how they have been represented in film, television and as cultural phenomena through music.

The characterisation in film and media demonstrates the different sides of white working-class identities. The social realism films of the 1950s and 1960s, such as *Saturday Night and Sunday Morning*, created a multidimensional portrait of the working class at work and at home rather than the generally limited, compliant and comedic interpretations that preceded its release. The films were pioneering and progressive because they were concerned with political issues and they challenged conventional narratives, including immigration, race and miscegenation. One such film, *A Taste of Honey*, based in early 1960s' Salford, explores the relationship between a white woman and a black man and the subsequent pregnancy, which highlights the prospect of being a single parent with a dual-heritage child in an intolerant Britain. Social realism or New Wave British cinema created a new framework to consider white working-class experiences. This could be viewed as a positive development given the societal changes that were taking place in the country.

Part of the post-war change in Britain was shaped by colonial immigration, primarily from the Caribbean and Indian subcontinent. This challenged notions that English identity was largely based on whiteness. Alongside the dismantling of the British Empire, the themes of immigration and multiculturalism provided the foundation for popular television programmes in a country that was marked in the 1960s by a consumer thirst for television. The emergence of *Till Death* provided sharp satire on the issues of class and identity but created a space and legitimacy for crude racist language to be aired on peak-time British television. Based on the relationships within a white working-class family, it nevertheless promoted the first fully fledged racist on television. It seemed that Alf Garnett was the personification of the English bigot but his extreme views gave the show a huge television audience. The association of whiteness, class and racism became embedded in the popular consciousness through these types of programmes.

More recently, films such as *This is England* portray working-class culture and communities in a more nuanced way, returning to some of the frameworks deployed by social realism in the 1950s. While addressing and celebrating the difference and diversity within the skinhead gang, the film does not refrain from discussing neo-fascist politics and racist violence. This is perhaps seen at its most extreme by the speech made by Combo in which he berates the impact of immigration on the lives of ordinary white working-class communities. *This is England* starts by showing the white working class embracing black culture and music and then descending into the dystopian vision of white nationalism before pulling back to recognise the limitations of such an approach.

In film and television, the white working class slipped from being viewed as multifaceted to being framed by its opposition to race and immigration. The impact of the 1958 Notting Hill riots and Enoch Powell's 'Rivers of Blood' speech were examined. Media reporting focused on the white working class as being antagonistic, violent and laying claim to an English identity that was based on whiteness as much as class. By viewing Teds as being loutish thugs and instigators of the 1958 riots, where the Dockers and Meatporters went on strike and marched to Parliament in support of Powell, the white working class were framed as racist and resistant to change.

Countering cultural and populist projections is challenging. The grassroots alchemy of music provides an opportunity to rebalance the common-sense assumptions of white working-class communities and multiculturalism. Punk, in its formative period at least, was viewed as a working-class and white subculture that, through the music of bands such as The Clash and songs like 'White Riot', attempted to show common cause between established and emerging communities. The narrative is complicated and layered given the association and trajectory of skinheads from being immersed in Caribbean culture (as shown in *This is England*) to demonstrating a white nationalism and support for political parties like the National Front. If punk was ambiguous in demonstrating a progressive whiteness, then 2 Tone showcased the importance and value of multiculturalism. The emergence of 2 Tone in working-class Coventry, together with explicit anti-racist messaging, helped to rebalance white working-class culture as being progressive and inclusive. As stated in the chapter, *"it was cerebral music"*.

The importance of culture, consumption and representation is central to this book. Reviewing a selection of films, television programmes and music genres, as well as popular events in post-war British history, cannot lead to a definitive answer on the issues of white working-class identity and racism. Yet, it should at least support the view that the white working class should not be fetishised as being racist or non-racist. The reality is that the white working class is similar to many other social groups in society in terms of having fluid identities that are constructed and reconstructed by many different factors. White working-class identities may take on the character of Arthur Seaton, Alf Garnett or Combo, or they may be shaped by the music of The Clash and The Specials. The white working class simply reflects policy and political contradictions that riddle the debates on immigration and race. Social realism in films and musical expression shows the everyday lived experiences of these communities rather than top-down projections by the media and government. In this way, the counterbalancing should be welcomed.

Notes

[1] Speech to Conservative Group for Europe (1993), available at: http://www.johnmajor.co.uk/page1086.html

[2] *The Guardian*, 'Junior Murvin has died but the story of Police and Thieves lives on'. Available at: http://www.theguardian.com/commentisfree/2013/dec/04/junior-murvin-died-police-and-thieves-jamaican-reggae

3. See *The Independent* (2014), available at: http://www.independent.co.uk/news/business/make-or-break-british-manufacturing-began-the-eighties-with-an-inevitable-shakeout-it-started-the-nineties-leaner-fitter--yet-fighting-to-survive--another-downturn-less-shattering-but-harder-to-throw-off-david-bowen-tells-a-tale-of-two-recessions-1491464.html

FOUR

International perspectives on whiteness, class and politics

Introduction

Debates on white working-class perspectives on multiculturalism and change resonate in Britain. National themes such as belonging and identity in a country that is being reshaped by immigration have become key political issues. Deindustrialisation, the marginalisation of the white working class, 'backlash' against multicultural policies and the emergence of whiteness, class and nationalism are not restricted to Britain. Indeed, research commissioned by the Open Society Foundation on 'majority communities' and integration identified common issues across countries in the European Union (EU). This has been further entrenched after the success of many extreme Right and nationalist parties at the 2014 European elections. Across the Atlantic in the US, the white working class has followed a trajectory that is not so different from perspectives closer to home. Comparing the similarities between different places may support a more rounded analysis of the British context, thereby helping to come up with strategies that could lead to an informed debate.

Underlying the discussion is the reality that white working-class views on multiculturalism will be very different in the UK to different countries in Europe and even more so in the US. Variations in terms (white working class may be understood in the US and the UK but does not fit easily into a European context), legislation (citizenship rights by birth as in the US or by application as in the UK) and politics (the long march to power of the Front National in France compared to the recent insurgency of, and popular support for UKIP in the UK and the Sweden Democrats in Sweden, or the model of the non-electoral group of the Tea Party in the US). The countries also vary considerably in terms of population size, composition and difference, as well as ideology and culture. Initially, it seems that there is little value in making a comparison between the experiences of white working-class communities in the US, Europe and the UK. Nonetheless, on closer inspection, the comparison may not be quite so far-fetched as there are common experiences between countries, including the loss of jobs primarily held by the working class, the demonisation of the working class and their sense that they have lost their identity with their own country, and the 'backlash' effect towards immigrants.

This chapter will reflect on the white working class, identities and the upsurge of political support in three different settings: the Sweden Democrats in Sweden; the Tea Party in the US; and UKIP in Britain. While the Sweden Democrats share much with UKIP in terms of putting themselves forward as the authentic voice of the working class, being anti-politics, being anti-EU and highlighting the impact of immigration on Swedish/British identity, the Tea Party is different because of its libertarian influence and support from the middle class as much as from the working class. Based on a selective and critical review of the literature and using, in part, fieldwork data from a range of studies, the analysis also demonstrates that the white working class should not be reduced to being a hostile group towards multiculturalism.

The white working class, multiculturalism and rise of the radical Right in Europe

In 2014, the Open Society Foundation published a series of research reports on white working-class communities in six cities (Aarhus, Amsterdam, Netherlands, Berlin, Stockholm, Lyon and Manchester) and countries (Denmark, the Netherlands, Germany, Sweden, France and the UK) in Europe (OSF, 2014). The context for conducting the studies was the success of radical Right parties at the 2014 European elections, when they came first in the UK, Denmark and France. In addition, there has been considerable economic change in Europe, with a move away from manufacturing to service industries. White working-class communities were the focus for the studies because they were viewed as providing the core basis of support for radical Right parties and have seen jobs lost because of economic restructuring. In each place, white working-class communities have also been subject to ridicule by the media as being welfare-dependent and resistant to change.

The Open Society Foundation research underscored key themes discussed in this book, such as the problems of defining the white working class. As noted earlier in Chapters One and Two, deciding who the working class is has been a point of contention for many decades, with new attempts to include cultural as well as occupational and economic considerations (Savage et al, 2014). Defining 'white' has also been subject to scrutiny because some view the term as a racial construct (Dyer, 2006) while others engage into a crude reductionism based on behaviours (Murray, 1996). Finally, in Britain (ONS, 2012), Europe (OSF, 2014) and the US (Frey, 2011), the demographic trends show increasingly diverse countries with significant growth in the population categories in the 'mixed' section. The confusion in defining the white working class was recognised by the Open Society Foundation, who used 'majority populations' (OSF, 2014: 9). Even this term is problematic because white working-class communities may not be in the majority in some cities and neighbourhoods. For example, white working-class residents were not the majority population in Aston in Birmingham, which was one of the case study areas used in the Joseph Rowntree Foundation research discussed in Chapters Five and Six (Beider, 2011). In the context of the comparative study across six European countries, the Open Society Foundation used 'majority' in terms of birth and citizenship rights now and in the past: 'it was defined as individuals who are citizens of the country where the research was taking place and born in that country and whose parents also were born in the country and citizens of that country' (OSF, 2014: 9).

Beyond definitional challenges, the research studies also referenced the concerns about immigration and the impact on national culture and belonging that were discussed in earlier framing chapters and are highlighted in later fieldwork chapters. National, city and neighbourhood context varied but many of the white working-class people interviewed framed immigration as being social change which could be unsettling.

> Many saw immigration as a threat to the sense of community and national identity. Language, dress, behaviour and the perceived unwillingness of immigrants to associate with the wider community were cited as barriers to communication, interaction and a shared sense of community. (OSF, 2014: 67)

Immigration, together with government policy that promoted multiculturalism, was viewed as being disconnected from the experiences and priorities of white working-class communities, who felt that politicians did not give them a voice on the issues of social change. The threats to national identity, as well as more local identity, were seen as both cultural (language, dress and behaviour) and economic (housing, jobs). Again, the type of language used in the

Open Society Foundation research overlaps with research conducted in the UK (National Community Forum, 2009; Beider, 2011, 2014).

White working-class disconnection from political institutions, deepening concern about the impact of immigration on national culture and identity, and worries about job security go beyond Britain and UKIP. Across Europe and in the US, political movements and parties have succeeded in mobilising support at national elections and shaking the political establishment.

Some of these interventions are not new. For example, in France, the rise of the Front National has long played a significant role in national and local politics, getting to the second round presidential run-off in 2002 and coming first in France at the 2014 European elections. Similar to many right-wing parties, the Front National seeks to represent the interests of the 'left behind', who feel that their way of life is being threatened by immigration and big government. The party has also attempted a political facelift under its leader, Marine Le Pen, who has softened some of the overtly racist rhetoric of her father and previous leader, Jean-Marie Le Pen. The Front National talks about protecting not white identity, but French culture, and focuses on how the political elite has led to France having too many immigrants. Specifically the target is Islam and how it challenges societal norms. The political makeover, representing those who feel excluded from mainstream political parties and pointing to the impact of immigration on diluting national identity, are typical paths followed by far Right parties in Europe.

The success and rejuvenation of the Front National is party based on speaking to two different types of constituencies, which has been highlighted by research commissioned by the national TV station, France 24. Taking a slightly different view that white working-class voters are the core support, the research pointed to the Front National formula for winning support in the north and east of Paris and along the Southern Mediterranean coast. In the former, the Front National has successfully mined concerns about immigration among working-class voters, but in the south, support comes from the self-employed and retired, who, while worried about immigration, are also against high taxation and government interference (France 24, 2013). Nonetheless the theme of people who compose part of 'Forgotten France' has become part of Marine Le Pen's leadership. In 2013, she toured small towns and villages in order to connect with people who had been left behind by the political elites in the French government in Paris and in the European Commission in Brussels. The idea was to extend support to working-class voters who had traditionally supported the

French Socialists using a plan based on attacking political and economic elites – the aforementioned failing politicians, faceless bureaucrats and uncontrollable multinational companies – as well as the embedded message on immigration. In 2014 and also local elections, this paid dividends, with the Front National winning in previously strong Socialist areas. Patrick Cathala is the type of voter that the Front National won over in 2014. A middle-aged male who used to work in construction but found his job being undercut by cheaper migrant labour, he blames the government, the European Commission and migrants for the predicament: 'I'm unemployed because firms prefer to hire workers from Romania, Bulgaria, Portugal or Spain. They're letting all those people in. What am I supposed to do?'[1]

The Front National has been described as a 'prototype of the populist radical right party' (Mudde, 2013). As a political organisation, the party has a track record of success in influencing political debates and wining at local, national and European elections. In contrast, the surge of support for the Sweden Democrats is relatively recent. The party was formed in 1988 as *Bevara Sverige Svenskt* (Keep Sweden Swedish), an organisation with strong links to neo-Nazi and white supremacist movements.

Sweden is regarded as a model of modern social democracy, with a generous welfare state and being welcoming to refugees and asylum seekers. The country is projected to admit 80,000 refugees over the coming years in the context of a population of 9.8 million (Duhan, 2014), and a universal welfare state to protect against unemployment, illness and supporting maternity and paternity leave is well-established (Esping-Andersen, 2013). Yet, well before the Swedish model of supportive migration and the welfare state, the country also recorded a significant membership of the Nazi Party in the interwar period (Ramalingam, 2012). In the post-1945 period, Sweden was firmly locked into building a modern country and democracy based on principles of equality and inclusiveness as a reaction to and move away from any association with Nazism and its position of neutrality during the Second World War (Ruth, 1984). The principles of equality extended across gender to include an open immigration policy and supporting multiculturalism in Swedish society. In contrast with Britain, these have become inculcated into the body politic in the way that issues of immigration have been debated by the media and politicians. In fact, multiculturalism has become part of the agreed norms in Sweden. As Ramalingam (2012: 10) observes:

> The mobilisation of anti- immigrant attitudes is thus understood not just to be deviant, but as an outright threat … aversion to anti-immigrant sentiment in Sweden is visible in the unwritten codes of conduct dictating the public debate on immigration policy … established parties in Sweden have deliberately chosen to not exploit the immigration issue and that party elites have not responded to the reality of anti-immigrant policy views prevalent among Swedish citizens … the topic of immigration in Sweden has generated its own set of permissible discourses and notions of political correctness.

The implication is that the high-minded approach to tolerance and active support for a multicultural Sweden by the political establishment is being conducted by a remote and disconnected elite far removed from the localised impact of immigration on working-class Swedes, whose neighbourhoods are experiencing churn and who are also competing with newly arrived migrants for welfare benefits, schools and housing. It is in this political context that the Sweden Democrats emerged as an anti-immigrant, anti-Muslim and pro-nationalist party and accessed a seam of popular discontent over the impact of multiculturalism on Swedish culture. This has translated into electoral success, challenging the social-democratic status quo in Swedish politics. The new insurgents captured 1.4% of the national vote in 2002, 5.7% in 2010 and 12.2% in 2014 (Ramalingam, 2012; Duhan, 2014;).

Similarities exist with both UKIP and the Front National. The Sweden Democrats have sought to erase their Nazi origins and symbolism and cultivate an imaginary as a party that speaks up for working people on issues that have been ignored by the political establishment. Just as Marine le Pen and Nigel Farage have modernised the Front National and UKIP, respectively, in their own image, Jimmie Akersson and his colleagues have championed the Sweden Democrats as a movement that respects and understands the lived experiences and the values of Sweden.

The rise of the Sweden Democrats was framed by modernisation of the party. Racist sentiments among activists led to expulsions and Akersson attacks not the concept of diversity in Sweden, but the practice of multiculturalism and its forced political correctness onto a majority by a liberal elite, on behalf of a newly arrived minority. Indeed, multiculturalism has been set up as a threat to not only Swedish identity, but also the cherished Swedish welfare state because hard-pressed taxpayers fund unemployed immigrants and their integration into society. Further, the Sweden Democrats have portrayed Muslims and Islam as undermining gender equality because of the way in which women are subjugated. Just as the Front National speaks to working-class communities in Northern France and middle-class business people in the Southern Mediterranean, or UKIP has broadened its appeal from people who wanted Britain out of the EU to representing the interests of working-class communities who lost out through immigration and the Labour Party's move to the political centre, the Sweden Democrats are seeking to deepen support through anti-immigration rhetoric, particularly about the way in which Islam is incompatible with core Swedish values of equality.

Support for the Sweden Democrats comes from a number of areas, but in the main, from white working-class men who have not been to university. In an analysis of the 2014 voting patterns, more than 16% of Sweden Democrats were former supporters of the larger Social Democrats and were largely working class (Duhan, 2014). They are not necessarily the neo-Nazis who were involved when the party was first founded, but rather working-class voters who viewed the political mainstream as not speaking about the issues that concerned them. The Sweden Democrats do not explicitly discuss whiteness. Rather, proxy terms such as culture and identity refer to the need to be vigilant against the threats of immigration and especially Islam. Yet, whiteness is a part of the Swedish nation. It is largely composed of people who are homogeneous and share similar social norms. According to Hübinette and Lundström (2011), the success of the Sweden Democrats has been by giving primacy to whiteness across different type of white communities who were themselves migrants to Sweden from Southern and Central Europe. Building on the work of Roediger (1991), whiteness is a site of privilege that becomes something to be preserved against visible minority communities. Even in a country that has a well-funded welfare state and socially liberal policies, whiteness becomes shaped by a longing for the past – Old Sweden – and protecting the civil liberties present in New Sweden. Both are under pressure from the arrival of Muslim-based immigration:

> The Sweden Democrats' longing for 'old Sweden' is expressed as a wish to return to the time when there were no ethnoracial conflicts and no non-Western 'patriarchal excesses', while what is under threat for the white anti-racists is the image of Sweden as an anti-racist country and for the white feminists the image of Sweden as a feminist country. In the end, all these self-images risk feeling

threatened by the presence of non-white, non-Christian, and non-Western migrants. (Hübinette and Lundström, 2011: 50)

Nostalgia and melancholy are evident in references to 'old Sweden' before open immigration policies and Sweden's now established position as a progressive and forward-looking society. 'Old Sweden' was noticeably more conservative and Christian in outlook, as well as being largely white. The call by the Sweden Democrats to protect culture looks to the past and seeks to recreate key aspects in the 21st century through policies such as dramatically reducing immigration, promoting assimilation into Swedish culture and rejecting multiculturalism. References to the past help to position the Sweden Democrats as cultural shields against the interference of newly arrived Muslims. The slogan 'Give us Sweden back' speaks to how immigrants and political elites have allowed the common norms of Sweden to be compromised.

The Sweden Democrats also appeal to a different type of white constituency that is removed from working-class males. These are social liberals who want to protect the progress made on women's rights and sexual orientation against the impact of new immigrants who may take a different view on the role of women and sexual orientation. Preserving 'New Sweden' in terms of civil liberties and strengthening social programmes in a rebooted welfare state expands the potential support for the Sweden Democrats. It is almost a return to the founding objectives of the Social Democrats but framed within an anti-immigration and nationalist message. It is only people who can demonstrate a 'Swedishness' who will be able to access new welfare programmes. Verifying whiteness and alignment to cultural tropes helps to demarcate immigrants as the outsiders in both the 'Old Sweden' and the 'New Sweden'.

The white working class and the Tea Party

Rick Santelli, a Business reporter with the American TV network CNBC, was angry with the government mortgage bailout policies initiated by the new Obama administration, which were viewed as supporting sub-prime lenders. In February 2009, from the floor of the Chicago Stock Exchange, he railed against federal (or national) government helping 'losers' with taxpayers' money and called on capitalists to organise a 'Chicago Tea Party' to dump securities into the local Chicago River:

> The government is promoting bad behaviour.... This is America. How many of you want to pay for your neighbor's mortgage, which has an extra bathroom, and can't pay their bills? Raise your hand! President Obama, are you listening?... we're thinking of having a Chicago Tea Party in July. All you capitalists want to show up to Lake Michigan, I'm going to start organizing. (Williamson et al, 2011:26)

It is important to note that the starting point for the social movement known as the Tea Party was on the floor of the stock exchange of America's third-largest city, with the focus on protecting the system of capitalism from supporting those in need. At its inception, this was a top-down intervention defending vested interests.

So, how did the Tea Party become framed as a grassroots revolt of hard-working, largely white communities against an overreaching national government? The concept and reference to the 'Tea Party' evokes revolutionary memory for many Americans. In 1773, an East India Company ship was delivering a shipment of tea to Boston. The British government legislated that tax would be levied at entry to the American colony rather than at origin in order to support the business fortunes of the East India Company, which was being adversely impacted by competition from other suppliers in Europe. Viewing this as another example of unfair colonialism, a protest was organised that led to the tea shipment being dumped overboard in Boston Harbour and the assertion that no tax would be paid.

Historically, the Boston Tea Party has been viewed as the first systematic act of defiance against the British Empire and the spark that led to the Revolutionary War and the birth of the United States of America in 1776 (Carp, 2010). The point being that the use of the term 'Tea Party' crystallised popular defiance against the perceptions of unfair taxation on hard-working communities. The difference between 1773 and 2009 is that rather than sending in messengers to tell people in other cities such as New York and Philadelphia about the popular protest in Boston, the internet enables instant communication to a global audience. As Williamson et al correctly point out:

> Across the country, web-savvy conservative activists recognized rhetorical gold when they saw it. Operating at first through the social-networking site Twitter, conservative bloggers and Republican campaign veterans took the opportunity offered by the Santelli rant to plan protests under the newly minted 'Tea Party' name. As seasoned

> activists organised local rallies, the video of Santelli quickly scaled the media pyramid ... being widely re-televised; and receiving public comment within 24 hours from the White House Press Secretary, Robert Gibbs. (Williamson et al, 2011: 26)

Creating the impression of an anti-government and grassroots movement was supported by the internet but also the media, especially right-leaning news organisations such as Fox TV. In a recent publication documenting the rise of the movement, DiMaggio recounts a leading supporter commenting that 'there would not have been a Tea Party without Fox' (DiMaggio, 2011: 224). The more interesting role has been played by the liberal media, such as the *New York Times*, which has viewed the Tea Party as a mass movement or uprising with more press coverage than the Occupy Wall Street or anti-war movements. The increased levels of noise created by the media spectacle helped to bring together the different Tea Parties across the country to organise a national protest on 15 April – Tax Day – 2009. The *New York Times* reported that more protests were organised in 750 cities while the independent pollster Nate Silver suggested that more than 311,000 people attended the various events, ranging from 15,000 people in Atlanta to 12 people in Fort Plain, New York State.

The burgeoning growth of the Tea Party reached an early peak with the march on Washington DC on 12 September 2009. This time, the *New York Times* suggested that it was the largest conservative rally ever to have taken place in the capital. In less than eight months from Santelli's broadcast, the Tea Party had captured a mood in US politics that grasped at the revolutionary spirit of 1776. Protestors had expanded their range of demands to include lower taxation, small rather than big government, individual freedom against gun control and legislation for the Affordable Care Act. This range of issues is captured in the following excerpt:

> A sea of protesters filled the west lawn of the Capitol and spilled onto the National Mall on Saturday in the largest rally against President Obama since he took office, a culmination of a summer-long season of protests that began with opposition to a health care overhaul and grew into a broader dissatisfaction with government. On a cloudy and cool day, the demonstrators came from all corners of the country, waving American flags and handwritten signs explaining the root of their frustrations. Their anger

stretched well beyond the health care legislation moving through Congress, with shouts of support for gun rights, lower taxes and a smaller government.

In the next section, a critical analysis will delve more deeply into the Tea Party movement and will focus on: the connections and links between white and white working-class grievances; the changing norms and concerns that the government is not looking after their interests; gaining a better perspective on whether the Tea Party is really something new or simply the latest in a long line of conservative and neoliberal movements; and to what extent the emergence of the Tea Party was linked to the historic election of Barack Obama, the US's first black president.

Hamill (1969) wrote a paean for the forgotten white working class:

> The working-class white man spends much of his time complaining almost desperately about the way he has become a victim. Taxes and the rising cost of living keep him broke, and he sees nothing in return for the taxes he pays…. His streets were the last to be cleaned in the big snowstorm…. His neighbourhood is a dumping ground for abandoned automobiles…. He works very hard, frequently on a dangerous job, and then he discovers that he still can't pay his way; his wife takes a Thursday night job in a department store and he gets a weekend job, pumping gas or pushing a hack. For him, life in New York is not much of a life.

In charting the mix of growing economic insecurity, political disconnection and concerns about a changing and different society, Hamill helps us to connect to some of themes that have underpinned the rise of the Tea Party since 2009. Recent and detailed opinion polls showed that Tea Party supporters are 89% white and pessimistic about the prospects for the country. They also tend to be older (75% over 45 years old) and men (59%), although women compose a significant block of supporters (41%). The poll confirms research in that Tea Party supporters are white, angry and resentful. This seems to suggest that there has not been a great deal of change since Hamill's *New York Magazine* article in 1969: 'The working class white man is actually in revolt against taxes, joyless work, and the double standards and short memories of professional politicians, hypocrisy and what he considers the debasement of the American dream' (Hamill, 1969).

The Tea Party is assumed to be a white working-class revolt but the evidence is conflicting. Some suggest that Tea Party supporters are working-class (68%) and this compares to 70% for the population as a whole. Another poll suggests that Tea Party supporters are actually middle-class rather than working-class. A better framing of class-related to the Tea Party is to consider the impact that the 2008 economic recession had on many American families. This led to growing levels of economic insecurity, downshifting and hardship to middle-class or working families who had previously been insulated by economic growth.

It could be argued that the Tea Party only came to prominence after and because of Barack Obama's election victory in 2008. The campaign had been based on the premise of progressive change built on a broad-based coalition of interests, including the professional elite, young people and communities of colour. The focus was on the federal government playing an active role in supporting vulnerable communities, an expansion of affordable health care and increased rights for same-sex couples. There was also a great deal of focus on and commitment to withdrawal from international wars and holding big business accountable. This was not the agenda that appealed to white voters and, not surprisingly, they did not support Obama in the same number as the progressive coalition.

So, to what extent should the Tea Party movement be regarded as a racist response to the election of a black president? Since the first protests in 2009, there have been accusations of open displays of racism at Tea Party gatherings. In contextualising overt racism, Zeskind (2012: 501) states that those who follow the Tea Party have not come to the terms with the fact that the country is changing from a majority to a minority white country, and with the election of Obama:

> from the beginning, the self-evident signs of racial animus have been omnipresent at Tea Party events. Posters at rallies and protests demeaned the president in specifically racial terms, depicting him as an African witchdoctor … there were placards where white people depicted themselves as racial victims, as slaves or worse … one woman carried a homemade sign that read 'Obama + Marxism = Slavery'. One of the most infamous … was carried by the founder of the 1776 Tea Party network … 'Congress = Slaveowner, Taxpayer = Niggar'.

It can be argued that Obama's presidency has become a lightning rod for white resentment, as evidenced by the outright displays of racism at Tea Party events and rallies just noted. This can be further explored by attacks on civil rights organisations such as the NAACP [National Association for the Advancement of Colored People] after it had accused the Tea Party of racism. It was variously denounced as promoting 'reverse discrimination', making 'more money off of race than any slave trade ever' and diluting the term 'racist'. The suggestion that racism has been overplayed or that it does not exist at all echoes strongly among white people in general and Tea Party members in particular. In the *New York Times* CBS Poll conducted in 2010, 63% of Tea Party supporters as opposed to 39% of white people agreed that 'we had gone too far in pushing for civil rights' (Zeskind, 2012: 503).

The sentiments against civil rights organisations and criticisms of equality of opportunity seep through Tea Party perspectives on fiscal responsibility and low taxation. It is debatable whether underlying racial narratives would have been as evident if Obama had not been elected president. It seemed that his victory in 2008, as well as his re-election in 2012, created an opportunity for racism and resentment to be aired. In claiming victimhood, Tea Party supporters have provided a rationale for organising as a social movement. As Zeskind (2012: 503) states: 'Thus Tea Partiers define themselves as "victims" of the civil rights movement and President Obama, who broke the white monopoly over the White House. They became the "slave" and the "niggar" memorialized on their poster boards'.

Victimisation and racialisation can be seen in Tea Party attacks on welfare. As discussed, the organisation has firmly embedded itself on the side of 'hard-working' Americans who have been let down by establishment politicians in Washington DC. The sense that one should not be dependent on the state to provide welfare and support, but should work hard, look after one's family and strive for independence, has been part of the American credo since 1776. In this context, welfare and being viewed as a 'freeloader' can be used as a proxy for viewing some communities of colour as having a sense of entitlement.

The dividing line between 'working' and 'not working' is laced with racial undertones. In one respect, it builds on the rhetoric of 'welfare queens' used by Ronald Reagan, former president and heroic figure for many Tea Party members because of his espousal of low taxes, freedom and patriotism. The cumulative resentments go beyond direct racism and associating welfare as a proxy for communities of colour. It is the very nature of what the US was, and what it will become, that is, the transition into a minority white country by 2043, with the number of white births in 2012 being a minority for the first time in the country's history. This should be regarded as more than simply a demographic transition. It is laced with deeply held views of dispossession and disconnection with societal norms that are deeply embedded in the American psyche, such as English as the common language, assumptions of the free market and the recognised role of government. An African-American president and the white population in the minority lead to an anxiety of not belonging.

In meeting the challenge of deep-seated societal change, the Tea Party movement has embraced symbols of Revolutionary America and adopted quasi-nationalism. The rhetoric is fixated on American exceptionalism or the theory that the US is different (with the inference being better) than other countries because of its economic and military power and grounded values of laissez-faire economics, individualism and small government. The Tea Party's historical narrative does not provide space for minorities, who are soon to become the majority in the country. However, the symbolism of being drenched in revolutionary fervour has been an important marker of difference from established political organisations. It has been argued that the nationalism of the Tea Party divides people into 'insiders', who deserve to become citizens, and outsiders, who do not:

> Nationalism is an ideological construction through which individuals and social movements can produce a notion of collective identity on a particular territory. It seeks to answer the question of who is in, and who is out of the people, the nation, and who has rights of citizenship in the state … it does follow inexorably from the assertion that there are 'real Americans' and others not so real. (Zeskind, 2012: 504)

The nationalism, resentments and 'othering' culminate in Tea Party views on immigration. These are universally hostile, with more than 40% of supporters stating that they would like legal immigration to be restricted. This seems strange for a country that had been built on the basis of immigration. Furthermore, 97% of supporters are opposed to illegal immigration. Some supporters have questioned whether US citizenship should be bestowed to children born in the country to illegal immigrants. This would go against the 14th amendment of the Constitution but Tea Party supporters state that 'birth tourism' is a significant problem and leads to a situation where illegal immigration becomes endemic. It has been suggested that the strategy is based not so much on curbing illegal immigration, but on preventing the sense of dispossession felt by Tea Party members.

The discussion demonstrates that while the Tea Party movement leads on the issues of low taxation and small government, the issues of race and immigration are part of the appeal of the social movement. Racialised discussion based on crude stereotyping against Obama, using welfare as a proxy for minorities and a hard-line stance on immigration are all examples that promote a nationalist fervour that excludes people who are not white and conservative. As such, it is the first mass-based popular movement since the Ku Klux Klan that has mobilised white Americans on the basis of dispossession and reclaiming a country. Zeskind has analysed the intersections of the Tea Party and race. He suggests that its slogan of 'Take it Back' not only is about government and taxation, but also refers to a country that has been lost to minorities and illegal immigrants. He forcefully contends:

> Tea Party ... embrace ... that non-Anglo-Saxon immigration has caused the downfall of the country is a way beyond the mantra of debt, taxes and fiscal policy that Tea Party leaders have claimed is their calling card. It puts the Tea Party nation in the company of those white nationalists who have promoted a more complete theory of white dispossession. (Zeskind, 2012: 503)

The themes of the dispossession of white communities and, at the same time, reaching back to the organisational memory of the American Revolution is a recurring theme for conservative or right-wing social movements in the US. To this extent, the Tea Party seems to be the latest in a long line of protests characterised by white leadership that has its origin in the Goldwater presidential campaign of 1964. This sought to mobilise white working communities and business interests against the social reform agenda of black emancipation embodied in the Civil Rights Movement led by Martin Luther King. The rhetoric was about taking back the country and battling the incipient sense of loss of a country and culture:

> The ideology of grassroots Tea Party adherents fits with the long-standing, well-documented connections between opposition to federal entitlement programs and espousal of racial stereotypes.... Even more broadly, since the Civil Rights era of the 1960s, the Republican Party and popular conservative mobilization have expressed strong opposition

> to strong federal government interventions in social and
> economic life, often viewing such interventions as intended
> to force racial integration and provide special help to people
> of color. (Williamson et al, 2011: 34)

Finding connections between culture, mood and protest between
the 1960s and 2000s supports an understanding of the growth of the
Tea Party. White America was under sustained challenge 50 years
ago. The norms of hard work, free enterprise and racial segregation
were challenged by the rise of the counterculture of 'tuning out', the
relaxation of social codes, the rise of popular music and legislation to
end racial discrimination. Alongside this was increasing voice against
the war in Vietnam. Rapid change threatened conventional ideas and
the American Dream. Hamill recounts this in the *New York Magazine*
article on the disengagement of the white working class. His encounters
with low- and semi-skilled workers in diners, bars and in their front
gardens pointed to resentment and disgruntlement. African-Americans
were squeezing their beliefs and culture out while they were being
treated with disdain by the political elite.

The discussion thus far has focused on the Tea Party as a populist,
white response to deep-seated societal changes, racial resentment and
big government. Some have suggested that the white working-class
bedrock that did not support Obama in 2008 or 2012 has found a
voice to register long-held grievances. This perspective runs the risk
of reducing white communities to default supporters of the Tea Party
and pathologises their experiences. As Levison (2013) argues, the white
working class is a complex constituency. Scoping and defining this
group not as the 'blue-collar brutes' discussed previously, but people
who compose up to 40% of the labour force and far removed from
pathological stereotypes:

> They are not the desperate and jobless workers who 'shaped
> up' in front of the factory gates every day to beg for work as
> factory workers did during the great depression. Many make
> decent money and vast numbers work as small independent
> contractors rather than hired employees. Nor do most
> working class men still talk and act like the inarticulate,
> hulking laborers portrayed by Marlon Brando in the 1950s
> and Sylvester Stallone in the 1970s. But they are united
> by sociological traits and cultural values that define many
> aspects of their social identity. Unlike the affluent fofthe
> highly educated they see themselves as 'real Americans'

who are 'just getting by'. They are 'hardworking', 'practical' and 'realistic'. They believe in 'old fashioned traditional values' … and real world experience rather than advanced education. These characteristics have not basically changed since the 1950s. (Salam, 2013)

Far from being supporters of the Tea Party, white working-class communities demonstrate a gradation that is not often credited to them. They are actually supportive of government interventions to bolster employment and health care because this is perceived to be supporting the family through increased levels of economic security and health provision. This constituency also supports meeting the needs of the poor, or redistributive policies. Unlike the Tea Party, and on closer inspection, the white working class want greater accountability of big business, especially in the wake of the 2008 recession.

Despite taking a generally progressive stance on government intervention, Levison (2013) notes that the white working class hold hard-line views on immigration. Does this specify cultural conservatism alongside being progressive on economic issues? In an earlier part of the chapter, we emphasised the direct and indirect racism and resentment in the messaging of the Tea Party. White working-class views on immigration could partly be linked to disgruntlement, but also to the increased levels of competition in the labour market from new migrants.

Does the Tea Party represent the views of the white working class? Culturally, sociologically and politically, this group has been framed and pathologised as being discontent and disconnected, having suffered more than most from the last recession. The Tea Party would like to claim this important constituency as strong supporters but the evidence points in another direction. The white working class is nuanced and diverse and takes a range of positions on government intervention, free trade and social policies that would be at odds with much of the Tea Party programme. It is all too easy to fill a vacuum in research with simple reductionism about the white working class, and this should be resisted.

Finally, the rise of the Tea Party in the US has led to comparisons with UKIP in the UK. Like the Tea Party, UKIP has messaged itself as being a populist, grassroots organisation that is taking on the political establishment who have failed to provide Britons with a successful economy, have not addressed the 'problem' of immigration and, most importantly, have allowed the European Commission to increase its influence on domestic policy.

The comparisons are compelling and UKIP has marketed itself as the 'People's Army', holding to account a disconnected, corrupt and unrepresentative political class that has greatly expanded the size of government and is out of touch with ordinary people. Despite attempts to portray UKIP as a white working-class movement, the reality is that much of its support comes from disgruntled former Conservatives, the white working class who have traditionally voted for the Right and those who have not bothered to vote for anyone before. The 2014 gains made in largely white working-class communities in the North and Midlands need to be viewed alongside its relative lack of support in large towns and cities.

There are similarities between the Tea Party and UKIP that need to be explored. In particular, they both exploit a mood among the white working class that they have suffered losses, which they measure in terms of jobs, identity and nation. They suppose that government, by supporting policies such as multiculturalism, has ignored and ridiculed the white working class and given priority to minority communities. Fundamentally, UKIP, like the Tea Party, is concerned with looking back to a past of British hegemony and norms that were shaped by whiteness. Immigration is viewed as being problematic, not just because of competition with white working-class people in the labour market, but because of the changing face of Britain in terms of cultural identity. This is not so much a revolt of the white working class as a new Battle of Britain in the 21st century.

Conclusion

Analysing white working-class communities and multiculturalism is beset with challenges. Ideology, legislation and the way in which white working class communities are defined are problematic. Yet, beyond these admitted constraints, similarities can be discerned in how the discussion is shaped and linked to the rise of radical Right parties and movements. The Open Society Foundation (OSF, 2014) gave a detailed account of the perspectives of white working-class communities in six different countries across Europe, showing common and emerging themes between groups. Discussion of the rise of the Tea Party in the US also intersects with these themes. Taken together, three common factors underpin the experiences of white working-class communities across different countries.

The first factor is criticism of existing political elites who have become disconnected with the views of communities. In Sweden and Britain, both the Sweden Democrats and UKIP have mined a deep seam of disdain with mainstream politicians. This has been manifested in terms of representation and fit. For example, UKIP claims to be the most working-class party in the country, making a distinction between members who are drawn from 'ordinary' backgrounds as opposed to the 'extraordinarily' privileged backgrounds of those who hold office in the main parties. In 2015 the leaders of the Conservative, Labour and Liberal Democrat parties graduated from the universities of Oxford and Cambridge and then worked in the Houses of Parliament and European Commission as political advisors. They are cast as insiders who cannot connect with working-class communities because their lives have followed a different path. In the US, the Tea Party has emphasised that the individuals it has supported who are elected to Congress come from a different background to Senators and Representatives, who are professional politicians or lobbyists. The disconnection with white working-class communities can also be related to the issues that are covered by elected representatives. Principally, support for positive action in the US or multiculturalism in Britain and Sweden is indicative that politicians have lost touch with the daily concerns and issues of working people. The rise of the Sweden Democrats has been partly predicated on this because they have successfully claimed that mainstream politicians are unwilling to discuss the issues of race and immigration that worry many Swedes. By raising anxiety about immigration, or the challenges of making a multicultural society work, the Sweden Democrats connect with an important strand of working-class opinion.

Second, invoking the past as a way of mobilising working-class support has been deployed to varying degrees of success across different countries. Viscerally, this can take the form of winning *our* country back, which takes collective memory to a time and place when the country was successful either economically or militarily. More importantly, this presaged the type of global migration drawn from Asia and Africa seen over the last 20 years. *Our* can be seen as a proxy for when countries and neighbourhoods were white – pre-immigration – and when governments were increasing the supply of manufacturing jobs, affordable and quality housing, and stable neighbourhoods. In this way, current white working-class insecurity regarding jobs, housing tenure and neighbourhood change can be placed on immigrants and disconnected political elites, contrasting with a past place that was so much better. For example, UKIP supporters in the media suggest that there was no popular sanction for the government-imposed model of multiculturalism that has led to working-class communities losing out on welfare and work. In Sweden, the Sweden Democrats slogan is 'Getting our Sweden Back', which again puts forward the idea of the country as being homogeneous and white. Britain and Sweden are different in this respect to the US, where the country has a strong narrative of being built on immigration. Invoking the past deployed by the Tea Party is about lowering taxation and diminishing the role of government in the lives of ordinary people. In addition, the Tea Party regularly puts forward the perspective that white communities lose out in jobs because of affirmative action measures that promote minorities.

Third, in Sweden and Britain, the Sweden Democrats and UKIP have distanced themselves from a racist narrative in order to position them as being respectable and patriotic organisations. Indeed, both accept the reality of multiculturalism and readily showcase minority candidates. Political makeovers of this type are not simply about flushing out members with Nazi or racist sympathies, but also about appealing to class politics and especially speaking on behalf of working-class communities who have been placed on the margins of society. The Tea Party in the US also seeks to position itself as a protector of working-class interests, although, in reality, its members are middle-class and it is backed by wealthy individual financiers.

Adding an international dimension to white working-class perspectives on multiculturalism increases our understanding of the key themes that have been covered in this book: disconnection and lack of voice; economic marginality; and being viewed as being resistant to immigration and social change. Globalisation means that the international flow of capital and people is likely to increase rather than diminish. In particular, immigration cannot be restricted by border controls in the UK, in Europe or in the US. Political and policy framing should shift to the impact of change on local communities and how future narratives need to be inclusive. This is about a progressive agenda on immigration, but also about creating space for white working-class views to be heard rather than ridiculed.

Note
[1] BBC (2014), available at: http://www.bbc.co.uk/news/world-europe-27404016

FIVE

A reactionary voice: nuanced views on multiculturalism

Introduction

This will be the first of two chapters based on research conducted in three different cities in England. There are two substantive points that have been made so far in this book: first, there has been a top-down framing of the white working class as being antagonistic to multiculturalism. (Haylett, 2001; Sveinsson, 2009; Rhodes, 2010; Beider, 2014); and, second, the voice of the white working class has not been directly heard, being mediated instead through politicians and the media, leading to a negative construction (see Murray, 1996; see also *The White Season* and *Till Death Us Do Part*). In addressing these frames and in reconfiguring the representation of white working-class communities in the debates on multiculturalism and social change, it is important to create a space for their perspectives. Communities that view themselves as lacking voice, whether real or perceived, need to be given a platform in order to engage and be challenged on issues of multiculturalism and change.

This and the following chapter are based on two research projects undertaken sequentially. The first of these was supported by the Joseph Rowntree Foundation (JRF), with fieldwork undertaken between July 2009 and March 2011. The rationale was to gain views on community cohesion and social change from white working-class communities, who had been marginalised in the discussion of these subjects. It has already been noted that white working-class communities had been the subject of policy frames addressing disadvantage and exclusion, such as the National Strategy for Neighbourhood Renewal launched by the Labour government in 2000 (DCLG, 2001). Varying levels of alarm about this segment of society being outside of mainstream norms was well-established by commentators (Murray, 1996) and also in the media (Sveinsson, 2009). Despite the white working class being active participants in key events on race relations in the post-1945 period, including the Notting Hill riots in 1958, the Smethwick election result in 1964, Powell's 'Rivers of Blood' speech in 1968 and the Northern riots in 2001, they were either absent or marginal in government publications. For example, in the report of the aforementioned riots of 2001, the white working class were relegated to secondary actors behind the rush to put forward the thesis of entrenched racial segregation leading to 'parallel lives' (Garner, 2007). In the 1958 riots and the political events surrounding Smethwick and the 'Rivers of Blood' speech, the white working class were viewed as angry, resentful and racist (Crossman, 1991; Olden, 2008; Schofield, 2013). They were either constructed as unwitting and silent victims or as raging racists, with little flexibility between these extremes. Given this, the JRF and subsequent project wanted to create a space for a more measured depiction of whiteness, class and perspectives on community cohesion and multiculturalism that had been hitherto afforded. The report was published in 2011 (Beider, 2011).

The second of the two projects was sponsored by the Open Society Foundation (OSF), with fieldwork conducted during 2013. This was after the 2010 general election and in the midst of the cutbacks in public spending under the new Conservative–Liberal Democrat Coalition government, both of which led to significant redundancies in the public sector. There had been a level of criticism from the new government that multiculturalism had been propped up by the state (see Cameron, 2011). As a result, local government had less capacity to implement community cohesion policy after 2010. Indeed, the new government's statement on multiculturalism and cohesion, *Creating the conditions for integration* (DCLG, 2012) emphasised the importance of non-state actors in driving forward the strategy. The JRF project focused solely on white working-class communities and their views on community cohesion. The OSF study considered the views of low-income white and Muslim communities on cohesion and integration, and how they may be able to work together for common benefit on grassroots projects. The report was published in 2014 (Beider, 2014).

Apart from being undertaken at different times and having slightly different aims, the research projects were located in different places. The JRF study identified white neighbourhoods in global, industrial and provincial cities. These were Somers Town in London, Aston in Birmingham and Canley in Coventry. The OSF project was based in Walthamstow in North-East London and consolidated previous research on *Muslims in London* commissioned by the OSF (OSF, 2012). Both projects adopted the same definition of the white working class. That is, people who had identified themselves as white in the 2001 Census and fitted the socio-economic categories of C2, D and E, previously discussed in Chapter One of this book. In Chapter One of the book, we noted the problems in defining the white working class and the trend to looking at wider classification based on networks and culture (Savage et al, 2014). Definitional challenges and limitations are noted in both reports.

Partnerships were established with community organisations (Somers Town, Aston) or community activists (Waltham Forest, Canley) in order to recruit white working-class residents. Snowball sampling then helped to generate interviewees, who formed the basis of focus groups. In total, there were 100 residents interviewed in the JRF project. The pool of participants was split almost equally in terms of gender and there was equitable representation across different age groups. The OSF project was smaller as it focused on a single area. Here, there were 31 white participants, with 21 women and 10 men. Again, there was good representation across age ranges. The research projects deployed a qualitative methodology of focus groups, study days and case study interviews. These studies give an insight into the views of 131 white working-class residents across four different neighbourhoods on multiculturalism, cohesion and social change. To this end, the analysis that will be discussed in this and the following chapter consolidates the perspectives of recent studies in terms of the disconnection from politics and the lack of voice on policy (Garner, 2007; National Community Forum, 2009; Rogaly and Taylor, 2009; Pearce and Milne, 2010).

The themes that will be discussed in this chapter include: a critical appraisal of national frames; such as community cohesion and integration; views on multiculturalism and social change; and how white working-class identity is framed by the residents themselves. Most of the data are drawn from the JRF project, which reconnect with earlier discussions in the book.

Perspectives on community cohesion

The concept of community cohesion was understood by local stakeholders. Policies and strategies were in place and interventions to support cohesion had been put into practice. There are differences in how community cohesion is advanced. In Camden, the term used is 'social' rather than 'community' cohesion. A stakeholder responded that there was no clear origin for the subtle difference but he thought that it was for political reasons: *"My guess is that at the time the Cohesion team was formed, we had a Lib Dem–Conservative administration in Camden and 'Community' cohesion was seen as a term more associated with Labour?"* (Somers Town stakeholder, male). This seems to suggest that community cohesion was developed and implemented under a Labour government and may reflect some of the issues associated with political ownership. A social cohesion advisory group was established with the aim to 'promote more integrated and harmonious communities in the borough; improve access to public and community spaces and buildings to facilitate greater interaction between diverse communities; integrate new arrivals, including refugee communities, into local communities and democratic life' (Camden Local Strategic Partnership, 2007).

However, it should also be pointed out that Birmingham and Coventry had Conservative-led administrations during the course of this project and both use the term 'community cohesion'. Local stakeholders accepted the term but had varying levels of concerns. Principally, these were related to the difficulties in applying the concept of community cohesion, as well as understanding the content. For example, Somers Town and Canley stakeholders had a variety of responses:

> "*Community cohesion is really nebulous and very difficult for anyone to engage with.*" (Somers Town stakeholder, male)

> "*Less political correctness – we have gone too far. My dad was Latvian. Community cohesion is part of that political correctness and it alienates and divides people. Even communities have issues with it – they don't want to be tarred with the same brush. That stuff about not having Christmas and having a winter festival instead – Indians I know are aghast at it.*" (Canley stakeholder, male)

However, local stakeholders seemed to be frustrated that the term was being imposed by national government with very little flexibility in relation to local circumstances. In practice, community cohesion manifested itself in different ways across the neighbourhoods. For example, community cohesion was shaped by the local authority in Coventry but the focus was on equality and access in order to enable people to come together. Explicit is criticism of previous approaches on community cohesion that focused on particular groups rather than the broadest possible approach to engage all groups:

> "*Partnership and community cohesion strategy were all rubbish and missed the point. Most of the focus is on asylum seekers and so on – it's not just about responding. An issue is about ongoing dialogue with new communities seen as wanting special routes*

into the council, there needs to be access across the board, everyone should have a route – not just special cases or groups." (Canley stakeholder, female)

Camden stakeholders stated that local strategies hold the key to improving community cohesion. This is partly because it may be seen as a remote concept and also that residents have to live with the challenges and experiences of different groups in Somers Town. They need to be empowered to work with community organisations and come up with grassroots approaches:

"Communities have to lead on integration and cohesion work. The council can't do it because it is detached. Having local people from the area doing community work gives it a head start and lends it immediate credibility. People aren't going to trust someone who turns up with a suit and a briefcase." (Somers Town stakeholder, male)

These comments suggest that community cohesion can be negatively perceived as part of political correctness, inflexible and imposed by national government. Instead, there is a need for greater flexibility and grassroots interventions in neighbourhoods.

The role of local community organisations

The project wanted to explore the role of locally based community organisations in supporting cohesion on the ground. In particular, this included acting as a conduit to bring people together, generate greater understanding and increase tolerance. This is emphasised by the following stakeholder with reference to the value of community organisations: *"It is an important conduit for people to come together because of reducing prejudice"* (Somers Town stakeholder, female). Community organisations were viewed by some stakeholders as important in building cohesion, supporting civic society and holding stakeholders to account. In each study area, we observed organisations that adopted or were supporting this role, for example: Somers Town Community Association organising activities that cut across race, gender and class, such as childcare and catering; Westwood School in Canley teaching students about respect and tolerance as part of mainstream lessons; and in Aston, the work of Aston Pride New Deal for Communities [NDC] on community engagement and representation. Despite this work, stakeholders had a range of concerns about community organisations.

Coventry stakeholders were concerned about the level of apathy in Canley. It was reported that there were not enough community organisations to liaise with the local authority and undertake work to build community cohesion or, indeed, support other activities. Community development workers and councillors had attempted a range of activities to engage local communities but these had been, at best, only partially successful. The view was that people only organise to protest against change rather than to support a proactive agenda:

> *"They don't come together, don't come to meetings unless we planned to knock it down, a proposed name change for the club brought them all out. We shouldn't drive communities. I couldn't think of anything that would pull them in – only the usual suspects."* (Canley stakeholder, male)

Interestingly, this Canley stakeholder believed that residents wanted minimum interference and only reacted when the status quo was threatened. This is similar to the complaints about community cohesion, which was viewed by some as a top-down model of national government intervention. The stakeholder dilemma in Canley may be summarised in the following quotes:

> *"There is a need for an overriding organisation. There are a lot of ad hoc things going on."* (Canley stakeholder, male)

> *"An organisation promoting Canley, would it work? No – if we ran it from here [city], we would be interfering, if we ran it from there [Canley], they wouldn't do it."* (Canley stakeholder, male)

There was much discussion by residents about the importance of pubs and clubs as places of community interaction. Canley has both, but these were not regarded as vibrant places. Rather, they were failing institutions that amplify the problems of community engagement in the area:

> *"In Canley, there are three pubs. A family steakhouse – it's dragged itself up, challenged groups and gangs. The [X] improved by becoming the [X]. It was taken over by devout Christians that kicked out the cliques, but in doing so, kicked out its bread and butter. The social club struggles, the smoking ban didn't help. I don't know how it is going to maintain itself, after the smoking ban, they scrubbed it so it was bright and cheery, six months later, it is the*

same old four playing dominos, it's a shame. The [X] is run by a little group of people, quite tight – a suit and tie would clear the place, it's a pub going nowhere fast." (Canley stakeholder, male)

It is important to note that these are all commercial enterprises not supported by government, although the social club has received some public funding.

In contrast, Camden has many community centres and organisations that are supported by local authority funding. They are viewed as an important part of the civic engagement of different groups across the area. Some, such as Somers Town Community Association, are generic and appeal to all sections of the community. However, others are more specific and are seen to appeal to sectional groups. Many residents in Somers Town perceived that minority groups received preferential support and funding for community organisations that the white working class could not access, such as the Asian Women's Centre. The theme of community organisations supporting sectional interests in Somers Town had been raised by the local authority. The agenda of a social cohesion meeting posed the question as to whether community centres contributed to, or prevented, community cohesion (Camden Local Strategic Partnership, 2007). Some stakeholders were mildly critical of community organisations, believing that they had become too focused on internal debates and processes rather than on building community cohesion: *"How mixed are the groups in community centres? Local interest is about running organisations and decision-making structures"* (Somers Town stakeholder, male).

Specifically on community organisations, and white working-class engagement in particular, Camden stakeholders pointed to Connecting Communities funding, which supported work with these groups, such as convening meetings of men in Somers Town and outreach work in pubs in the neighbourhood. A stakeholder did suggest that in contrast with new communities, the expectation of some white working-class communities was that Camden Council would resolve problems. For example, the following quote suggests that new communities may be more dynamic: *"The Congolese community pull together and have an after-school club"* (Somers Town stakeholder, female).

Aston Pride NDC had a remit to regenerate part of the area from 2001 to 2011. Much of the focus was on supporting community organisations and organising activities that could bring people together, as well as deliver services. Regrettably, local stakeholders recognised that the Aston Pride boundary excluded most white residents in the area. This led to the perception, recounted by residents elsewhere in this report, that the regeneration agency only met the needs of minority groups.

In fairness, Aston Pride worked closely with the Flood Action Group. Most, but not all, of the active members were long-established white residents living in the Witton area. The flooding caused by a local underground river had galvanised local residents to form an action group that lobbied the local authority for help and support with fixing damaged properties. The group continued to work together, accessing wider support from the local authority, for example, members worked with Aston Pride to refurbish Witton Community Centre, which was reopened in 2010 as a space for meetings and activities.

One Aston stakeholder suggested that more could be done to increase the voice of white communities in Aston. The community carnival, held annually in July, was successful in bringing together different groups, although there was a major issue in that some groups were not represented, creating resentment among those affected: *"The white community is active but don't feel they are represented. You could say that the Witton Flood Action Group gave a voice to this group but also had lots of other people"* (Aston stakeholder, male).

Despite the ending of Connecting Communities and uncertainty about government spending and policy interventions, the challenges of community cohesion remain. There was a clear division in the awareness of community cohesion between stakeholders and residents, with the former able to understand its core meaning and discuss how cohesion was developed in each research site. These were individuals who were partly responsible for developing and implementing policy. The majority of residents had not heard of the term 'community cohesion', but a few had and knew its meaning.

Discussion with both stakeholders and residents demonstrated a number of challenges with community cohesion as a concept and its perception and usefulness as a model of intervention. Many stakeholders found community cohesion to be a problematic concept. Some associated the term with a top-down approach to community development. It was nebulous in the sense that both 'community' and 'cohesion' can have different meanings depending on locality, ideology and the composition of communities. The following stakeholder comment is typical of the findings:

> *"People just glaze over. It's an expression of forced mixing of communities on people from a height. Not mixing from the bottom up. It's only sociologists and council staff that use the term. It's not an experience, community cohesion; you don't hear people asking*

about cohesion. You hear them asking if so and so went to the village fete." (Canley stakeholder, male)

In this context, community cohesion was regarded as a generic instrument imposed on local authorities, neighbourhoods and residents by national government.

Policymakers appeared to have an understanding of the key tenets but recognised limitations in application. Its association with national government and its cross-cutting reach leave the concept exposed at a time of dramatic reductions in government spending:

> *"Community Cohesions equals authority, it's a negative. It's not necessarily about race ... working class are quite a tolerant group of people, in Coventry, we have Polish, Ukraine, Asian, Irish, West Indian, Somalian"* (Canley stakeholder, male).

Stakeholders welcomed new and practical interventions to support community renewal. Many suggested that community cohesion happened in these neighbourhoods prior to the concept being instilled into government policy.

After a decade of policy guidance and local interventions, there is a still reluctance by national government to recognise how difference is manifested. As seen in resident debates, difference is a lived experience for many people. Difference couched in terms of immigration and competition for resources such as housing may lead to a racist discourse. Community cohesion was viewed as shutting down discussion about the composition of communities:

> *"We close down debates about race ... conflict is not always bad and difference can be good and leads to change."* (Somers Town stakeholder, male)

> *"It affects them in the same way as us.... It's the worst expression to use, it disenfranchises 90% of the people."* (Canley stakeholder, male)

We learned from the project that community cohesion presented a conundrum to stakeholders. It was viewed as being a government instrument that forced different communities to work together. However, on the positive side, there was recognition of its influence in shaping policy, although it was not seen as easy to implement. Local stakeholders gave examples of what they thought were community cohesion initiatives in the study areas. These ranged from working with schools on hate crime (Coventry), supporting new arrivals (Birmingham), promoting a city as belonging to a broad spectrum of people (Coventry) and organising street festivals (Camden). This is summed up in the following stakeholder quote in response to listing community cohesion activities:

> *"Positive images campaign city-wide. It doesn't matter where you are from and what you like, we all come from Coventry now, the feedback from BME [black and minority ethnic] groups around a sense of belonging was very positive; neighbourhood management, community engaged is what it's about, a citizen rather than a customer; far Right activity, racism, DNA testing promotion, we are different to how we see ourselves; schools – spent more Prevent money; targeted activity – the gentle stuff."* (Canley stakeholder, female)

Our findings demonstrated that the real issues and challenges within neighbourhoods are not so much about bringing people together on common and shared norms, but about accepting the value of difference and how this is manifested within the arena of power and conflict, such as competition for social housing or support for community projects. This resonates with resident findings discussed later in the report. Here, residents felt that their views were muted compared to other groups. Concerns were not being listened to by government. More than this, conflict over resources, such as social housing in Somers Town and Canley, pointed to cohesion challenges: principally, that the concept had become preoccupied with cultural explanations (see Chapter Two) and less about difference and conflict. This view is summarised by a stakeholder who has responsibility for delivering cohesion policy: *"Groups of people have issues and they want to make themselves distinct from other groups. We are going against this by smothering over differences. Conflict is not really bad and difference is good, although it is a challenge"* (Somers Town stakeholder, male).

In contrast to local stakeholders, most residents had not heard of community cohesion. This is not altogether surprising because it is not an outward-facing concept. It could be contended that definitional challenges regarding community cohesion should only concern those who work directly in policy. The minority of residents across the three areas who stated that they understood the concept suggested that it was about bringing people together:

"Using community centres to bring people together, varieties of cultures, positive ways of bringing people together." (Aston resident, male)

"Yes, I have heard of it as I go to a lot of meetings, it's about networks of activities, local people working together to improve things." (Canley resident, female)

"It's everyone getting together, working together, bringing down barriers to include everyone; race, culture, it all being welcome." (Somers Town resident, female)

Although most had not heard of the term, they were prompted to think further about its meaning. There was a consensus that community cohesion was about bringing people together. Beyond this basic assumption, there was very little recognition of norms and shared spaces. Rather, the opposite was the case. Much of the discussion with residents was focused on how government policies on race and equality at local and national level had not connected with white working-class residents. These policies were a proxy for political correctness. In short, some residents viewed equality of opportunity as simply supporting minority groups at the expense of the majority. Political correctness was raised on a number of occasions during the course of the project and was seen as diminishing the rights of white working-class communities:

"It means that we do what they want." (Aston resident, male)

"Segregating groups – like [X] – the Asian women's centre. Everyone should have access – they segregate themselves and whatever funding they get, they kept. It's PC [political correctness] to throw money at them." (Somers Town resident, female)

We could be sanguine about the fact that many residents did not know about community cohesion. After all, this was developed by government and largely discussed by the policy and academic communities. A more substantive point relates to policy disconnection with white working-class communities. Despite attempts to build community cohesion in Aston, Canley and Somers Town, people felt disenfranchised. The perspectives of white working-class communities had been excluded from debates on immigration, race and community.

Moreover, government (and community cohesion was framed in this way) seemed uninterested and favoured minorities instead.

Residents wanted to increase interaction with different people in their neighbourhood. The focus was on creating spaces for community interaction to take place. For example, people in Coventry lamented that the Canley Carnival had not happened for many years and that community development work had declined: *"The carnival in Canley stopped 20 years ago, the community centre in St Margaret's closed. People are not prepared to do something for nothing. Most people now take rather than give back. It really has gone downhill"* (Canley resident, female). Community interaction was recognised as being beneficial. It seems that the basis for valuing diversity is predicated on the role of neutral spaces and institutions such as community organisations, schools and street festivals. These are embedded in the community, trusted and credible, and largely non-political. Thus, community organisations encountered during the research were valued for providing services such as advice on welfare issues, access to childcare and signposting services. Similarly, schools focus on improving educational outcomes for young people and families living in disadvantaged communities, while festivals provide a space to participate freely in a range of arts and cultural activities. These are examples of community advocacy that is provided freely and fairly to all groups within a neighbourhood:

> *"My son is the only white kid in his class – he is seven this year – he loves it – his sister and one other are the only white kids in the school. Mainly black, Somalian, Asian and mixed race – they like it – we have only had one incident where someone shoved dirt in his face. I think it's good for him."* (Aston resident, female)

> *"Brilliant. It's community-based so no one cares; it's about being good people. We have had lots of Kosovans and Chinese move into the area."* (Canley resident, female)

> *"In the school I was working in, a lot of Bengali and Somalia community, you might have five British working-class whites in the whole school. We did a lot of work, weekly events – got a whole group going for everyone – it didn't feel agenda-based. If you keep the fairness going, everyone was equal to come and get on."* (Somers Town resident, female)

Community interaction took place in each of our research neighbourhoods but at an informal rather than formal level. In shops, junior schools and in parks, people met each other in routine situations. In this way, community cohesion was placed as a series of routine interactions set against the everyday life of a neighbourhood. It is organic. Residents expressed the desire for these conversations with people who are different with regard to race and class, or both:

> "The places people meet each other are the doctor's surgery, the market, the pub. That's where you'd bump into someone in the street and hear that so-and-so's just died, or got married, and you'd get all your information that way – you wouldn't have to read it in a Journal." (Somers Town resident, female)

Local stakeholders understood the concept of community cohesion but did not feel that it had been helpful in terms of application. Some viewed it as central government interference and this was picked up by residents who complained about political correctness and the unfairness of government policy on race and equality of opportunity. The fieldwork shows that people perceived local authorities as not wanting to hear what they have to say, or giving them any input into decision-making.

The research findings demonstrated that national policies such as community cohesion need to be reconfigured to focus on the grassroots experiences of communities. Most importantly, there is a need to connect policy to the day-to-day experiences of people living in these types of neighbourhoods. A disconnect between policymakers and people seems to exist and appears to be deepening. Beyond this, community cohesion has to move from being perceived as a top-down model of government intervention to one that engages with the routine lives of people. Community interaction happens in informal and neutral spaces in a myriad of ways. Residents want to be engaged in a bottom-up debate about communities, change and the future

The construction of whiteness and class

Across the three areas, there was consensus that the term 'white working class' was not about social or economic categorisation, but acceptance of a values-driven framework. In this context, values seemed to be fixed, exclusive and bounded, but class was permeable, dynamic and open. These communities were keen to differentiate themselves from others on the basis of both class and race, and wanted to reclaim white and working-class as an identity that should be valued by government and society as a whole. It was something to be proud of and had little in common with stereotypes.

An important and interesting theme emerging from fieldwork was the construction of whiteness. As discussed earlier, much of the commentary on this group is unflattering. A point of convergence depicts white working-class communities as a feckless group, which is resistant to change, problematic in terms of social norms and behaviours, and living in annexed council estates that are mired in unemployment, high teenage pregnancy rates and poor educational performance (Murray, 1996). Of course, stereotyped assumptions have been attributed to many communities, and not simply from the wider media.

There is very little research on the perspective of residents and activists giving a grassroots view on the themes of white working-class communities and community cohesion. This is a considerable weakness The studies gave these groups a voice, which was especially important at the time of the general election, when many felt disenfranchised.

The research demonstrated that there was another type of social construction being developed in terms of ethnicity and class. Many of those who participated were eager to differentiate themselves from others who shared the neighbourhood. It should be emphasised that the discussion was not exclusively about minority communities, although this was the most important theme across the study areas. Debates focusing on newcomers included students (in Canley and Somers Town, as well as Aston) and middle-class householders (in Somers Town and, to an extent, Canley), who were seen as eroding neighbourhoods. The threat to neighbourhood cohesion and, to a lesser extent, working-class values was not simply fixed on migrants or immigration, but also encapsulated encroachment from middle-class gentrification and the expansion of universities, both leading to a reduction in the availability of affordable housing.

As we have seen, working-class communities have been framed within negative cultural connotations as being work-shy and unable or unwilling to embrace demographic and economic changes. Yet, residents were angry about the projection of such values placed on their neighbourhoods and the people who lived in these places. There was acceptance that a minority of residents led a lifestyle that was dependent on benefits, crime and dysfunctional families. These were viewed as outside the working class and, in many cases, were met with a withering reaction. In one of the areas, this was a stronger factor, with recognition of criminal families having an element of control and influence:

"Looking at the whole area, the bottom end has changed, the middle area is quite stable. Over the road is very different. Lots of subcultures. It's crazy! Talking at the micro-level of three or four streets. It's a bit frightening just how ingrained it is – a very divided area." (Canley stakeholder, male)

"The urban myth is that Canley is where the most criminal families live, it is where the drug trade is run from. There is an element of truth. There are parts of Coventry that are white, working-class and less isolated and removed than Canley." (Canley stakeholder, female)

These comments are typical of much of the discussion about stereotypes. The reality is that a very small number of people conform to commonly held white working-class images. These are largely located in distinct parts of the neighbourhood (as is the case with Canley) or in specific housing developments (Somers Town). There is a need to accept that disadvantaged neighbourhoods are neither the idyllic vision of working-class culture nor the dens of iniquity of popular portrayal. As ever, the reality is rather different from these two opposite and extreme perspectives. Residents and other interviewees were nuanced in the way that they defined areas. The Canley quotes demonstrated recognition that problematic perceptions exist but, at the same time, emphasised the importance of separating sub-neighbourhoods and residents. In the same way that publications on the white working class have been criticised for generating pathologies or 'Othering' (Sveinsson, 2009), residents were inclined to differentiate themselves from other groups and neighbourhood areas that were problematic. They were not perceived to be part of the working class.

Attempting to define the term 'white working class' became an important feature of the discussions during the course of the research. For methodological reasons, we suggested a social economic category of groups C2, D and E living in areas in the neighbourhoods in the top 20% of the Index of Multiple Deprivation used by government. It was clear from the outset that the definition needed refining, and our discussions with both residents and stakeholders helped to advance the notion of the white working class. White ethnicity was viewed by some residents as being exclusive, fixed and bounded. However, some of the residents interviewed had non–white relatives, and white migrant groups such as Polish workers who had moved to the UK after EU expansion in 2004 were regarded as being problematic because of the adverse impact on the availability of affordable housing. Class was much more difficult to define. It was permeable, transitory and unbounded.

It should be noted that a small proportion of those interviewed in the community study days and focus groups had family members who were drawn from minority backgrounds. This was not a blunt one-dimensional group. Rather, it was multifaceted and expressed that difference could be beneficial. Some raised and celebrated the concept of '*a melting pot*', or a fusion of different communities, as something that should and could be embraced. On the subject of integration, it was seen as a matter of simply joining in and being part of a community. For example, in one area, the pub is owned by a Sri Lankan landlord who is a popular figure in the local community and whose wife was welcomed to the country when she relocated in 2010:

> "*I grew up around Birmingham; I have coloured black friends and I've got a bit of Indian in me but I don't know much about that culture.*" (Aston resident, male)

> "*I can't be racist as I have seven half-Bengali step-children… there is no division because this is their home.*" (Somers Town resident, male)

> "*I come from a Welsh rural community, grew up on a farm – became a lorry driver for many years – at the end, I was a manager, but I still see myself as working-class.*" (Somers Town resident, male)

These individuals continued to regard themselves as working-class because of values based on reciprocity and mutual support. The key point to be made here is about whiteness and 'othering'. As discussed in Chapter One, some have suggested that white working-class groups have been cast as a distinct 'other' in society (Nayak, 2009; Skeggs, 2009). Residents interviewed during this project viewed themselves as a group in class and ethnic terms, even though, in some cases, the latter was more complex. Ethnicity was implicit in the discussions while class was more explicit. Groups identified themselves as white and working-class.

The normative assumptions about the white working class leading to the layering of negative cultural stereotypes were acknowledged and resented by participants across the research sites in two distinct ways. First, there was a sweeping assumption that everyone living in these areas was feckless and helpless against the reality that many people worked and sustained families despite challenging economic and social circumstances. Second, and related to the first, there was an assumption that the white working-class are a lumpen proletariat:

> "*They think that we are all on the giro. They think we are all the same.*" (Aston resident male)

> "*I may be from the 19th floor of a tower block, 30 and have a child, but I am not stupid! I see the news. My father's got O and A levels and all that. I get fed up with being seen as thick.*" (Somers Town resident, female)

There was an eagerness to put forward another type of social construction of the white working class. People highlighted the importance of intrinsic and bounded values. These were principles and core beliefs that people were born into and that could not be traded. They emphasised a strong work ethic, respect, collective values and reciprocal support. Repeatedly, residents emphasised these values as an important part of identity and, crucially, as something that differentiated them from other groups by ethnicity and class: "*It is about who you are. It is about identity*" (Somers Town resident, male); "*Working-class is not about money. It's about people who have always worked, live in a council area and grown up with working-class values*" (Canley resident, female).

The point made was that being working-class means having a values system based on respect for yourself and others. Indeed, those who do not work and did not display these values were frowned upon:

> "*The benefits culture isn't working-class. It's not the unfortunate ones that need benefits that are the problem; it is the deliberate exploiters of the system who don't want to work. They are an underclass and at odds with the working class.*" (Somers Town resident, male)

> "*We are not low-class, I'm working-class.*" (Aston resident, female)

The bounded set of egalitarian values is important and helps the group to self-identify. Rather than being presented as a dependent community that had lost its way, participants across study areas emphasised a framework or code of working-class principles. In this way, identity could be maintained. People could understand, in a common-sense way, that they were similar. Thus, newcomers were not seen as being part of this value system. Most of the discussion and debate focused on minority communities, but not exclusively. Newcomers could also be composed of middle-class people gentrifying Somers Town or students moving into Canley. Differentiation was most marked by how some established minority communities were viewed as uninterested in hard work, reciprocity and respect. This was emphasised in most of the discussions. These minority groups were regarded as being dependent on public subsidies and abusing the welfare system to the detriment of the working class. In Canley, some residents spoke about the adverse impact of Polish migrants moving into the area:

> *"I used to vote Labour, I won't even vote now because they let in so many Poles and other foreigners, they get all the work, and Labour did nothing!"* (Canley resident, male)

> *"And the Poles have been put here. On the bus [the driver], they don't even know where they are going. There will be more when the new houses go up. There are loads of Poles and Somalians, some Asians."* (Canley resident, female)

Concerns about white migrants in Aston were also expressed, but these were about cultural norms, as well as problems in private sector housing allocation and the impact on the neighbourhood: *"The private landlords are filling their houses with Somalis, Poles, illegal immigrants. My husband's the only one who clears our entry"* (Aston resident, female). This suggests that the problem of community cohesion and white working-class communities may not be associated with race. In addition, British white working-class identity is based on values that some newcomers may not share.

Students were also seen as being problematic. The short-term nature of lettings gave rise to neighbourhood churn and led to deterioration in neighbourhoods: *"And there are a lot of students, a lot of the buy-to-let go to students – and they aren't here for long and they don't care. Some of them are very untidy. The foreigners are the same"* (Somers Town resident, female). The following quote from a resident in Aston recounts the problems of living in the neighbourhood: *"Rubbish that the Asians leave around – fridges and mattresses. White students are bad as well – I saw rats in bags of rubbish they left outside"* (Aston resident, female).

In Canley, proximity to the University of Warwick leads to increased housing pressures as students access housing. Some of these are international students. This leads to the conflation of students and foreigners having an adverse impact on the area. For example, asked a second time about the adverse impact of living in Canley, the following quotes suggest that students are seen as being problematic:

> *"Foreigners – loads of Chinese in the last five years buying houses and renting them to students."* (Canley resident, female)

> *"I've lived here for 34 years in the immediate area and there are a lot of students, unruly children that break fences. I will leave as soon as I can. I hate it."* (Canley resident, female)

Problems associated with white minorities, such as Polish migrants, or other groups, such as students, were raised in all three study areas. Moreover, a few of the residents involved in the research were from white minority backgrounds, for example, Greek. This suggests that white working-class communities may not be quite as bounded and homogeneous as described earlier. Hence, the challenges are not simply about ethnicity, as Poles are deemed to be white but present issues in terms of integration, housing and employment. In addition, students are also viewed in a negative way in terms of cohesion and restricting access to housing. Both groups are seen as a distinct 'other' separate from working-class values and culture.

The definition of the working class shows that ethnicity is of key importance. People cannot belong if they do not have a certain values set. It was almost viewed as a non-transferable birthright that guides and supports throughout a life course. Of course, ethnicity is a wider and more nuanced concept than race and is applicable in this context. Fixed and bounded values, alongside ethnicity, appeared to be the key determinant of being white working-class, although this is challenged by research conducted with a similar group discussed in Chapter Six (see also Beider, 2014). There is much less certainty when the discussion turned to the issue of defining class. Some participants thought that it was more about employment or tenure: *"Working-class is literally someone working and providing for their family"* (Canley stakeholder, male); *"When I was a kid, I thought it meant people who couldn't afford to buy a house"* (Somers Town resident, female).

Here, working-class is not about being bounded, but could encompass any working or waged person with a family in any neighbourhood. Alternatively, it could mean all those who are in rented accommodation. Class becomes an elastic term, leading to many different interpretations: *"Our working definition is traditional – a group of people from those on benefits to blue-collar, all semi-skilled or unskilled labour groups"* (Canley stakeholder, female).

In contrast to working-class values, there was no agreement about the definition of class. Policies such as the 'Right to Buy' introduced by the Thatcher government in the 1980s weakened the notion of tenure as a key building block of working-class identity. This was not raised in any of the sessions convened during the project as a strong indicator of being working-class. On the contrary, buying a council house was viewed as leading to increased prosperity:

> "Best thing Thatcher did – it gave a good opportunity to the poor."
> (Somers Town resident, female)

> "I teach and so know a lot of the residents from that area – they own their own house, own other houses, rent them out to students … they still describe themselves as working-class." (Canley stakeholder, male)

Class becomes permeable and transitory. It is interesting to compare this to the very clear sense of cultural identity and the powerful understanding of a values system that helped to frame identity. This is fixed and bounded. Hence, from the fieldwork, and in these three areas, the social construction of the white working class is strongly influenced by positive cultural values, just as much as by economic factors. However, and in contrast to much of the policy debates, culture is not shaped by a negative pathology. Again, there is a disconnection with how working-class communities have been constructed by aspects of government policy, the media and research. The contrary appears to be the case: a strong sense of right and wrong, earning a wage, and mutual support and reciprocity. Residents were proud of their roots and identity.

Retrospection and the search for ideal neighbourhoods

People looked to the past to inform their future neighbourhood. Nostalgic and idealistic accounts of people and place littered the discussions and may be related to discussions in previous chapters about the 'heroic' working class that helped to build the foundations for post-1945 prosperity. Not surprisingly, the hankering for the past was especially (though not exclusively) evident from the retired residents interviewed. There was much retrospection about how life used to be, and what it had become. A social construction of a neighbourhood largely populated by white working-class communities was created during discussions. A sense of nostalgia permeated through the debates

136

across the study areas. This was especially strong in Somers Town and Canley but was also referenced in Aston. Community organisations and informal spaces such as the pub, festivals and shops developed a symbolic importance as places where communities had come together. Neighbourhoods had changed and generally not for the better. New communities were seen as exacerbating neighbourhood decline not only in terms of increased competition for resources, but also in terms of the closure of pubs and clubs. Of course, it should be added that these were not necessarily neutral spaces, but contested by class and gender, as well as ethnicity. Recreating neighbourhood spirit was perceived to be difficult and required newcomers to adapt and change to accepted norms.

A key concern was the extent to which residents wanted to build community cohesion – the sense of shared space, norms and connections between different groups of people in the same and contiguous neighbourhoods. There was a great deal of retrospection about the idealised neighbourhood. Participants lamented the loss of institutions such as the public house or street market that helped people to informally interact. There was a general agreement about the need for people from different backgrounds to interact but concern was expressed about the limitations created by cultural difference. In short, culture and race were important in idealising neighbourhood and immigration, with Muslim communities viewed as being especially problematic. It was felt that this group was reluctant to integrate into 'societal norms' compared with other groups, which may be the result of perceived cultural differences.

Participants had mixed views about their neighbourhood. Some, especially in Somers Town, enjoyed living in the area. This was partly due to its proximity to key transport hubs allowing easy access to the West End. In addition, residents remarked that Somers Town continues to possess a community spirit based on reciprocity and mutuality, as embodied by activities run by Somers Town Community Association. The working-class values discussed previously remained important in bringing people together. Many had a nostalgic view of neighbourhoods when these values were self-evident and, crucially, before the impact of immigration (in Aston and Somers Town) or economic change (Canley). The imagery was of cohesive neighbourhoods where people would informally look out for each other's children and for each other. Community institutions such as shops, pubs and clubs were important in the retrospection, as was the view of people earning a good wage and accessing decent housing. The sense of life as it was is summed up in the following stakeholder quotes:

"Coventry 1960s' car factory workers were labour aristocracy; well-paid, good housing, the salt of the earth type. Like the mining village mentality of everyone working together and East End gangs ... the Krays were always good to their mother! The blitz spirit is a myth but you get the idea of people in the same boat." (Canley stakeholder, female)

"Somers Town was lost a long time ago. It had everything you would associate with a working-class culture – a street market, greengrocers, fish shops – but these had disappeared by the 1980s." (Somers Town stakeholder, male)

Retrospection and nostalgia are a heady mix. Participants spoke about the sense of neighbourhood change and focused on the decline of community organisations. These were places where people interacted, shared information and found out what was going on in their neighbourhood. In this context, the decline of pubs, social clubs and shops was symptomatic of reduced opportunities to come together. Rather than considering wider factors, such as the much cheaper option of buying alcohol from supermarkets, the ban on smoking in public places and high rents, participants were quick to blame non-drinking Muslims (in Aston and Somers Town), people who had gentrified the area (Somers Town) or students (Canley) for the decline in pubs and clubs:

"Pubs used to be what brought people together, but they've closed now mostly. Used to be good old knees-up pubs, family pubs where you knew people and you kept on eye on each other's kids playing outside. It's not about people not being able to afford a drink though, it's cos a lot of the new people don't drink, that's why they are closing." (Somers Town resident, female)

Neighbourhood change was seen as preventing white working-class communities from coming together. More than this, there is the simplicity of the past seen through common norms and the sharing of common spaces such as pubs and clubs. Many of those interviewed associated immigration with the decline of pubs. Further, it was even worse that many pubs had been transformed into housing developments, which were viewed as helping minority communities rather than the white working class into housing, and community centres (again, for minority communities).

Apart from anger at the demise of key spaces, residents also suggested that this loss had diminished opportunities for different communities to come together. Informal spaces for interaction such as street markets and more formal organisations such as community centres had also been transformed because of demographic change. Concern was expressed that community organisations simply served sectional interests and were not open to white working-class communities:

> "People used to all mix in pubs but they [Bengalis] don't drink. They end up in Bengali-specific centres while our pubs are closing and we get resentful ... why can't there be a Women's Centre and why does it have to be an Asian Women's Centre instead?" (Somers Town resident, male)

> "The people – used to be a garden competition every year, and there would be such beautiful gardens, people would really try – there's no pride anymore. People cared for each other in the past – you didn't worry if they'd think you were gonna be nosey: if they were sick, you'd knock on their door and see if you could help with the kids, bring them food, whatever. Nowadays, people just go into their houses and shut the doors – people are more afraid." (Canley resident, male)

The sense of a community pub with someone on the piano and people joining in may be a romanticised vision. Some residents remember them as largely male-only domains associated with regular skirmishes and fist fights. In addition, people pulling together and looking after neighbours may be based on selective and edited narratives. Retrospection sometimes blurs the collective memory. The view could be gendered, although it needs to be emphasised that women who were interviewed also spoke about the loss of community pubs, social clubs and shops.

A more substantive point was made related to the reallocation of space for specific minority use. Supporters of community cohesion would question the need for these types of facilities since they help to embed separateness and may increase tension between different communities (CIC, 2007). There was certainly a great deal of resentment towards the change of space for this purpose. This being said, a much broader view was that local authorities need to clearly demonstrate how investment would help to bring communities together and meet specific needs. Discussion with residents showed that this has yet to win over white working-class communities given the frequent references to being not valued and being last in line for social housing.

In each of the three study areas, people acknowledged that places had undergone change. Many thought that this had not been beneficial. Neighbourhoods were more diverse, less cohesive and more fragmented. Immigration was viewed as leading to neighbourhood decline, overcrowding in housing and transforming once stable areas into places that were now difficult to recognise. Despite all this, people stressed that they did not want to be perceived as racist. Indeed, in many cases, they did not blame minority communities, but government, at a national level, for a perceived lax approach to immigration, and at a local level, for not addressing key issues such as access to social housing. Resentment was largely fuelled by how public resources were allocated.

The debates on minority communities were nuanced. At a neighbourhood level, different communities were seen as adding to the richness of a community, for example, in terms of an increased choice of eating establishments, an improved retail offering and extended business hours (Asian-owned shops were praised). Beyond this, Caribbean communities were seen as integrating into neighbourhoods and not viewed as problematic. There were similarities in terms of language, faith and culture: *"The African Caribbeans are very integrated – where the Somalis and the Poles are at the other end of the scale"* (Aston resident, male); *"Caribbean races mix with white communities … it will be a melting pot, which will be a good thing"* (Somers Town resident, male).

People also recognised that minority communities had lived in these neighbourhoods for several decades and were Brummies, Coventrians and Londoners. However, white working-class communities still regarded Pakistanis, Bangladeshis and Somalis as not doing enough to integrate into neighbourhoods. They were largely viewed as being outside the framework of working-class values discussed previously in terms of both ethnicity and class. Some residents suggested that the problem related to the Muslim culture as being outside the norms of living in the UK. Specifically, concern was expressed about the views and status of women, the propensity to have large families (and thus access social housing), and the introduction of mosques into a community, which created problems with street parking. In Somers Town, the local mosque was a converted house on a busy residential street and was perceived as causing significant problems related to parking and pedestrian access. Thus, some residents felt that although change was sometimes necessary, addressing the impact of change was much more challenging.

Conclusion

Some may regard the quotes taken from the fieldwork to be an affirmation of the view that white working-class communities are, indeed, racist, are against social change and fully justify the label of 'working-class brutes' ironically used by Hamill in his description of low-income white New Yorkers back in 1969 (Hamill, 1969). The discussion, in part, is unedifying. White working-class perspectives are coated with resentment, anger and concern about the erosion of identity as a result of government actions and immigration.

Yet, there is another view that has been hidden in policy and academic debates. This is of a people who accept and embrace multiculturalism, whose very identity has been shaped by difference and diversity as a lived experience, and who reject top-down constructions of community cohesion and the framing of working-class communities as problematic. The voice here is measured and progressive and some distance from the chaotic lumpen proletariat described in the opening chapters of this book or personified by the racist character Alf Garnett in *Till Death* or the people associated with Wibsey Working Men's Club in Bradford, as depicted in *The White Season*.

The rejection of community cohesion comes as no surprise given its association with government, which has been viewed somewhat scornfully since the parliamentary expenses scandal in 2007. In these circumstances, multiculturalism would have been viewed with suspicion. More important is the everyday integration that people recognise and describe. White working-class communities speak openly about the impact of multiculturalism: minority communities are neighbours, friends and family members. These lived experiences of diversity are a powerful riposte to commentators who portray white working-class communities as being detached and as supporting extremism.

The chapter demonstrates that white working-class views on multiculturalism, community cohesion and integration run along a continuum. Resentment about the allocation of public resources, particularly housing, political representation and being given a voice all need to be addressed. There is a need for a more robust intervention, one that addresses government's failure to connect with marginalised communities who have been neglected by the changing political calculus that largely focuses on middle-class concerns. In addition, there is also a need to create the type of economy that delivers jobs for working communities. Unfortunately, there is little hope that either of these changes will be implemented in the short term.

SIX

Integrated and equal: similar challenges and opportunities

Introduction

This second fieldwork chapter will largely be based on data from the Open Society Foundation (OSF) study derived from interviews in Waltham Forest. The discussion will address white working-class anxiety about fairness and equity from government in relation to public benefits, such as social housing, and about the ability to have a voice in public affairs. Again, some of the discussion with participants appeared to be underpinned by racist language indicative of the micro-'clash of civilisations' that based political debates on community cohesion and integration. Yet, the interviews also revealed a more progressive view that supports both multiculturalism and the dynamic sense of identity. The complexity of views, sometimes reactionary and at other times progressive, may be symptomatic of the way in which national debates have been played out, especially since 2001, when measures were taken to reduce immigration, as well as to build cohesive neighbourhoods and common national values. Britain is represented in near-crisis terms, as almost a country under siege, with its borders needing to be secured and a reaffirmation of identity advanced by the media and commentators. It is no surprise that local debates conducted with communities, who are often framed as victims of change, become racialised.

Fairness and equity

One of the central concerns of this book is the disconnection of white working-class communities from political institutions. This chapter attempts to identify some of the reasons for this detachment from established ways of conducting politics and the consequent resentment. One explanation given was that the white working class do not feel that they have been treated fairly by government. In employment, social services, community development and, most notably, housing, a strong and consistent view was expressed that residents lost out to minorities and new migrants. A related narrative in the fieldwork and also in some of the wider literature was that white working-class communities have been politically marginalised and ignored. This was linked to themes on the politics of resentment discussed earlier in Chapters One and Two (Rhodes, 2010; Kenny, 2011).

Being treated unfairly was most vividly seen in the specific debates on social housing. Many were proud to be social housing tenants and resented the portrayal of these neighbourhoods as council estates beset by social problems. Indeed, social housing tenants were largely content with their housing; it was affordable, regulated and maintained. In short, social housing was seen as an important resource and as identified with the working class. Many saw social housing as a right that was being denied to them by the local authority or housing associations.

It is not surprising, then, that access to social housing became a touchstone of wider concerns about neighbourhood change. The commonly held view was that minorities and immigrants were preferentially allocated social housing in each of the study areas. This allocation was changing 'neighbourhood character', or, to put it more simply, Somers Town and Canley, in particular, were becoming ethnically diverse and associated less as being white working-class neighbourhoods. Loss was personal and recounted through personal testimonies. A pattern emerged. Residents claimed that they were told by the local authority that they did not have high priority on social housing waiting lists only to see a minority family being allocated to a social housing unit. In reality, Camden Council (Somers Town) or Whitefriars Housing Association (the arm's length housing body that Coventry City Council transferred its housing stock to) were simply following agreed lettings policy and meeting housing need. On the ground, it appeared that these communities were being housed ahead of white working-class residents:

> "If you've got five kids, then you get a big house and the only people that have five kids nowadays are the Bengalis and the Somalis and so they get all the big places." (Somers Town resident, female)

> "I was told I didn't have enough points – they haven't been here two minutes and they get a house, we have to wait years. Why should we have to?" (Canley resident, female)

> "My cousin is black. She was here for two years and now has a beautiful house. I have been here for eight years … I don't. I'm still here. It's about skin colour." (Aston resident, female)

The inference is clear. The housing system disadvantages white working-class communities and their values and favours everyone else, but primarily minorities. In each of the research sites, there was a lack of awareness of council policy and media-fuelled speculation related to the process of housing allocation and the points system. This system was not determined locally, but was part of a broader housing and social policy, a policy that recognised minority communities and immigrants as having the greatest housing need. In addition to this, the impact of housing policies such as the right of tenants to buy council housing at a discounted rate and the subsequent problems of replacing social housing stock exacerbated the problem.

The 'buy-to-let' boom created by the loosening of credit entities may be responsible, even if unintentionally, for reducing neighbourhood cohesion. Private sector landlords, unlike their counterparts in the social housing sector, are not driven by the need to promote neighbourhoods that are stable and thriving. Rather, the overriding objective is to maximise profit. Furthermore, at least two of the research sites for the Joseph Rowntree Foundation (JRF) study, Aston and Canley, could be described as reception housing markets. Although the London housing market is characterised by affordability challenges, it could also be argued that some parts of Walthamstow, which formed the basis for the OSF study, could also be viewed as an affordable market for migrants moving to London. The areas provide an opportunity for those with limited income to rent or buy a property but these factors did not seem to resonate with some of the residents, who viewed housing as crystallising the sense of loss and disconnection discussed earlier. They expressed dissatisfaction with housing allocation and saw housing policies as giving newcomers an advantage that was not deserved. They also felt that their voices were not being heard when they did raise issues related to this perceived problem.

Interestingly, the stakeholders interviewed understood the problems associated with accessing decent housing. As they saw it, there were two key challenges. First, housing regulation was predicated on priority need. It was evident that other groups had greater need for this resource than white working-class communities. This was largely due to greater household size, or other social needs among the minority families. Second, there was very little that the local housing department could do about what was perceived as unfair in the private sector. Landlords were able to charge and let properties to a range of tenants and the local government has no influence on these decisions. Problems with accessing affordable housing, combined with the depletion of housing stock, emphasised the powerless position of white working-class communities. Residents expressed a view that social capital was being eroded. Specifically, young people could no longer afford private sector housing, nor could they access social housing. Thus, housing was the vessel that directly demonstrated the concerns of residents: the breaking up of families, the loss of networks and a dilution of the core values that bound residents together. The inability to address these concerns or provide solutions was blamed on government policy and the social change that resulted from increased immigration into the country: *"If you can't get on the housing list and you aren't a priority case, then you have to move away and that breaks up families. None of my children and grandchildren live around here"* (Somers Town resident, female).

Policies on housing were seen as unfair. The perception was that housing organisations rewarded groups even though these groups were perceived as adding little or no value to neighbourhoods. The contrast between cohesive and values-driven working-class communities and resistant minority communities, as well as other groups such as students, was telling. A message was being relayed that dependency and failure would be rewarded: *"I was told that unless I was an alcoholic or a druggie, then I wouldn't get a place"* (Somers Town resident, male).

Housing was symptomatic of the wider concern about the future of white working-class communities. These residents viewed themselves as hard-working, values-led communities that had missed out on housing opportunities because of an unfair system. They could not compete for housing when it came to family size or social problems, which were viewed as the gateway to securing an affordable form of tenancy.

Despite the vehemence of the discussion on access to social housing, many accepted that neighbourhoods were multicultural and understood the benefits that this would bring to the neighbourhood. The wider debate on multiculturalism and social change revealed a range of competing views. For the most part, white working-class residents welcomed increased levels of diversity and difference. However, the practice of equality opportunity for some was seen as leading to adverse outcomes. This was intensified by the perception that government at the local and national level was uninterested in their views. The white working class was without voice and no one was advocating on their behalf:

> *"Equal opportunities are anything but. We are bottom of the pile now."* (Somers Town resident, male)

> *"Aston Pride's ran by Asians for Asians."* (Aston resident, male)

> *"And the England flags, the council are worried about the political
> correctness of it. It's England – if we can't be proud in England
> …"* (Canley resident, female)

People rejected the view that they were racist or had a dislike of
foreigners. Rather, the blame was placed on 'political correctness',
which was viewed as preventing free discussion around the issues of
identity, race and neighbourhood. Before continuing, it is important
to attempt to unpick the notion of 'political correctness' and what it
means in contemporary Britain. The term encapsulates children being
'forced' to celebrate community festivals such as Eid and Diwali, the
appointment of minority staff at the council for tokenistic reasons,
and renaming streets after anti-colonialist leaders. In this way, 'political
correctness' is white people being told to do something to appease
the views of a minority. Many thought that political correctness had a
stifling effect on people as they did not want to be thought of as racist
or saying something that was deemed inappropriate

> *"It's not a problem them being here, just the rights they have over
> us."* (Canley resident, female)

> *"Minorities now hide behind the race card. When Camden Town
> was full of Greek and Irish people, it wasn't like that. Everyone
> mixed and fitted in. The new lot don't do that."* (Somers Town
> resident, male)

In countering some of the views articulated in the fieldwork, it is
important to state that political correctness has become a pejorative
term that becomes dismissed too readily by some parts of the media
(eg the influential right-wing British newspaper, *The Daily Mail*),
commentators and the research community (see Goodhart, 2004).
However, there is also a need to emphasise the factors contributing
to the emergence of race equality policies. They came about because
evidence showed that minority communities were facing discrimination
as a result of their ethnicity (Daniel, 1968). During the 1970s, racist
language was mainstreamed into society by its use in peak time UK
TV programmes such as *Till Death Us Do Part*. Hence, equality policies
have played an important role in addressing discrimination and racism
and should not be viewed as political correctness. There is a need for
free debate but this should not be to the detriment of the progress
made since 1975 and 1976 (the passing of the Sex Discrimination and
Race Relations Acts, respectively). White working-class communities

need to feel that they may voice their concerns and fears, but they must do so within a framework of equality of opportunity and permissible behaviours. More than this, as previously mentioned in this book, programmes such as *Till Death* and *The White Season* created an unchallenged space for concerns about social change and the impact of multiculturalism to be presented to an audience of millions.

Residents viewed equality of opportunity as part of government interference in private domains. Predictably, they were resistant to interventions because the benefit that these policies would bring to neighbourhoods was not clear. They were tolerant of diversity and understood this as the reality of living in a modern Britain based on fairness that applied to all groups. Many had no problem living alongside people of different backgrounds:

> "My street is a microcosm.... Next door is Polish, then Indian, then African and then an obese white family and an Irish woman a little further. There is no hostility. Everyone largely muddles along." (Aston resident, male)

> "I've found them some of the nicest people, but if I listen to what other people say, I wouldn't have even spoken to one." (Canley resident, female)

> "People and the media call Somers Town racist but it isn't. We never even used to notice the differences. When I was at school, about 60 years ago, a Greek boy who spoke no English at all started and we were told by the teacher to be kind to him ... and we were. He still lives round here now. The indigenous population has always been accepting and we never felt threatened. Some people are threatened now but everyone is scared to say anything for fear of being called racist. I stuck up for black people ... recently a black guy had to stick up for the white groups ... in a housing meeting because it would have been seen as racist if a white person had said what he said. It has gone full circle." (Somers Town resident, male)

We have noted that a sense of loss, resentment and lack of voice may, in some cases, become linked with multiculturalism and social change. Access to social housing has been used as the metaphor for neighbourhood change, which is deepened by the perception that government does not listen to the views of the communities represented in the JRF and OSF research studies. In part, the resident narratives echo some of the language associated with Enoch Powell in his 'Rivers of Blood' speech in 1968. Yet, there is a much more progressive view of multiculturalism which shows that the white working class are not all supporters of extremist views. It is this variation that is lost in the heated discussion of the white working class and multiculturalism.

The reality of multiculturalism

Multiculturalism for white working-class communities in the research sites was not an option, but a reality. This weakens the policy approach of community cohesion and integration that supported the idea that multiculturalism was at fault for people leading 'parallel lives' (Home Office, 2001). The projection of segregated communities in conflict and not binding to societal norms has been influential at both national and local authority level. However, resident focus group discussions and stakeholder interviews in all of the research sites suggested a different and much more complex pattern.

Community conversations with the white working class intimated different types of social interaction and relationships. For some, it related to being neighbours and providing space for mutual support, whereby home became a space for micro-integration. Contrary to conventional wisdom, the experiences were generally positive: *"I love it, I love it. My house comes in and it's like the United Colours of Benetton. There's Asians, there's blacks, Asians, mixed race, white, Irish, everything, gingers, everything"* (Waltham Forest, white female). Beyond the home and the neighbourhood, the reality of difference was encountered in the workplace, school and college. People were pragmatic and realised that they could not and would not live in isolation. This was especially telling in the case of young, white working-class participants who did not differentiate between people on the basis of ethnicity. In London, and especially East London, there was recognition that you could not select friends and acquaintances based on skin colour, faith or culture: *"It's everything round here. Like, it'll be a mixed group fighting someone else in their group that they don't like or someone from another area"* (Waltham Forest, young white male).

To a lesser or greater extent, communities accepted and even celebrated multiculturalism. People enjoyed living with difference and social relations developed in a number of domains. White working-class communities had been living in the same neighbourhoods as immigrants since at least 1945. Many individuals from minority communities were born, educated and worked in the same locality, where their white peers certainly regarded them as British.

For some individuals, social interaction between different communities was an embedded and natural part of their everyday life. Difference was the norm and diversity was celebrated, not merely tolerated. It should be noted that these routine interactions took place despite the challenges and pressures that had affected integration from international and local events since 2001. Additionally, there was a retreat from multiculturalism after the publication of the Parekh Report (2000). In this context, the residents who were interviewed showed themselves to be remarkably resilient and progressive given that these are generally low-income communities in competition with each other for scarce public resources during a period of difficult economic circumstances. This is very different from the portrayal in recent publications (Goodhart, 2004; Ford and Goodwin, 2014).

We have seen so far that a social construction has developed around white working-class communities. The focus of the discussion on policy is on a cultural rather than economic framework, depicting these communities as being hostile to immigration and change (see Sveinsson, 2009). However, the fieldwork shows a much more variegated perspective. Residents were concerned with the pace of neighbourhood change but the majority of those who participated viewed cultural diversity and difference as being positive. There is an acceptance that cities such as Birmingham, Coventry and London have attracted migrants for many decades. Initially, these may have been drawn from different parts of Britain, but more recently, people have come from around the world. Increased knowledge and awareness of different groups is being played out against a background of competition for scarce resources, such as jobs and social housing. Despite this, there was a willingness to start local conversations between groups in order to support understanding: *"We need these people to come into our culture and educate us about theirs. They don't do that but we can learn from them and people do want to"* (Somers Town resident, female).

The white working-class neighbourhoods in the fieldwork sites were, in reality, comprised of different groups and communities. They are from cities that have played an important role in attracting migrants to live and work in urban areas. In 2001, Canley was more than 90% white, though this is changing rapidly because Coventry has attracted students, immigrants and refugees from around the world. In Aston in Birmingham, Somers Town in North London and Waltham Forest in North-East London, multiculturalism is an important part of neighbourhood life and its existence results in a pragmatic understanding of neighbourhood change. For example, Somers Town has experienced cycles of immigration, with Jews, Irish and Greek newcomers. Similarly, Aston has been a reception housing market to immigrants from the Caribbean and the Indian subcontinent. This is also the case for Waltham Forest, which has a large Pakistani community and emerging Somali and Polish communities. Multiculturalism and 'everyday integration' (Institute of Public Policy Research, 2012) happens in a routine and grassroots way, with people sharing space, services and facilities. Often, the commonality of experiences of diversity is related to improved services, cultural richness or simply letting people get on with their lives:

> "When the Indians came, they took all our corner shops over but the majority were friendly, spoke English. We accepted that they were prepared to open longer hours than us." (Somers Town resident, female)

> "It is fascinating working here; I was the only white person in the office to begin with, now there are five of us. It has been an interesting change, I had a couple of weeks of culture shock, being such a visible minority, but there is a cultural richness here, before too long, there are no ethnic issues, after the initial surprise, it's just about people are people and not skin colour." (Aston resident, male)

Given the sometimes virulent content of contemporary political debates on immigration, it is especially noteworthy that working-class communities continue to celebrate aspects of multiculturalism and unanimously disapprove of right-wing extremist politics. Social interaction with individuals from different communities was the norm for many in the low-income white focus groups. Young people who had experienced this close sense of difference throughout their lives did not perceive this as a problem. Rather, it was a by-product of growing up in a multicultural neighbourhood:

> "My cousin has just been born today, mixed-race." (Waltham Forest, young white male)

> "I've got a Pakistani cousin that's just got married ... like, I don't even know them but, yeah, it's my uncle's daughter innit? She doesn't keep in contact with the family ... like, I've just found out." (Waltham Forest, young white male)

Multiculturalism is a positive lived experience for the majority of white working-class residents in the fieldwork. Nowhere is this asserted with greater clarity and purpose than when a white participant in Waltham Forest, responding to suggestions that the white working class may be attracted to supporting far Right and extremist groups such as the British National Party (BNP), unequivocally retorted: *"That's a load of shit. I'm not being funny but it's a multiracial community, no one's racist around here ... I mean, it's a multiracial community"* (Waltham Forest, white female 1).

Of course, the limitations of a qualitative methodology are well-known. Skewed sampling, lack of representation and taking individual perspectives are some of the weaknesses of this type of methodological approach. However, it creates an opportunity for depth and a richness of data that is missing from survey approaches. The Waltham Forest fieldwork told a story of a white working-class community that was supportive of multiculturalism and lived the experience of social change as an everyday reality. Immigration does have an impact on jobs, housing and social cohesion, but the views of white working-class communities cannot be framed as being uniformly hostile. The opinions expressed by those interviewed have rebalanced the debate.

Overlapping identities

Earlier in the book, we explored the problems associated with defining 'white' and 'working class' and noted that these are constructed in different ways to meet short-term policy and political objectives. Whiteness, in particular, is a shifting term. With the retreat of multiculturalism, we advanced the view that white working-class identity, which has sometimes been seen as 'dirty whiteness', was washed in the framework of viewing Muslims as the 'enemy within'. The fieldwork studies show that whiteness is implicit but complex. Residents interviewed were concerned not only about the impact of established minorities, but also about white newcomers, such as Polish migrants and university students, who were viewed as not sharing values or contributing to the neighbourhoods. Whiteness and class may interchange with being British or English and this is sometimes transparent and inclusive and other times opaque and closed, depending on policy and political narratives. In this section, we will discuss these concepts within the context of the OSF project based in Waltham Forest.

Discussions about British identity are yet another example of the complexities of social change, which are often blunted and simplified by cohesion and integration policy. The much-celebrated citizenship tests, or common norms, did not arise in community conversations. Instead, participants spoke about the inclusive and multifaceted frame of identity. Being different was not viewed as being problematic to a British identity. For example, young people spoke powerfully about British identity, which they linked to being born or brought up in Walthamstow: *"British, it doesn't mean that you're white at all ... you're in this country and you're meant to be here, you don't need to be white to be British"* (Waltham Forest, young white female). Britishness appears to be an inclusive identity beyond the reductionism of phenotype and place that has often underscored national narratives. The views offered by communities who took part in this study seem to underscore a modern Britain as a diverse and multicultural environment that has little resonance with superficial appearance and more to do with respecting legal frameworks and codes of behaviour. To this end, newly emerging groups such as Polish and Lithuanian migrants were regarded as not acclimating to the country or being British, even though they presented as white. Concerns about collectivised behaviour, jobs and the strain on health and educational services were shared by some of the interviewees. It could be argued that identity was an earned right and not automatic. Moreover, there was concern about the failure of newly arrived migrants to respect social mores as pedantic as putting out rubbish on the correct day, which was emblematic of a respect towards local customs and, more broadly, Britain itself. As we have noted, integration is a lived experience but so, too, are perceived micro-aggressions that may be conflated into common-sense narratives. The importance of learning English as a proxy for identity, whether one is British or working-class, cannot be underestimated. White working-class communities felt that language was important in demonstrating a willingness to integrate and build commonalities with established groups. New migrants were viewed as outside British identity but many felt that in 20 years, they would be accepted within the country. For the moment, new immigrants were viewed with a level of suspicion.

White working-class communities were concerned with the lack of respect shown by new communities. For example, disrespect for the cleanliness of the community and local social mores were a significant problem in Waltham Forest and many felt that the new Polish communities were to blame: *"Every time I walk the kids to school, there's plenty of dog poo everywhere and, like, people just throw their beds out ... if you go down the alleyways ... it's just piled up with rubbish everywhere"* (Waltham Forest, white female). New migrants were associated with contributing to environmental problems and not taking the initiative to integrate. In the OSF study, white working-class communities seemed to agree that Eastern Europeans were not considered British, as were established minority communities: *"So what about new people who have been moving in, like Polish people? They're not English"* (Waltham Forest, young white male).

The perception of everyday micro-aggressions by newly arrived migrants, such as spitting and burning poppies leading up to Remembrance Sunday, became conflated with wider debates on integration. Spitting in public was associated with minority communities and was viewed by some white working-class participants as a key cultural marker. A small personal act becomes inculcated with identity and respect:

> *"They should respect their country; they go spitting everywhere ... they should keep the floors tidy. I mean we can't go round and spit in their country can we?... They get chucked out the country."* (Waltham Forest, young white male)

> *"I don't think it's changed over the years. I remember someone spitting in the playground in that school when my son was there and my son was 21 this year, and they spat in the playground and I went mad. I said, like, with no disrespect, like, 'There's no reason for spitting on the floor'. I went in, and he wasn't the headmaster then, and they went, 'It's cultural'. I said 'Hold on a minute', I said, 'let me get this right, because in some countries it's cultural to give birth in a field, but you wouldn't want me to do it in your playground would you?'"* (Waltham Forest, white female)

The burning of poppies before Remembrance Sunday was another example of the lack of respect for social mores. This occurred near the Royal Albert Hall in Kensington, London, in November 2011, although media reports suggested that a now-banned group, 'Muslims against Crusades', conceived of it in Walthamstow. This made an impression on the young white people taking part in the sessions: *"I remember hearing about a load of Asian people burning the poppies or something. That pissed me off"* (Waltham Forest young white male). This act was viewed as something graver than simply breaking the law. Young people saw it as a symbolic act by some Muslim Britons to show a lack of respect for British history and tradition. The custom of spitting, the importance of learning to speak English and the act of burning poppies are all construed as being problems related to cohesion and integration. They evoke imagery that does not fit well into the policies and frameworks that are set out by government, and they seem to be litmus tests for conflict or integration between communities. Though spitting and burning poppies are extreme acts, and the large proportion of minority communities speak English, these disparate encounters become part of the community memory. Minorities are thought to support these outlier positions.

Similarly, the importance of migrants speaking English seemed to have struck a chord with white working-class participants. It was not only seen as being a primary means to support integration, but also viewed by white working-class groups as causing problems when minority communities spoke in their mother tongue. Specifically, speaking another language in a public space was deemed as showing lack of respect or even rudeness:

> "I think the only thing I get fed up with is when they talk in their own language in front of you. It's not even about learning English, it's just the simple fact that if you're standing there talking to an English person, in pure English, and then the same conversation turning round to your Turkish friend or whatever, you're still standing there and you're just like don't know where to look really."
> (Waltham Forest, white female)

Some participants suggested that learning and communicating in English leads to mutual respect and understanding. Of course, this fails to recognise that increasing numbers of households speak many different languages. Here, competency in English appears to be more than simply communication and part of a set of rules that enables cohesion and integration to take place. There was a view that core British identity is predicated on the ability to speak the majority language. In this context, new migrants such as Poles and Somalis were not perceived as British, in contrast with Caribbean and Pakistani communities in Waltham Forest.

New groups have not had the opportunity to interact and be accepted as part of the diversity of Waltham Forest. They were regarded as problematic with regard to increased competition for jobs and housing, as well as for placing a burden on the welfare system. The perceived economic threat posed by new migrants at a time of recession led to many of the negative comments. These new migrants were viewed as being a separate entity from the established norms of multiculturalism, which had developed over many decades. The welcome was not extended, nor were they viewed as supporting the codes and respect that both white and established minority communities implicitly observed.

Racialised discussion of the impact of new immigration peppered the focus groups, alongside the championing of Waltham Forest as a diverse and multicultural area. This appears to be a contradiction but could be placed in the context of national political narratives on immigration. At the national level, successive governments have attempted to restrict immigration but, at the same time, promote integration. Controlling the influx of immigrants into the country while encouraging shared norms and values is a difficult balancing act to achieve politically. Furthermore, given the national political leadership, which was perceived as lacking, it is not surprising that views on immigration in Waltham Forest appeared to be divergent and contradictory. White working-class residents in Waltham Forest, like their peers in Canley, Aston and Somers Town, alternately accept multiculturalism, label new migrants as problematic, or blame the government for local problems in Waltham Forest.

Government interventions such as community cohesion have focused on the lack of cross-cultural contact as being problematic. In short, communities were seen as living 'parallel lives' apart from each other even though they share the same urban space. The experiences in Waltham Forest demonstrate that culture and interaction are close, sometimes dense and personal. The participants in the OSF study had lived alongside and with minority communities for many years. Thus, positing conflict between communities as a 'clash of cultures' has to be deconstructed; policy, which continues to be framed by this narrative, is unlikely to meet its objectives. The norms of diversity and culture may be traced to the well-established patterns of migration in East London. Others include access to jobs, an accessible housing market, and established links through community infrastructure and the residents of that community. However, many places, such as Canley and Somers Town, which may have previously been viewed as closed, white working-class neighbourhoods, are viewed in a much more diverse way.

A common policy and academic assumption is one that views white working-class communities as a homogeneous group. This theory goes further by ascribing collective behaviours. Both notions are problematic. Recent research demonstrates that communities are different and multifaceted in terms of tenure, employment and place, which may lead to nuanced findings on integration and cohesion. The JRF and OSF studies found that participants were diverse not only in terms of these classifications, but also in terms of ethnicity. A matrix of social, educational and work relationships with minority communities was the norm, and this shaped some of the views on common challenges and opportunities related to difference and grassroots coalition-building.

'Everyday integration'?

It has been noted that residents interviewed enjoyed, for the most part, living in a multicultural area. Moreover, there were numerous instances of intercultural contact between white working-class and minority communities. Low-income white communities spoke about their close personal and family relationships and these highlighted diversity.

While it is clear that multiculturalism is an important part of what attracts people to live in Waltham Forest and other research sites, this is at the superficial level rather than being 'hard-wired' into the community. Despite well-established cohesion and community engagement interventions, different communities did not have an extensive embedded set of social networks and friends. Most continued to associate with immediate friends and family living on the same street, or in the same neighbourhood.

In this way, it could be argued that community cohesion has not worked. Those interviewed were not interested in government-instigated attempts to come together in order to develop shared values. While the experiences in Waltham Forest are far removed from the community cohesion rhetoric of 'parallel lives', with communities entrenched in a segregated and symmetrical pattern of living, their lives may be characterised as ones of soft rather than hard integration.

Everyday, or 'soft-wired', integration was a common theme in Waltham Forest. Participants engaged with different communities in a variety of public spaces: schools, workplaces, the market and park. However, this did not always lead to strong and meaningful relationships outside these settings. Social bonds and networks were not dense, but should the lack of 'hard-wired' integration really be presented as a problem? The focus groups showed soft contact in different spaces where ordinarily people would interact. Increasingly, modern society seems to be composed of fleeting encounters. For example, people in Waltham Forest would describe routine friendly encounters with friends:

> "If I see someone that was black or of a different culture to me, but I know them, I'll go over and start speaking ... if they ain't got nothing on, I'll tell them to come ... wherever we are, when we see our mates, then we get together." (Waltham Forest, young white male)

In the Waltham Forest study, white working-class communities had a strong attachment to place. This was about not simply multiculturalism, but also proximity to family and friends. Access to support networks in the local area was repeated many times in discussions. This may reflect the fact that unlike middle- and high-income families that may be able to afford such services as childcare, people in low-income communities have to rely on the informal support of their family and friends. There was a general view that Waltham Forest was a good place to live. Low-income white communities had lived in the area either from birth or for a very long time. Some had moved to Waltham Forest because it was seen as a good place to raise their families. This is seen in the following quote, which emphasises the point that despite social and economic challenges, the borough continued to be viewed in a positive light:

> "When I first moved here, it was a really, it's not a bad area now compared to a lot of places, but when I first moved here, it was a really, really nice area to live in. There wasn't a lot of street crime; there weren't a lot of problems locally. It was a nice area to live in, the people were nice." (Waltham Forest, white female)

The white working-class focus groups demonstrated the importance of the social capital generated by the connections between family and friends. Reciprocal support for each other and looking after children was an important part of the discussion for white women:

> "Oh yeah! Everyone does watch everyone's backs, do you know what I mean, even if you, even if there's an indifference, you still go, 'Oh there's an issue with so and so, or your kids', ... do you know what I'm saying? If there's an issue, people do that round here, they do tend to watch each other's back even though they've had their own disagreements and whatever over their time." (Waltham Forest, white female)

Both of the communities that participated in the focus group study viewed Waltham Forest as home and had similar drivers in arriving at this conclusion. At various stages, people spoke about the importance of the area, which provided a network of family and friends who provided extended and unconditional support. This level of grassroots community activism could be harnessed to develop new types of local leaderships embedded in the neighbourhoods. Diversity and difference were embraced as part of the lived experience in Waltham Forest. It was an incentive for regarding the borough as a good place to live, giving an infrastructure of community organisations, places of worship and shops. However, this should be qualified. New arrivals, especially the range of different groups from Eastern Europe, were not viewed as being inside this cosy framework.

Grassroots community interaction does not necessarily require the government to intervene by bringing communities together. Earlier, in both the Waltham Forest study and the areas that formed the basis of the JRF project, we noted the levels of frustration from white working-class communities about the perceived 'political correctness' associated with government interventions on race. The resentment was founded on the sense that white working-class communities were being told by a remote and disconnected government to act or behave in a way that may leave them in a disadvantaged position. Not surprisingly, they reacted against these types of imposed policies. In contrast, multiculturalism was viewed as much more fluid and organic. It need not be forced or hard-wired into people: *"I think the government causes half the problems with stuff like that to be truthful … but you see what I'm saying, they force the issue, which makes an issue that there shouldn't be in the first place"* (Waltham Forest, white female).

The role of the government should not be to direct people to interact with each other, a practice that was viewed as the basis of community cohesion, but rather to encourage informal interactions in public spaces. Many participants discussed the positive impact of community festivals such as the Mela and leisure time, with an emphasis on play and food. This was more than the derided 'saris and samosas', which was seen as representing multiculturalism (Alibhai-Brown, 2000). The events that white working-class communities discussed had an everyday resonance to their lives and a capacity to mobilise people across communities because they created opportunities and incentives to celebrate: *"Because we used to go the Lloyd Park Asian one* [Mela]*, and that was brilliant with the curries and all that and the mixed foods"* (Waltham Forest, white female).

The catalytic role of informal grassroots events bringing together different groups is in sharp contrast to the inflexible, top-down frameworks of community cohesion and even the recently supported policy of integration based on localism. The view of focus group participants was that the government should be the facilitator and not the driver, sponsoring local groups to deliver. This does not mean that the government should not have a role, particularly when racism is present. It is important that racism, in all its forms, be addressed and the Equality Act 2010 provides the legal framework and incentive to encourage and promote good relations. In short, oversight and legal remedies are examples of the hard-wiring of integration while community interaction at festivals and engagement in national events like the 2012 Olympics are examples of soft integration.

The realities of multiculturalism seem to be in contradiction to much of the national narratives developed since 2001. Of course, problems exist in terms of competition for public resources, such as housing, accessing representation or increasing the white working-class voice in local politics. However, it does not readily follow that communities are in conflict with each other or that they are living parallel lives. Rather, people interviewed in Waltham Forest, as well as those in the JRF study, demonstrated the positive experiences of living in a diverse area. They did not particularly want to meet to talk about difference, but rather to address local challenges affecting the community. There was agreement on the importance of creating public spaces for people to congregate organically for leisure, cultural and sporting activities. Local authorities should use these platforms as opportunities to facilitate grassroots interaction rather than the top-down directives that have marked much of the policy on community cohesion.

Political disconnection

White working-class people revealed a jaundiced view of politics at the local and national level in the focus group discussions. The general opinion was that they had neither voice nor influence with political representatives. In both the JRF and OSF studies, discussions with local stakeholders revealed that low-income white communities had not been the focus of either cohesion or, indeed, preventing extremism work. Some of the white participants felt that minority communities had a voice in contrast to white working-class communities. They saw them as having local councillors, funded community organisations (with extensive networks with the local authority) and an infrastructure of faith-based organisations. It was felt that there was no shortage of individuals or institutions that could advocate on behalf of minority groups. It was much more difficult to identify a similar community infrastructure for white working-class communities. The sense of a forgotten community is summarised in the following:

> "I'm not being racist here, but I don't think, like, whereas the Turkish people, they'll have their family and they'll all get together and they're doing events and then you've got everyone else who are doing their own events with their own kind, white people, they just sort of, like, that's it!" (Waltham Forest, white female)

160

This person celebrated living in a multicultural Waltham Forest. However, she was reflecting the sense that white working-class communities could be viewed as the forgotten minority within cohesion and integration frameworks. This was not necessarily the fault of the local authority, which was simply taking guidance from national cohesion policy. For example, low-income white communities were merely referenced in the Connecting Communities programme in 2009 (DCLG, 2009).

The goal of building grassroots responses to integration has been further compromised by views on local political leadership. Participants believed that this leadership had failed local communities. As noted earlier, white participants felt that local equality interventions had been mired in political correctness. Nationally, there was severe criticism of government policy and politicians. Young white people disagreed with the cohesion framework which suggested that people clustered within their own groups rather than with each other:

> "That's the problem with the government because they don't get out from behind that big chair to look in the real world and see what goes on and they don't know what goes on and us kids do, we know what goes on." (Waltham Forest, young white female)

Political disconnection, mistrust and a lack of credibility are not the basis for building links between communities. The OSF research suggested a need to create opportunities for new organisations and individuals to work with the local authority on these issues. National and, indeed, local political institutions are blemished and it will require significant and thoughtful investment to deliver inclusive and progressive engagement. Despite these comments, it could be construed that the challenge is not simply about improving knowledge between communities, but addressing the wider disconnection that institutions have with white working-class communities.

At a profound level, the commentary reflects broader tropes in the cohesion and integration debates. First is the impact of socio-economic change and displacement as a result of immigration. The transformation from being a majority to a minority community aggravates people's loss of voice with institutions such as schools and local government. Second, the white working-class perception that preferential treatment is given to minority communities, such as taking time off for religious festivals, echoes some of the debates in the media. Third, there was concern that government was forcing an issue onto communities and identifying a problem that may not have existed with cohesion and integration policies. The reality, which the political leaders missed, is that participants actually valued living in a multicultural society.

It may be that cohesion and integration policy under successive governments has failed to understand that it is often the more basic, personal issues that really matter to local people. Furthermore, there was a general reluctance by government to consider these views because it was thought that those in opposition to multiculturalism held views based on ignorance or racism. The problem for community cohesion and integration policy is that they are framed nationally and do not travel well or have the currency of language to advance cohesion and integration at the grassroots level.

Across the OSF focus groups with white working-class communities there was a view that community cohesion and integration were linked to political correctness. These terms were used pejoratively and made it difficult to discuss the impact of multiculturalism in Waltham Forest. More problematic was the perception that the needs of minority groups were favoured over the needs of low-income white communities. The idea that political correctness supported the needs of minority communities was a recurring theme: *"Well, if a white, not being funny, if a white person said anything about Asians, you're racist straight away"* (Waltham Forest, white female).

In many of the groups, education and specifically schools became the nexus for anger and frustration related to political correctness. In contrast to the perceived protection afforded to minority communities (and, in particular, their children) from racist comments, white children did not have the same rights, and were often labelled as racist. Preferential treatment for minority children and their parents was viewed as both embedded and endemic in recounted interactions with teachers and politicians alike:

> *"I'm going back to when my son was at primary school and we went in there and it was like, I can't even, oh it was the Golden Jubilee I think it was, and they went 'Oh, we're having a Caribbean Carnival', I was like, 'Okay, but it's the Golden Jubilee. So that should be bunting and de de de de de' and as I said, I come from a multicultural family so I ain't got a problem with black or white, but even the black people in the school were saying like, they force an issue all the time, they make things an issue, do you see what I'm saying? The government go 'Oh well you can't do', and the next thing was Mary was making Joseph a curry, like seriously; she wasn't making him a curry was she? That wasn't in the Bible. She didn't make him a curry."* (Waltham Forest, white female)

Political disconnection, contradictory views on immigration and multiculturalism, and respect for social mores suggests that national and local interventions have not made the impact that they perhaps should have after over a decade of investment and policy framing. This points not only to the challenge of the content and message, but also to the agencies that are delivering the message. Government and local councillors seem disconnected from the communities that they seek to represent.

The communities that took part in the fieldwork across the different sites are viewed by some critics as parochial in their views, resistant to change and de facto supporters of the BNP or, indeed, the United Kingdom Independence Party (UKIP). Yet, the acceptance of this assertion would be a mistake. Rather than being categorised as racist, many simply want fairness and equality. The participants were keen to engage in conversations with different communities and even identified ways in which people have or could come together to build meaningful and more natural cohesion. Intense competition for resources and a loss of employment and other opportunities did not impede the formation of an environment in which residents could develop nuanced views on diversity and change. Finally, there was an active distaste expressed towards voting for the BNP and other extreme right-wing organisations. Furhtermore, voicing concern about issues that directly impact their lives and communities should not be perceived as leading automatically to support for the BNP or participating in racist violence.

Conclusion

The second of the two fieldwork chapters has been largely based on the OSF study of white working-class communities in Waltham Forest in North-East London. This builds on the previous chapter in reiterating grassroots support for multiculturalism and reconfiguring white identity as being fluid and inclusive.

In the first part of the chapter, the importance of being treated fairly was emphasised. This was related to housing and jobs, but also in more general terms regarding a lack of voice in local politics. In contrast to minority communities, white working-class communities felt that their claims were not taken seriously. They believed that they had no representation and some viewed a bias towards minority communities. Again, this may be seen as the politics of resentment from a group that is getting smaller in number and feels threatened by increasing levels of diversity. Taken further, fairness is not really about an egalitarian distribution of resources, but one that entrenches privilege in housing and employment markets by basing housing, for example, not on need, but on cultural factors such as the 'sons and daughters'[1] policy for social housing. In the age of equality of opportunity, as codified in the Equality Act 2010, there can be no return to policies that discriminate against minority communities. Instead, fairness could be seen as the importance of challenging vested political interests and being clear about the way in which policies are transmitted. Fairness is not advanced by the clear breakdown of trust between people and their political institutions. In short, fairness and the impact of immigration is not just a white working-class problem, but an issue that affects all Britons.

The lived reality of multiculturalism is stressed by many interviewees. It is seen as being an asset to neighbourhoods and communities. In a similar way, being white and working-class is not so much about skin colour, but about values and where individuals have been brought up. To this point, white Polish immigrants were viewed as less British than established Pakistani communities. The former are viewed as a threat and are placed in an outlier category while the latter are seen as being legitimate members of the community and having a similar identity shaped by Walthamstow and the East End. In this context, being white and working-class is about values rather than ethnicity. It is inclusive to certain groups but outside the reach of others.

Despite the support for multiculturalism and inclusive views on identity expressed in this and the previous chapter, how can we explain the racialised language used by white working-class respondents in Waltham Forest and in Canley, Aston and Somers Town? Is this not evidence of the sentiments that may have been expressed by the Teds who attacked Caribbean migrants in 1958 or the Dockers who marched in support of Enoch Powell after he gave his 'Rivers of Blood' speech in 1968? There is no excuse for racism from whatever source. It need not be justified and should be condemned. However, the white working class are reflecting national tropes on race and immigration that have been set by political representatives during the post-war period. In this way, if immigration is considered problematic, then public opinion is likely to reflect this in interviews. Racialised discussion matches national debates but the lived and positive experiences of difference are a reflection of local reality. In these two studies, a gap exists between politicians and people, but also between national government rhetoric and the views of white working-class communities.

In this chapter, residents argued for the need to create spaces for people to come together on a grassroots basis as opposed to the top-down community cohesion model that was mired in strategies, frameworks and measurements, as well as driven by central and local government. It is also detached from the laissez-fair approach of the Conservative–Liberal Democrat Coalition policy of integration that expects people to magically come together and resolve the challenges of integration that it has to some extent created. At the everyday level, people interact as neighbours, students, work colleagues and consumers of culture. Residents expressed a positive view of events such as the 2012 London Olympics or local events where white working-class and other groups could come together. These were events through which the lived diversity of a country could be celebrated rather than a grand plan to discuss community cohesion or establish points of integration.

Support for a grassroots approach creates an opportunity to develop a different paradigm of community development. White working-class communities are neither the victims nor the aggressors per se, nor are they searching for an idealised community that existed in the past. They are building on the expectation that neighbourhoods in cities will be multicultural, and to this end, community-building needs to factor in dynamic notions of identity, culture and voice that are very different to the past or the current environment. Without such an approach, it is very likely that the white working class will continue to be misunderstood or, at a minimum, misrepresented in its approach to accepting and moving forward in a multicultural nation.

Note

[1] A housing policy that gives people born or brought up in an area extra points in the allocation of housing.

SEVEN

Reshaping white working-class identities: inclusive and progressive

Introduction

The motivation for writing this book was to rebalance the narrative about white working-class communities, multiculturalism and social change. As we have noted, the white working class have been reified as being either victims or aggressors as Britain transitioned into one of the most diverse societies in Europe during the post-1945 period. The evidence gleaned from fieldwork studies, secondary data and cultural representation shows a range of views. Yes, the white working class are sometimes victims and aggressors, as has been discussed, but they are also at the forefront of supporting immigrants and minority communities, as well as embracing multiculturalism. This latter story has been absent and has been drowned out by the welter of discussion and debate confirming the former stereotype. The need to consolidate a debate on reshaping white working-class identities as being both progressive and inclusive is challenging because of a certain path dependency in viewing these groups within a different framework.

Has conflict and antagonism taken place between the white working class, newly arrived immigrants and established minority communities? Selective incidents have been highlighted in the book, including the 1958 Notting Hill Riots and the 1968 'Rivers of Blood' speech, and these have then been conflated to prove that Britain cannot become a cohesive multicultural society. Indeed, the prime minister professed in 2011 that multiculturalism had failed. Proponents who are fatalistic on immigration and multiculturalism tend to forget or ignore the commonalities between white working-class and minority communities, not only in terms of a common class position, but also because they occupy the same cities and neighbourhoods. They also engage in interactions with non-white groups, through personal and professional relationships.

Despite this, white working-class communities continue to be framed by their opposition to immigration and multiculturalism, which makes it difficult to gain a more considered view with a full and accurate depiction. Throughout this book, the intent has been to move away from a simplistic reductionism, where the white working class need not be given a vaulted status or demonised as being the source of societal problems. In a racialised society, it would be a false perspective to suggest that the white working class is devoid of racism. Recent studies have revealed commentary that is racist and this has to be challenged rather than rationalised. Yet, the white working class are not the only group that takes part in racist discourse. Nor are they likely to be represented in political institutions or among political leaders that have legislated to bring about increasingly restrictive measures on immigration during the post-war period, or members of interview panels who recruit people into organisations and onto boards but fail to achieve minority representation on these entities. Finally, the working class is absent among university admissions systems, which foster a system where 21 colleges at Oxford and Cambridge did not admit a black student in 2013 (see *The Guardian*, 2013b). Racism and a pernicious culture against difference and diversity are entrenched in the white middle and upper class that populate politics, companies and universities. It is they who have power and influence and yet fail to support and embrace the practical meaning of multiculturalism. White working-class communities are absent from these decision-making roles, which impact the opportunities of the many. A sense of perspective is required.

Blaming multiculturalism

We have noted the definitional challenges with 'white' and 'working class' but also 'multiculturalism'. In the absence of clarity, this term, like the 'white working class', becomes used and abused in many narratives. Multiculturalism has been promoted in the relatively recent past despite becoming a noxious term as a result of political and media criticism since its zenith in 2001. For example, the promotion of London's candidacy for the 2012 Olympic Games emphasised the vibrant diversity of this global city. However, a year before, the British prime minister had derided 'state multiculturalism' while his German and French peers were claiming that the concept was dead.

In the book, we discussed how the prominence of multiculturalism has been linked to the downward fortunes of white working-class communities. It heralded identity politics during the 1970s and was fermented in the claims by minority communities for decent housing, social justice and political representation. The campaign for a better deal for those who did not have a voice resulted in the white working class being 'crowded out' in public policy and politics. After all, they had benefitted from access to social housing while immigrants were funnelled into poor-quality and unregulated inner-city private sector housing, were politically represented by the Labour Party in Parliament and the trade unions in the workplace, and had pubs and working men's clubs that were places of leisure and social activity. Multiculturalism and the new set of claims have been seen as jeopardising this worldview.

The politics of resentment and 'white backlash' were situated as white working-class responses to an impression that multiculturalism gave preferential treatment to minority communities at their expense. Access to decent housing, competition for jobs and the apparent support of the Labour Party to the needs of diverse interest groups embedded this perception. A bubbling discontent with the outcomes of a multiculturalism policy has been the framework of the resentment and the 'white backlash' thesis. Some suggest that it explains the reason why the white working class, and the electorate generally, have supported openly racist and nationalist parties like the British National Party (BNP) in 2009 and United Kingdom Independence Party (UKIP) in 2014. However, this supposition may be naive.

Multiculturalism has been in decline since the publication of the seminal Macpherson and Parekh Reports in 1999 and 2000, respectively. From its high point, it has been attacked by politicians, the media and commentators. New Labour's policy of community cohesion was ushered into public discourse in 2001 following riots in Burnley, Oldham and Bradford. Multiculturalism was buried as a policy framework with the telling phrase 'parallel lives' because it had led to increased rather than decreased segregation between white and minority communities. After the fatal 7/7 London bombings, there was discussion that the so-called 'home-grown' terrorists, who had killed innocent people on the transport network, had been born and brought up in England during a period of multiculturalism. The inference was that the policy had led to loyalties that placed faith ahead of country. Declining multiculturalism was a feature of New Labour and this trend continued with the introduction of the policy of integration under the Conservative–Liberal Democrat government that was elected at the 2010 general election.

The position of white working-class communities in the rise and fall of multiculturalism changed. Initially, in the halcyon early days of New Labour, they were viewed as being backward in their perceived opposition to multiculturalism, which was then regarded as a marker for a modern Britain. In the book, we discussed this idea in terms of the media portrayal of the suspects in the Stephen Lawrence murder inquiry. They were white thugs who lived in a closed and dangerous council estate in South London. It was almost as if the suspects were symptomatic of white working-class communities. They were an example of 'dirty whiteness' and hyper-visible as having no place in a modern country. However, as multiculturalism has receded and been replaced by a febrile new period of racialised discourse, working-class 'dirty whiteness' has been, to some extent, cleaned and white identity and the norms associated with this is the basis for national identity. Immigrants and Muslims have become the problematic 'other'.

Whiteness has been laundered by multiculturalism. In addition, class has been rehabilitated. This was initially signalled in 2009 by Connecting Communities, a programme ostensibly designed not only to address the impact of the recession on neighbourhoods across England, but also to counter the rising levels of support for the BNP in working-class areas. The importance of the white working class or 'left behind' voters also became prominent after the 2014 European elections with the success of UKIP. Class and its framing against the backdrop of immigration became an important part of political discourse after years in the political wilderness.

Instead of recognising the anger of the white working class in response to deindustrialisation, the decimation of working-class jobs and their political disconnection from mainstream political organisations, the white working class became the victims of multiculturalism.

In short, these factors were integral to the white working class's loss of identity and voice. The critique of multiculturalism should be challenged when the white working class are viewed solely as being socially conservative and against immigration. The layers that have been revealed by in-depth studies are discounted for a quick political fix. Racism is left unchallenged in working-class communities and throughout society because it represents the new age of discourse where racism has become almost legitimised.

Culture, identities and representation

One of the most powerful forms in shaping white working-class identity has been through film and television, as well as music. Being supported by influential work emanating from academic institutions such as the Centre for Contemporary Cultural Studies at the University of Birmingham, culture and subculture were used in the book to explore the depiction of white working-class identities. By selecting seminal moments, we attempted to construct how the white working class went from 'hero' to 'zero'.

Characterisations show the many parts of white working-class identities. Thus, social realism films, such as *Saturday Night and Sunday Morning*, helped to establish an image of working-class communities as having complex and interesting lives. There were a number of films during the late 1950s and 1960s that changed the paradigm by creating a platform in film to explore prescient political and social issues. Notably, *A Taste of Honey* explored the theme of miscegenation between a young white woman and older black man against the backdrop of Salford in the early 1960s. This was daring commentary, albeit at the start of a decade that witnessed many social reforms. It seemed to highlight a number of issues that are relevant to this book. First, there was recognition that a black presence was a part of Britain, as well as its working-class neighbourhoods and places of work. Second, interracial relationships between working-class white women and black men were becoming a reality. Third, there was an understanding that Britain's role as an imperial power was fading fast and challenges lay ahead in terms of managing social change and immigration from former colonies.

Social realism created a range of working-class characters that could be viewed as charismatic, such as Arthur Seaton in *Saturday Night and Sunday Morning*. This was a progressive development in presenting a different and multidimensional portrayal of working-class communities. A different and less positive character was created in a hugely popular TV programme launched in 1965. *Till Death Us Do Part* sought to portray in a comedic and satirical way the relationships in a working-class family living in the East End of London. This was referenced to the decline of British influence alongside the rise of colonial immigration and multiculturalism. The main character, Alf Garnett, expressed openly racist views on prime-time television using language that was justified as being used in reality by working-class communities. If Arthur was a cool anti-hero, it was evident that Alf was a loud-mouthed racist bigot who complained that the problems of the country rested with immigrants and immigration. *Till Death* represented the conjoining of whiteness, class and racism and was beamed on prime-time television to an audience of millions.

In the book, we discussed the return of social realism in later films such as *This is England*, which was screened in 2006 but harked back to a time 20 years previously. The portrayal of Britain in 1983 is unflattering. Beset by the vitriolic nationalism of the 1982 victory over the conflict with Argentina in the Falklands, and mired in economic recession, the film addresses issues related to white working-class identity, immigration and racism through the lens of a skinhead gang. Initially, the group are seen as diverse and embracing multiculturalism. The release of a former member, Combo, from prison marks a sharp detour into a much darker and racist narrative. The gang is split as some follow Combo's National Front-infused analysis of the adverse impact of immigration and multiculturalism on England. The film is littered with racist diatribe towards minority communities and violence aimed at an Asian shopkeeper. At its conclusion, *This is England* emphasises the pointlessness of nationalism and racism.

Cultural representations of white working-class communities as being racist and backward are unconvincing. The situation is made even more challenging by the way in which the media has portrayed this group in key events since 1945. Two were discussed as symptomatic of the problem. Increased levels of immigration in 1950s' Britain from its former colonies were needed to support an expanding economy. Many of these migrants found a home in areas of cheap accommodation, such as Notting Hill in London. During this time, the area was a largely decrepit and disadvantaged part of West London. It was also predominantly white and working-class. As violence erupted in 1958, the victims were seen as Caribbean immigrants and the aggressors were working-class white men. The subculture of Teds became viewed as young white racist men who instigated the 1958 riots. Again, 10 years later, in response to Enoch Powell's 'Rivers of Blood' speech, white working-class Dockers and Meat Porters went on strike in support of the apocalyptic vision of Powell and the impact of immigration. In both instances, the white working class were seen as being in the vanguard of racist violence.

Responding to the negative and 'zero' cultural representation, the medium of music was deployed. In the first instance, punk was seen as a white proletarian subculture that exploded in Britain in 1976. Leading bands of the genre such as The Clash were political and influenced by the politics of race and immigration. Songs like 'White Riot' demonstrated a bond between white working-class and black youth. However, the punk aesthetic was also influenced by Nazi symbolism and this, along with the skinhead Oi! movement and its association with racist parties such as the National Front and British Movement, clouded the view that it was a progressive intervention and representation of white working-class culture. Latterly, the rise of 2 Tone unequivocally showcased how music, culture and representation can be fused in a joyous celebration of difference. This was birthed in Coventry, a working-class city in the heart of the country, and was pioneered by a diverse group of musicians who promoted anti-racism in songs and music. It was a grassroots movement that continues to influence working-class culture.

Moving from hero to zero in cultural representation is not linear. However, film, television, media and music are critically important to the themes that are central to this book. The white working class need not be lionised or demonised. However, characters like Arthur Seaton, Alf Garnett and Combo show the divergent views of white working-class males. Some are racist and antagonistic, others less so. This group may also be represented by the music of punk and ska and bands like *The Clash* and *The Specials*. Cultural representation does not give us hero or zero, but, instead, shows a range of identities that are missing from research and policy contributions.

Across the pond and in Europe

White working-class loss, fears of immigration, political disconnection and search for an idealised past contributed to the rise of the insurgent parties of the nationalist Right across some parts of Europe and in the US. For example, this is seen in the growth of UKIP in Britain, the Sweden Democrats in Sweden and the upsurge of the insurgent Tea Party movement in US politics after the historic election of President Barack Obama in 2008. In all cases, these organisations were to the Right of the mainstream parties and put themselves forward as representing voters who had no voice. In some cases, such as in the UK and the US, the insurgents were influential in shaping the political agenda. Of course, the rise of UKIP in Britain reached a high when it emerged victorious at the 2014 European elections, while the Tea Party continues to be a vocal interest group inside the Republican Party.

Our discussion showed that similarities do exist beyond the specificity of national politics, history and ideology. For example, concern with the powers of the federal government in the US and the European Commission in Europe, the anti-politics strategy of the Tea Party and UKIP, and the resurrection of immigration as challenging norms of national identity and whiteness had been established over many years in both countries. The white working class has been seen as the basis of core support and yet the data suggests a middle-class engagement. The Tea Party has begun to fade in the US because of Republican mainstream challenge and recognition that the politics of fear regarding immigration does not make sense in a country that will be minority white by 2050.

Back in the UK, the lessons around support for UKIP are clear. Mainstream parties need to challenge the rhetoric of fear, as well as the assumption that the white working class is the core support. As we have seen in the book, there is an element of working-class voters who supported Powellism, and these are the residue who continue to vote for UKIP. Much more pressing is building a vision based on the future reality rather than a long-gone past.

The voice of the white working class

The fieldwork chapters attempted to give voice to white working-class communities. At one level, they may be viewed as simply confirming that this group is resentful and angry about issues of multiculturalism and change. Yet, an alternative view also emerges – one in which people support multiculturalism through a lived experience and reject top-down government policy on race. The voice here is considered and progressive.

Everyday integration exists, with white working-class and minority groups living together as family members, neighbours, work colleagues and students. As such, the lived experiences of multiculturalism are a strong argument against those who incorrectly suggest that white working-class communities are living 'parallel lives' separate and apart from minority communities. Of course, there is resentment and disagreement between white working class residents on the impact of immigration. On the other hand, the blame is not so much placed on immigrants, but on a disconnected and remote government that does not listen and assumes that white working-class communities fall into a reductionist stereotype, which has been challenged in the book.

In the first of the two fieldwork chapters, the importance of being treated fairly was stressed to interviewers. This was linked to a lack of voice in local politics. Compared to minority communities, who appeared to have community organisations and local representatives, white working-class communities made the point that they did not have organisations that addressed their needs. However, such a perspective can be challenged because their voice is heard in the media on a regular basis. The importance of fairness perhaps speaks more to the need for government to become even more open and transparent in the allocation of public goods such as social housing.

The second fieldwork chapter considered the views of white working-class communities in the Borough of Waltham Forest in North-East London. Again, multiculturalism is viewed as a lived reality and an asset to neighbourhoods and communities. Being British was not in any way linked to being white. Values of hard work, reciprocity, trust and support were seen in established minority communities in the East End but less so in newly arrived white migrants from Eastern Europe. This study showed that white working-class identity was diverse and inclusive of established minority groups. Those interviewed come across not as being closed or resistant to change, but as eager to engage in grassroots dialogue with different communities. These voices of white working-class residents challenge some of the conventional wisdom that has become embedded when we think of the interaction of these groups with the themes of immigration and social change.

The fieldwork chapters did contain viewpoints and expressions on multiculturalism that seem to echo the worst examples of white working-class resentment and anger, as seen in the Notting Hill riots and responses to the 'Rivers of Blood' speech. However, as we have stated earlier, these different, divergent and sometimes contradictory views are reflective of the way in which the politics of immigration and race have been conducted since 1945. Arguably, these matters have become even more toxic since the attacks of 11 September 2001, the emergence of community cohesion and the decline of multiculturalism. For example, the working class are no different to the majority of people interviewed in Britain about the need for greater restrictions on immigration. They need not be assumed to have more progressive or, indeed, regressive views on the subject. The fieldwork again shows the variety of views, with a strong agreement on the need to promote the local expression of multiculturalism.

Summary

Given the past and present, what of the future? It is risky to predict the prospect for white working-class communities and multiculturalism. Despite the difficulty, and reviewing some of the themes discussed previously, we start from the three premises based on economic, political and cultural frames.

First, considerable challenges abound in attempting to define the white working class based on a reductionist logic that is not fit for purpose. While the socio-economic categorisation on class became a mainstay in Britain for much of the 20th century and remained fixed in research and the popular consciousness, this categorisation has been challenged by new analysis that sees class as much more elastic, taking into account the extent of social networks and cultural preferences in forming alignments. This could be described as transforming class definition in a post-industrial society, when our sense of identity, belonging and even status becomes challenged. The meaning of class is shaped by representations in the media and television and this will likely carry on as an elastic definition of class is expanded for inclusivity and then constricted by the narrow and incomplete stereotype transmitted into millions of homes.

Second, the messiness of class is compounded by race. Some have suggested that the white working class do not have the privilege and power of white that is associated with other groups in society. Whiteness is invisible and is not the dominant norm that provides the benchmark against which people are measured. Rather, and as discussed, the whiteness of the white working class is seen and tangible, expressed in many different forms, with crass language, crude aesthetic tastes and living in annexed and dangerous council estates. This is a 'dirty whiteness' that is obvious and scorned rather than the 'clean whiteness' that is hidden yet celebrated.

Accepting that white working-class communities do not have access to power and resources has been mentioned at various times in this book. However, do we accept that the white working class does not have the privilege associated with whiteness? On balance, we are suggesting that this would be too bold of a statement. Whiteness has been, and continues to be, the dominant norm in British society. The white working class benefit from their ethnicity in a way that is denied to minority groups. Indeed, in almost every public policy domain, from health and housing to employment, it is minority groups that occupy the bottom rung in terms of statistical outcomes. Being a victim of 'stop and search' tactics by the police or being seen as a member of a suspect community is about race and racism and not simply class. In discussing and giving voice to white working-class communities, racism should not be wished away or relegated to being of lesser importance in public policy debates. It is very much alive in British society.

Third, the rise and fall of multiculturalism has been analysed in this book as leading to the recalibration of whiteness and class. In short, the increasing salience of multiculturalism helped to stratify the 'dirty whiteness' of the white working class while its demise could be viewed as resulting in a 'clean whiteness'. History has shown how this has been framed. At various times in the post-1945 period, concerns about immigration and the impact of difference have been used to create a convenient point for whiteness to become unified against a common enemy. British identity has been restated as being about white identity in terms of cultural norms and practices that have marked out immigrants and minorities as the outliers who needed to move towards core values, however poorly defined. The antagonism towards immigration, which has been a constant in British politics, appears to have become increasingly prominent in the recent period. Indeed, this has become the new normal in British society. Multiculturalism has been seen by some as playing a role in marginalising the white working class and its retreat is the basis for this group to assume an importance in society that had been lost. It is in this space that political parties like UKIP, feeding off the concerns about immigration and the loss of British norms and identity, have attempted a reverse takeover of progressive public discourse. Given the shield of racialisation, whiteness has become dominant.

Looking ahead

Globalisation and interconnectedness will continue to be important in shaping national and local public policy debates. In turn, the issues that have been central to this book – whiteness, identity, social change – will be impacted by immigration and the continuing transformation of Britain from being monocultural to a multicultural country.

Yet, at the start of a new century, characterised by the international movement of people and capital and the fluidity of space and identity, Britain appears to be moving in the opposite direction, as seen through its support for the protectionist agenda of ultra-nationalists and a hankering for a past that was never the reality. As we have noted, following the 2014 European elections, Britain made a type of history that it may come to regret. The nationalist and right-wing UKIP was victorious with 27% of the popular vote. This can be attributed to a strategy that fixates on white working-class voters who are angry about the impact of multiculturalism and the lack of traction that they have on the agenda of the mainstream political parties.

The success of anti-immigration parties should not come as a shock either in Britain or other countries in Europe. Gaining the support of the white working class has been achieved during the most severe economic contraction since the 1930s. In Britain, people have suffered as the country has experienced the most sustained fall in the standard of living in the post-1945 period. It could be described as moving from a period of relative security to one of profound insecurity.

Disconnection ...

It should be asserted that the success of UKIP has been signposted by some of the studies on white working-class communities discussed in this book. The extent of political disconnection and disdain for the group described as the 'political class' is palpable. This is more a problem for Labour than the Conservatives or the Liberal Democrats, for it has historically claimed to act in the interests of the working class and the white working class. Its transition into New Labour and the unprecedented success demonstrated by the convincing victories in 1997, 2001 and 2005 were partly the result of building a wider coalition of support.

The white working class were forgotten and regarded as being an anomaly in building a modern, international country. This group were politically homeless and viewed minorities as speeding ahead in terms of housing, jobs and political representation. Lack of voice, economic decline and disconnection from political institutions viewed as being impenetrable and mired in scandal presented a 'perfect storm' for UKIP to be cast as the unlikely saviour of the white working class. Similar to its peers in Europe and to the Tea Party in the US, UKIP has, for the moment, claimed a connection with and representation of white working-class interests. It is a new and shiny insurgence, but looks can be deceiving. Scratch this 2014 sheen and a very different party is revealed, one that commits to the type of free-market economic policies that led to the economic crisis, one that supports and advocates for restrictive laws on workers' rights, and one that has a deeply racist, homophobic and sexist political culture whose supporters identify not only with Margaret Thatcher and the Conservatives, but with Adolf Hitler and the Nazis.

... Reconnection

This book has shown the weak and fragmented response by political parties to the white working class. Again, this should not be surprising because Labour, in particular, has been concerned about the political consequences of being seen as weak on immigration policy. Richard Crossman (1991) recounts the fear that this issue created among Labour politicians in the 1960s and the worry that it could lose white working-class support. As was the case then, the response has been to call for greater restrictions on immigration, including closing UK borders. Attempting to reconnect with white working-class communities by speaking the language of the fatalists on immigration and social change is the equivalent of the Monty Python 'dead parrot'.

Britain has been debating the impact of multiculturalism and immigration for more than 150 years. Newly arrived immigrants – the Irish in the 1850s, Jews in 1900s, Caribbean communities and those from India and Pakistan in the 1950s and now Poles in the 2000s – have been greeted with the rhetoric of concerns about the pressure on working-class communities, housing, schools and jobs. Neighbourhood change locally and identity change nationally have been the political calling card of those who seek to make capital from fear.

Reconnecting with the white working class should be based on the reality of immigration, multiculturalism and 'everyday integration'. The questions that need to be posed have to include practical issues rather than overblown rhetoric. In the fraying of the welfare state, who are the people likely to look after elderly and disabled relatives in care homes or hospitals for wages that many would not find sufficiently attractive? Who selects, picks and packs the fruit and vegetables for the local supermarket that are an essential part of dietary requirements? Where do people go to get essential provisions after these supermarkets have closed in the evening? Who owns the Indian restaurant that you, your family and friends go to during the weekend? Studies of white working-class communities demonstrate that the positive benefits of multiculturalism are acknowledged and, in some cases, embraced. This is the lived reality. Reconnecting is about emphasising and making the case for the benefits of difference for everyday and routine life.

In appealing to white working-class voters, rather than pandering to narrow nationalist rhetoric, political parties need to connect and make the case for a vision of a modern, multicultural society that depends on the creativity and skills of all established and emerging communities in order to compete in an increasingly competitive global economy. Closed borders, insularity and virulent nationalism paint a pessimistic picture of a country as one that is going backwards rather than forwards. Political parties need to emphasise the loss of jobs, income and services, all of which are likely to have a disproportionate impact on white working-class communities, if the agenda of UKIP and its followers is translated into policy. The stark choice is between regression and progression. Thus, political parties need to find ways to connect with white working-class voters though a programme of radical, practical and reforming policies that emphasise inclusion rather than exclusion.

Rebooting

The disconnection of people from politicians and political institutions is visceral. In this context, it could be argued that the white working class have been sceptical of multiculturalism. This is not simply because of resentment and 'white backlash' against the 'favours rather than fairness' linked with minorities, but also because government has, in a top-down and bureaucratic manner, implemented these policies. Research findings on white working-class perspectives and multiculturalism show that the message of difference and diversity loses potency when delivered by discredited individuals and institutions. Rebooting work with white working-class communities does not mean that government should withdraw from the policies of cohesion, integration and multiculturalism. Anti-discriminatory laws need to be policed and policy frameworks set the parameters of debate. However, the state should in some circumstances be the facilitator rather than driver in local communities. This means that promoting the benefit of diversity and multiculturalism should not be the task of a remote institution or discredited politicians. Rather, trusted activists on the ground or working through community organisations rooted in the reality of the everyday lives of white working-class communities are the best way to connect with this group. This type of compact – people, organisations and government – gives the prospect of a radical and progressive politics that is different from the nationalist nostalgia of UKIP, Blue Labour or, indeed, the vacuous indifference of the Conservative–Liberal Democrat Coalition's policies of integration.

This type of rebooting is based on the premise that white working-class communities are as diverse as any other group in society. They have fluid identities that are shaped and constructed depending on different contexts. Some examples of these have been represented in the fieldwork studies presented and can also be seen through the cultural spectrum that we have viewed. There is a very strong possibility that coalitions of interest between white working-class and established and emerging minority communities can occur at a grassroots level and that they can be based on common concerns and aspirations. The rebooting is about building a practical and progressive majority coalition comprised of the young, women and minority voters, along with middle-class liberals and the traditional working class, in order to build a core of support through cities and towns. In this way, the white working class will challenge and free itself from the straightjacket that it has been forced into by reification. That is, it will move away from being insular, closed and resistant to change and multiculturalism and instead become the agency for shaping a new Britain based on new values. Given the racialisation of politics domestically and concerns about insecurity internationally, there has never been a more important time to fight for a progressive future.

References

Alibhai-Brown, Y. (2000) *After multiculturalism*, London: Foreign Policy Centre.

Amin, A. (2002) 'Ethnicity and the multicultural city: living with diversity', *Environment and Planning A*, vol 46, no 3, pp 959–80.

Back, L., Keith, M., Khan, A., Shukra, K. and Solomos, J. (2002) 'New Labour's white heart: politics, multiculturalism and the return of assimilation', *The Political Quarterly*, vol 73, no 4, pp 445–54.

BBC (2010) 'Profile of Gillian Duffy, the voter PM called "bigoted"'. Available at: http://news.bbc.co.uk/1/hi/8649476.stm

BBC (2014) 'UK European election results'. Available at: http://www.bbc.co.uk/news/events/vote2014/eu-uk-results (accessed 29 August 2014).

BBC News (2009) European election: United Kingdom result. Available at: http://news.bbc.co.uk/1/shared/bsp/hi/vote2004/euro_uk/html/front.stm

BBC Online (2001) 'Blair defends Blunkett on race comments', 10 December. Available at: http://news.bbc.co.uk/1/hi/uk_politics/1700370.stm

BBC Online (2007) Gordon Brown speech to the Labour Party Conference. Available at: http://news.bbc.co.uk/1/hi/uk_politics/7010664.stm

Bebber, B. (2014) 'Till death us do part: political satire and social realism in the 1960s and 1970s', *Historical Journal of Film, Radio and Television*, vol 34, no 2, pp 253–74.

Beider, H. (2007) *Neighbourhood renewal & housing markets. Community engagement in the US & UK*, Oxford: Blackwell.

Beider, H. (2011) *White working-class views of neighbourhood, cohesion and change*, York: Joseph Rowntree Foundation.

Beider, H. (2012) *Race, housing & community: Perspectives on policy and practice*, Oxford: Wiley-Blackwell.

Beider, H. (2014) *Building grassroots solutions to integration in Waltham Forest*, London: Open Society Foundations.

Bentley, N. (2007) *Radical fictions: The British novel in the 1950s*, Oxford: Peter Lang Pub Inc.

Benyon, J. and Solomos, J. (1987) *The roots of urban unrest*, London: Pergamon Press.

Blackhurst, C. (2014) 'Farage has made UKIP, not Labour, Britain's most working-class party: UKIP's grumpy blue rinse and harrumphing ex-army officer image is not the reality', *The Independent*, 3 April. Available at: http://www.independent.co.uk/voices/comment/ukip-not-labour-is-now-britains-most-workingclass-party-9236118.html

Bloemraad, I., Korteweg, A. and Yurdakul, G. (2008) 'Citizenship and immigration: multiculturalism, assimilation, and challenges to the nation-state', *Annual Review of Sociology*, vol 34, ss 8.1–8.27.

Blunkett, D. (2002) 'Integration with diversity: globalization and the renewal of democracy and civil society', speech given to Foreign Policy Centre, London.

Bonnett, A. (1998) 'How the British working class became white: the symbolic (re)formation of racialized capitalism', *Journal of Historical Sociology*, vol 1, no 3, pp 316–40.

Bonnett, A. (2008) 'White studies revisited', *Ethnic and Racial Studies*, vol 31, no 1, pp 185–96.

Bottero, W. (2009) 'Class in the twenty-first century', in K. Sveinsson (ed) *Who cares about the white working-class?*, London: Runnymede Trust.

Bourdieu, P. (1984) *Distinction*, London: Routledge.

Bourne, J. (2001) 'The life and times of institutional racism', *Race and Class*, vol 4, no 7, pp 7-22.

Bourne, J. and Sivanandan, A. (1980) 'Cheerleaders and ombudsmen: the sociology of race relations in Britain', *Race and Class*, vol 21, no 4, pp 331–52.

Bradley, H. (2014) 'Class descriptors or class relations? Thoughts towards a critique of Savage et al.', *Sociology*, vol 48, no 3, pp 429–36.

Brodkin , K. (1998) *How Jews became white folks and what that says about race in America*, New Brunswick, NJ: Rutgers University Press.

Brown, D. (2004) 'Subcultures, pop music and politics: skinheads and "Nazi rock" in England and Germany', *Journal of Social History*, vol 38, no 1, pp 157–78.

BSA (British Social Attitudes) (2013) *Social class: The role of class in shaping social attitudes*, London: National Centre for Social Research.

Burchill, J. (1977) '1976', *NME*, 1 January, pp 17–20.

Camden Local Strategic Partnership (2007) *Camden Local Strategic Partnership update on the Social Cohesion Advisory Group*, London: Camden Council.

Cameron, D. (2011) 'Speech to Munich Security Conference', Cabinet Office, London.

Cantle, T. (2005) *Community cohesion: A new framework for race and diversity*, London: Palgrave.

Carp, B. (2010) *Defiance of the patriots: The Boston Tea Party and the making of America*, London: Yale University Press.

CCCS (Centre for Contemporary Cultural Studies) (1982) *The empire strikes back: Race and racism in 70s Britain*, London: Hutchinson.

Centre for Social Justice (2013) *Requires improvement: The causes of educational failure*, London: Centre for Social Justice.

Chahal, K. and Julienne, L. (2000) *'We can't all be white'. Racist victimisation in the UK*, York: Joseph Rowntree Foundation.

Cheong, P., Edwards, R., Goulbourne, H. and Solomos, J. (2007) 'Immigration, social cohesion and social capital: a critical review', *Critical Social Policy*, vol 27, no 24, pp 24–49.

Childs, D. (2006) *Britain since 1945: A political history*, New York, NY: Routledge.

CIC (Commission on Integration and Cohesion) (2007) *Our shared future*, London: Department for Communities and Local Government.

Clarke, J. (1998a) 'Subcultures, culture and class – a theoretical overview', in S. Hall, T. Jefferson and R. Roberts (eds) *Resistance through rituals*, London: Hutchinson.

Clarke, J. (1998b) 'The skinheads & the magical recovery of community', in S. Hall and T. Jefferson (eds) *Resistance through rituals*, London: Hutchinson.

Clarke, K. (2011) 'Conservative Party Conference 2011: we must tackle "feral underclass", says Ken Clarke'. Available at: http://www.telegraph.co.uk/news/politics/conservative/8806128/Conservative-Party-Conference-2011-we-must-tackle-feral-underclass-says-Ken-Clarke.html (accessed 29 August 2014).

Clarke, S. and Garner, S. (2009) *White identities: A critical sociological approach*, London: Pluto Press.

Clarke, T. (2001) *Burnley Task Force report on the disturbances in June 2001*, Burnley: Burnley Borough Council.

Cohen, N. (2014) UKIP's rise threatens the Left as well as the Right: that Nigel Farage can speak to former Labour voters ought to be a matter of shame to the British Left and a call to arms', *The Guardian*, 1 February. Available at: http://www.theguardian.com/commentisfree/2014/feb/01/ukip-nigel-farage-rise-labour-no-good

Collins, M. (2005) *The likes of us: A biography of the white working classes*, London: Granta Books.

Coventry City Council (2008) *Coventry's Economy 1976 to 2026*, Coventry: Coventry City Council.

Crossman, R. (1991) *The Crossman diaries: Selections from the diaries of a cabinet minister, 1964–1970*, London: Mandarin.

Crown Prosecution Service (2014) *Hate crime and crimes against older people report 2012–2013*, London: CPS.

Cruddas, J. (2006) 'New Labour and the withering away of the working class?', *The Political Quarterly*, vol 77, pp 205–13.

Daniel, W. (1968) *Racial disadvantage in England*, Harmondsworth: Penguin.

DCLG (Department for Communities and Local Government) (2001) *National strategy for neighbourhood renewal*, London: DCLG.

DCLG (2009) *'Connecting communities', policy briefing*, London: DCLG.

DCLG (2012) *Creating the conditions for integration*, London: DCLG.

Dench, G., Gavron, N. and Young, M. (2006) *The new East End: Kinship, race and conflict*, London: Profile Books.

Denham, J. (2002) 'Promoting community cohesion', Speech given to the Industrial Society and the Runnymede Trust, London, 18 March.

DiMaggio, A. (2011) *The rise of the Tea Party: Political discontent and corporate media in the age of Obama*, New York, NY: Monthly Review Press.

Duhan, M. (2014) 'Stockholm syndrome: Europe's new Northern Radicals'. Available at: http://www.global-counsel.co.uk/system/files/publications/Global_Counsel_Stockholm_Syndrome_0.pdf

Duncombe, S. and Trembelay, M. (eds) (2011) *White riot: Punk rock and the politics of race*, London: Verso.

Dyer, R. (1988) 'White', *Screen*, vol 29, no 4, pp 44–65.

Dyer, R. (2006) *White: Essays on race and culture*, New York, NY: Routledge.

Eatwell, R. and Goodwin, M. (eds) (2009) *The new extremism in 21st century Britain*, London: Routledge.

Esping-Andersen, G. (2013) *The three worlds of welfare capitalism*, New York, NY: John Wiley & Sons.

Featherstone, S. (2009) *Englishness: Twentieth-century popular culture and the forming of English identity*, Edinburgh: Edinburgh University Press.

Foot, P. (1969) *The rise of Enoch Powell: An examination of Enoch Powell's attitude to immigration and race*, Harmondsworth: Penguin Books.

Ford, R. and Goodwin, M. (2014) *Revolt on the Right: Explaining support for the radical Right in Britain*, London: Routledge.

Fox, C. and Guglielmo, T. (2012) 'Defining America's racial boundaries: blacks, Mexicans, and European immigrants, 1890–1945', *American Journal of Sociology*, vol 118, no 2, pp 327–79.

France 24 (2013) *'Where are France's National Front voters?'*, 7 July. Available at: http://www.france24.com/en/20130807-national-front-fn-voters-elections-france-politics-le-pen-far-right-immigration-tax

Frey, W. (2011) *Melting pot cities and suburbs: Racial and ethnic change in metro America in the 2000s*, Washington, DC: Brookings Institute.

Fryer, P. (1984) *Staying power: The history of black people in Britain*, London: Pluto Press.

Garner, S. (2007) *Whiteness: An introduction*, London: Routledge.

Garner, S. (2011) *White working-class neighbourhoods: Common themes and policy suggestions*, York: Joseph Rowntree Foundation.

Garner, S. and Bhattacharya, G. (2011) *Poverty, ethnicity and place*, York: Joseph Rowntree Foundation.

Gillborn, D. (2009) 'Education: the numbers game and the construction of white racial victimhood', in K. Sveinsson (ed) *Who cares about the white working-class?*, London: Runnymede Trust.Gilroy, P. (2005) *Postcolonial melancholia*, New York, NY: Columbia University Press.

Glasman, M., Rutherford, J., Stears, M. and White, S. (eds) (2011) 'The Labour tradition and the politics of paradox', the Oxford London Seminars 2010–11, *Soundings Journal*.

Goodhart, D. (2004) 'Too diverse?', *Prospect*, February.

Goodwin, M. (2009) 'The contemporary radical Right: past, present and future', *Political Studies Review*, vol 7, no 3, pp 322–9.

Hall, S. (1995) 'The whites of their eyes: racist ideologies and the media', in G. Dines and J.M. Humer (eds) *Gender, race and class in media: A text – reader*, Thousand Oaks, CA: Sage, pp 18–22.

Hall, S., Jefferson, T. and Roberts, R. (eds) (1998) *Resistance through rituals*, London: Hutchinson.

Halsey, A.H. (1995) *Change in British society*, Oxford: Oxford University Press.

Hamill, P. (1969) 'The revolt of the white lower middle class', *New York Magazine*.

Hanley, L. (2007) *Estates: An intimate history*, London: Granta.

Hanley, L. (2011) 'Labour must bury working-class conservatism, not praise it', *The Guardian*. Available at: http://www.theguardian.com/commentisfree/2011/apr/19/labour-working-class-gillian-duffy

Harrison, M. (1995) *Housing, 'race', social policy and empowerment*, Aldershot: Avebury.

Hartigan, J. (2005) *Odd tribes: Towards a cultural analysis of white people*, London: Duke University Press.

Haylett, C. (2001) 'Illegitimate subjects? Abject whites, neoliberal modernisation, and middle-class multiculturalism', *Environment and Planning D: Society and Space*, vol 19, no 3, pp 351–70.

Hebdige, D. (1979) *Subculture: The meaning of style*, London: Routledge.

Heffer, S. (1999) *Like the Roman: The life of Enoch Powell*, London: Weidenfeld & Nicolson.

Hewitt, R. (2005) *White backlash and the politics of multiculturalism*, Cambridge: Cambridge University Press.

Hill, J. (1986) *Sex, class and realism: British cinema 1956–63*, London: British Film Institute.

Home Office (1999) *The Stephen Lawrence Inquiry, Report of an Inquiry by Sir William Macpherson of Cluny*, London: Home Office.

Home Office (2001) *Community cohesion: A report of the independent reviewing team*, London: HMSO.

Home Office (2004) *The end of parallel lives? The report of the Community Cohesion Panel*, London: Home Office.

Home Office (2005) *Improving opportunity, strengthening society*, London: Home Office.

Home Office, Office for National Statistics and Ministry of Justice (2014) *An overview of hate crime in England and Wales*, London: Home Office.

House of Commons Education Select Committee (2014) 'Underachievement in education by white working class children'. Available at: http://www.publications.parliament.uk/pa/cm201415/cmselect/cmeduc/142/142.pdf

Hübinette, T. and Lundström, C. (2011) 'Sweden after the recent election: the double-binding power of Swedish whiteness through the mourning of the loss of "old Sweden" and the passing of "good Sweden"', *NORA – Nordic Journal of Feminist and Gender Research*, vol 19, no 1, pp 42–52.

Huntington, S. (1993) 'The clash of civilizations?', *Foreign Affairs*, vol 72, no 3, pp 2–49.

Husband, C. and Alam, Y. (2011) *Social cohesion and counter-terrorism. A policy contradiction?*, Bristol: The Policy Press.

Ignatiev, N. (1995) *How the Irish became white*, New York, NY: Routledge.

Institute of Public Policy Research (2012) *Rethinking integration*, London: IPPR.

Ipsos Mori (2014) *Perception and reality: Public attitudes to immigration*, London: Ipsos Mori.

Jones, O. (2011) *Chavs: The demonization of the working class*, London: Verso.

Joppke, C. (2004) 'The retreat of multiculturalism in the liberal state: theory and policy', *British Journal of Socioogy*, vol 55, no 2, pp 237–57.

Joshi, S. and Carter, B. (1984) 'The role of Labour in the creation of a racist Britain', *Race & Class*, vol 25, no 3, pp 53–70.

Kaczka-Valliere, J. and Rigby, A. (2008) 'Coventry – memorializing peace and reconciliation', *Peace and Change*, vol 33, no 4, pp 582–99.

Kaufman, E. and Harris, G. (2014) *Changing places*, London: Demos.

Kenny, M. (2011) 'The political theory of recognition: the case of the "white working class"', *British Journal of Politics and International Relations*, vol 14, no 1, pp 19–38.

Kundnani, A. (2002) 'The death of multiculturalism', *Race and Class*, vol 43, no 4, pp 67–72.

Kundnani, A. (2007) 'Integrationism: the politics of anti-Muslim racism', *Race and Class*, vol 48, no 4, pp 24–44.

Kundnani, A. (2012) 'Multiculturalism and its discontents: Left, Right and liberal', *European Journal of Cultural Studies*, vol 15, no 2, pp 155–66.

Kymlicka, W. (2012) *Multiculturalism: Success, failure, and the future*, Washington, DC: Migration Policy Institute.

Lacey, S. (1995) *British realist theatre: The new wave in its context 1956–65*, London: Routledge.

Lawler, S. (2012) 'White like them: whiteness and anachronistic space in representations of the English white working class', *Ethnicities*, vol 12, no 4, pp 409–26.

Lay, S. (2002) *British social realism: From documentary to Brit grit*, London: Wallflower.

Levison, A. (2013) *The white working class today: Who they are, what they think and how progressives can regain their support*, Washington, DC: The Democratic Strategist.

Levitas, R. (1998) *The inclusive society: Social exclusion and New Labour*, Basingstoke: Macmillan.

Local Government Association (2002) *Guidance on community cohesion*, London: LGA.

Madood, T. (2007) *Multiculturalism: A civic idea*, London: Polity Press.

Malik, S. (2002) *Representing black Britain: Black and Asian images on television*, Thousand Oaks, CA: Sage.

Malpass, P. and Murie, A. (1999) *Housing policy and practice* (5th edn), Basingstoke. Macmillan.

Mandelson, P. (1997) 'Labour's next steps: tackling social exclusion', Lecture delivered to The Fabian Society, 14 August, London.

McLaughlin, E. (2005) 'Recovering blackness/repudiating whiteness: the *Daily Mail*'s construction of the five white suspects accused of the racist murder of Stephen Lawrence', in Murji, K. and Solomos, J. (eds), *Racialization: Studies in theory and practice*, Oxford: Oxford University Press

Migration Policy Institute (2009) *United Kingdom: a reluctant country of immigration*, Washington, DC: Migration Policy Institute. Available at: http://www.migrationpolicy.org/article/united-kingdom-reluctant-country-immigration (accessed 29 August 2014).

Mills, C. (2014) 'The great British class fiasco: a comment on Savage et al', *Sociology*, vol 48, no 3, pp 437–444.

Moore, T. (2013) *Policing Notting Hill: Fifty years of turbulence*, London: Waterside Press.

Mudde, C. (2013) 'Three decades of populist radical right parties in Western Europe: so what?', *European Journal of Political Research*, vol 52, pp 1–19.

Mullins, D. and Murie, A. (2006) *Housing policy in the UK*, London: Palgrave Macmillan.

Murji, K. and Solomos, J. (eds) (2005) *Racialization: Studies in theory and practice*, New York, NY: Oxford University Press.

Murray, C. (1996) 'The emerging British underclass', in R. Lister (ed) *Charles Murray and the underclass: The developing debate*, London: IEH.

National Community Forum (2009) *Sources of resentment and perceptions of ethnic minorities among poor white people in England*, London: Department for Communities and Local Government.

Nayak, A. (2009) 'Beyond the pale: chavs, youth and social class', in K. Sveinsson (ed) *Who cares about the white working-class?*, London: Runnymede Trust.

Neal, S. (2003) 'Scarman, Macpherson and the media: how newspapers respond to race-centred policy interventions', *Journal of Social Policy*, vol 32, no 1, pp 55–74.

Negus, K. (2002) 'The work of cultural intermediaries and the enduring distance between production and consumption', *Cultural Studies*, vol 16, no 4, pp 501–15.

ONS (Office for National Statistics) (2012) *England and Wales has become more ethnically diverse in the past decade*, London: ONS.

Olden, M. (2008) 'White riot: the week Notting Hill exploded', *The Independent*, 29 August.

OSF (Open Society Foundation) (2012) *Muslims in London*, New York, NY: OSF.

OSF (2014) *Europe's white working class communities*, New York, NY: Open Society Foundations.

Ouseley, H. (2001) *Community pride not prejudice*, Bradford: Bradford Vision.

Parekh, B. (2000) *Rethinking multiculturalism:Cultural diversity and political theory*, Basingstoke and London: Macmillan.

Parsons, T. (1977) 'Review of The Clash', *NME*, 9 April, p 13.

Patterson, S. (1965) *Dark strangers: A study of West Indians in London*, London: Harmondsworth Press.

Payne, G. (2013) 'Models of contemporary social class: the Great British class survey', *Methodological Innovations Online*, vol 8, no 1, pp 3–17.

Pearce, J. and Milne, E. (2010) *Participation and community on Bradford's traditionally white estates*, York: Joseph Rowntree Foundation.

Phillips, M. and Phillips, T. (1998) *Windrush: The irresistible rise of multi-racial Britain*, London: Harper Collins.

Phillips, T. (2005) 'After 7/7: sleepwalking to segregation', Speech at the Manchester Council for Community Relations, 22 September.

Pilkington, E. (1988) *Beyond the mother country: West Indians and the Notting Hill white riots*, London: I.B. Tauris.

Progress (2011) 'Labour isn't working'. Available at: http://www. progressonline.org.uk/2011/04/19/labour-isnt-working/

Putnam, R. (2007) 'E Pluribus Unum: diversity and community in the twenty-first century: the 2006 Johan Skytte prize lecture', *Scandinavian Political Studies*, vol 30, no 2, pp 137–74.

Qualifications and Curriculum Authority (1998) *Education for citizenship and the teaching of democracy in schools* (The Crick Report), London: Qualifications and Curriculum Authority.

Ramalingam, V. (2012) *The Sweden Democrats: Anti-immigration politics under the stigma of racism*, Centre on Migration, Policy and Society Working Paper No 97, Oxford: University of Oxford.

Ratcliffe, P. (2013) '"Community cohesion": reflections on a flawed paradigm', *Critical Social Policy*, vol 32, pp 262–81.

Rattansi, A. (2012) *Multiculturalism: A very short introduction*, Oxford: Oxford University Press.

Rattigan, N. (1994) 'The last gasp of the middle class: British war films of the 1950s', in W. Winston Dixon (ed) *Re-viewing British cinema, 1900–1992: Essays and interviews*, Albany, NY: State University of New York Press, pp 143–53.

Rex, J. and Tomlinson, S. (1979) *Colonial immigrants in a British city*, London: Routledge & Kegan Paul.

Rhodes, J. (2010) 'White backlash, "unfairness" and justifications of British National Party (BNP) support', *Ethnicities*, vol 10, no 1, pp 77–99.

Rhodes, J. (2011) '"It's not just them, it's whites as well": whiteness, class and BNP support', *Sociology*, vol 45, no 1, pp 102–17.

Ritchie, D. (2001) *Oldham independent review: One Oldham, one future*, Manchester: Government Office for the North West.

Roediger, D. (1991) *The wages of whiteness: Race and the making of the American working class*, London: Verso Books.

Rogaly, B. and Taylor, R. (2009) 'Moving representations of the "indigenous white working class"', in K. Sveinsonn (ed) *Who cares about the white working class?*, London: Runnymede Trust.

Rose, D. (1995) *A report on phase 1 of the ESRC review of social classifications*, Swindon: ESRC.

Rose, D. and Pevalin, D. (2001) 'The National Statistics socio-economic classification: unifying official and sociological approaches to the conceptualisation and measurement of social class', ISER Working Papers.

Rose, D. and Pevalin, D. (2003) *A researcher's guide to the National Statistics socio-economic classification*, London: Sage.

Rose, D. and Pevalin, D. (with O'Reilly, K.) (2005) *The National Statistics socio-economic classification: origins, development and use*, London: ONS.

Ruth, A. (1984) 'The second new nation: the mythology of modern Sweden', *Daedalus*, vol 113, no 2, pp53-96.

Sabin, R. (2011) '"I won't let that dago by": rethinking punk and racism', in S. Duncombe and M. Tremblay (eds) *White riot: Punk rock and the politics of race*, London: Verso.

Salam, R. (2013) 'The white working class matters', *National Review Online*.

Salewicz, C. (2006) *Redemption song: The ballad of Joe Strummer*, London: Harper Collins.

Savage, J. (2005) *England's dreaming. Sex pistols and punk rock*, London: Faber & Faber.

Savage, M., Warde, A. and Devine, F. (2005) 'Capitals, assets and resources: some critical issues', *British Journal of Sociology*, vol 35, no 4, pp 522–46.

Savage, M., Devine, F., Cunningham, N., Taylor, M., Li, Y., Hjellbrekke, J., Le Roux, B., Friedman, S. and Miles, A. (2012) 'A new model of social class? Findings from the BBC's Great British class survey experiment', *Sociology*, vol 47, no 2, pp 219–50.

Savage, M., Devine, F., Cunningham, N., Friedman, S., Laurison, D., Miles, A., Snee, H. and Taylor, M. (2014) 'On social class, anno 2014', *Sociology*, vol 48, no 3, pp 1–20.

Scarman, J. (1981) *The Brixton disorders, 10–12 April (1981)*, London: HMSO.

Schofield, C. (2013) *Enoch Powell and the making of postcolonial Britain*, Cambridge: Cambridge University Press.

Schwarz, B. (1996) '"The only white man in there": the re-racialisation of England 1956–68', *Race & Class*, vol 38, no 1, pp 65–78.

Searchlight (2013) 'Communities must build a common story and identity together', interview with John Denham. Available at: http://www.searchlightmagazine.com/archive/communities-must-build-a-common-story-and-identity-together-john-denham

Skeggs, B. (2004) *Class, self, culture*, London: Routledge.

Skeggs, B. (2005) 'The making of class and gender through visualizing moral subject formation', *Sociology*, vol 39, pp 965–82.

Skeggs, B. (2009) 'Haunted by the spectre of judgement: respectability, value and affect in class relations', in K. Sveinsson (ed) *Who cares about the white working-class?*, London: Runnymede Trust.

Skey, M. (2011) *National belonging and everyday life: The significance of nationhood in an uncertain world*, New York, NY: Palgrave Macmillan.

Small, S. and Solomos, J. (2006) 'Race, immigration and politics in Britain: changing policy agendas and conceptual paradigms 1940s–2000s', *International Journal of Comparative Sociology*, vol 47, no 4, pp 235–57.

Solomos, J. (2003) *Race and racism in Britain* (3rd edn), Basingstoke: Palgrave Macmillan.

Standing, G. (2011) *The precariat: The new dangerous class*, London: Policy Network.

Standing, G. (2014) *A precariat charter: From denizens to citizens*, London: Bloomsbury.

Sveinsson, K. (2009) *Who cares about the white working-class?*, London: Runnymede Trust.

Szreter, S. (1984) 'The genesis of the Registrar General's social classification of occupations', *British Journal of Sociology*, vol 56, pp 31–48.

The Daily Telegraph (2007) 'Enoch Powell's "Rivers of Blood" speech', 6 November. Available at: http://www.telegraph.co.uk/comment/3643826/Enoch-Powells-Rivers-of-Blood-speech.html

The Daily Telegraph (2009) 'Government has neglected white working class, says John Denham', 30 November. Available at: http://www.telegraph.co.uk/news/politics/6691426/Government-has-neglected-white-working-class-says-John-Denham.html

The Daily Telegraph (2014) 'Mass immigration has left Britain "unrecognizable", says Nigel Farage'. Available at: http://www.telegraph.co.uk/news/politics/ukip/10668996/Mass-immigration-has-left-Britain-unrecognisable-says-Nigel-Farage.html

The Guardian (2007) 'A message to my fellow immigrants', 20 May. Available at: http://www.theguardian.com/commentisfree/2007/may/20/comment.politics

The Guardian (2013a) 'Stop and search: on the streets with the police', 20 October. Available at: 2013 http://www.theguardian.com/law/2013/oct/20/stop-and-search-streets-police

The Guardian (2013b) 'The absence of black students diminishes the greatness of Oxbridge'. Available at: http://www.theguardian.com/education/abby-and-libby-blog/2013/dec/04/black-students-absence-diminishes-oxbridge

The Guardian (2014) 'Labour MPs urge leadership to curb free movement within EU', 1 June. Available at: http://www.theguardian.com/politics/2014/jun/01/labour-mps-urge-curb-eu-free-movement-open-letter-ed-miliband

The Huffington Post (2014) 'Local elections a warning for Labour that the white working class is "pissed off" and voting UKIP', 23 May. Available at: http://www.huffingtonpost.co.uk/2014/05/23/local-elections-ukip-labour-party_n_5379912.html

The Independent (2010) 'Labour was "in denial" over immigration says Burnham'. Available at: http://www.independent.co.uk/news/uk/politics/labour-was-in-denial-over-immigration-says-burnham-1981433.html

The Observer (2008) 'She "loved Shannon to bits". But she had her kidnapped. Inside the dark, dangerous world of Karen Matthews', *The Observer*, 7 December. Available at: http://www.theguardian.com/uk/2008/dec/07/shannon-matthews-kidnap-trial

The Observer (2010) 'We were wrong to allow so many eastern Europeans into Britain'. Available at: http://www.theguardian.com/commentisfree/2010/jun/06/ed-balls-europe-immigration-labour?guni=Article:in%20body%20link

The Runnymede Trust (2000) *The future of multi-ethnic Britain* (the Parekh Report), London: Profile Books.

Thompson, E.P. (1964) *The making of the English working class*, London: Victor Gollancz.

Tomlinson, S. (2013) 'Immigration, immigration, immigration', *Renewal*, vol 21, no 4, pp 66–73.

Travis, A. (2002) 'After 44 years secret papers reveal truth about five nights of violence in Notting Hill', *The Guardian*, 24 August.

Trilling, D. (2012) *Bloody nasty people. The rise of Britain's far Right*, London: Verso.

Trilling, D. (2014) '10 myths of the UK's Far Right', *The Guardian*, 12 September.

Tyler, I. (2008) '"Chav mum chav scum": class disgust in contemporary Britain', *Feminist Media Studies*, vol 8, no 1, pp 17–34.

Walters, P. (2012) *The Story of Coventry*, Stroud: The History Press.

Webster, C. (2008) 'Marginalized white ethnicity, race and crime', *Theoretical Criminology*, vol 12, pp 293–312.

Wellings, B. (2013) 'Enoch Powell: the lonesome leader', *Humanities Research Journal*, vol 19 , no 1, pp 45–59.

Williamson, V., Skocpol, T. and Coggin, T. (2011) 'The Tea Party and the remaking of Republican conservatism', *Perspectives on Politics*, vol 9, no 1, pp 25–39.

Worley, M. (2013) 'Oi! Oi! Oi! Class, locality, and British punk', *Twentieth Century British History*, vol 24, no 4, pp 606–37.

Zeskind, L. (2012) 'A nation dispossessed: the Tea Party movement and race', *Critical Sociology*, vol 38, no 4, pp 495–509.

Filmography

A Taste of Honey (1961)
Blackboard Jungle (1955)
Kes (1969)
Nils by Mouth (1997)
O Dreamland (1953)
Passport to Pimlico (1949)
Room at the Top (1958)
Saturday Night and Sunday Morning (1960)
Secrets and Lies (1996)
The Bridge Over the River Kwai (1957)
The Cockleshell Heroes (1957)
The Dam Busters (1953)
The Loneliness of the Long Distance Runner (1962)
The White Season (2007)
This is England (2006)
This Sporting Life (1963)
Till Death Us Do Part (1965)
We are the Lambeth Boys (1959)

Index